To Bob —

Best wishes to a fellow WWII veteran of the 97th Division —

*H. Stanley Neff*

# UNFORGETTABLE
# J O U R N E Y

## A World War II Memoir

A teenage soldier writes home describing training,
combat in Europe and occupation duty in Japan.

# H. Stanley Huff

**Bridgeford Press**
Fort Wayne, Indiana

Published by BRIDGEFORD PRESS
P.O. Box 5251
Fort Wayne, Indiana 46895-5251

Publisher's Cataloging-in-Publication Data
Huff, H. Stanley.
    Unforgettable journey: memoirs of a World War II combat infantry-
    man / H. Stanley Huff. -- Fort Wayne, Indiana : Bridgeford Press,
    2001.
        p.   ill.   cm.
    ISBN 0-9701980-0-0

    1. Huff, H. Stanley.   2. World War, 1939-1945—Personal
    narratives, American.  3. World War, 1939-1945—Campaigns.  I. Title.

| | | |
|---|---|---|
| D811 .H84 | 2001 | 00-104505 |
| 940.54 /21 | dc—21 | CIP |

PROJECT COORDINATION BY BookPublishing.com

03 02 01 00 ◇ 5 4 3 2 1

*Printed in the United States of America*

*To my wife, Alda*
*My children, David, Sandra and Nancy*
*And my grandchildren, Kristi, Adam, Emily and Nikki*

# CONTENTS

## PART III: THE EUROPEAN WAR

## PART IV: THE JAPANESE OCCUPATION

## PART V: REFLECTIONS

# PREFACE

I N MARCH 1946, I WAS A FEW DAYS WEST OF SEATTLE ON ONE OF the famous liberty ships turned out at the rate of one a day by the Kaiser Shipyards. After leaving Yokohama, we had encountered a frightening typhoon including a monumental tidal wave. The tiny troopship was tossed around like a cork. At times it seemed to point straight down and the propeller actually came completely out of the water. When we were thrown into a trough, the ship shook so violently that we feared it would split in two. With clenched teeth, I thought of the irony of drowning at sea after having survived the dangers of combat.

After a couple days of terror, however, the storm passed and the rest of the trip was uneventful. The sky and the peaceful blue water were beautiful but they became monotonous after more than two weeks at sea. There was a chilly March breeze—not only the natural winds of the Pacific but also from our moving ship. You could smell the salt in the air with every breath.

Just five months past my twentieth birthday, I had traveled over 50,000 miles in the military. As I sat on deck for hours contemplating my life, dreams of the exciting new life I was about to begin alternated with memories of all that had happened to me in the previous 29 months.

How alone I had felt riding the bus to Indianapolis for induction. The months of training in the United States. That first night in a foxhole in Europe, listening to real bombs bursting around me. Many close calls with death. My days lost behind German lines. That night in a newly captured German castle. And, finally, six months of occupation duty in Japan, a country of immeasurably different culture, where we, the conquering army, were treated with deference and where we lived what was in many ways a life of luxury.

My thoughts drifted from the war to the present and on into the future. Although I was coming home with a Combat Infantryman's Badge, a European Theater Ribbon with two Battle Stars, an Asiatic-Pacific Occupation Ribbon, and a Bronze Star, along with an assortment of other ribbons and decorations, I was really interested only in getting out of the Army! For months I had dreamed about the change from soldier to civilian again. I was definitely going to college, since the GI Bill would pay my expenses. But where would I go? What would I study? I thought about the girls I had been corresponding with and whether I would continue to date them, whether I might get serious with any of them.

Without knowing it, I was reviewing my passage from teenage boy to adult. To a large degree, I had grown up in the Army, in battle. This is the story of that maturing.

When she died a few years ago, I found that my mother had kept nearly 250 of my wartime letters. My dear wife, Alda, encouraged me to use them to write a book about my days as a soldier. This book, then, is the result of my efforts to put my World War II adventures in print.

# ACKNOWLEDGMENTS

M<small>ANY PEOPLE HAVE MADE IT POSSIBLE FOR THIS BOOK TO BE</small> produced:

My grateful thanks to my mother, Dora E. Huff, who meticulously saved most of my wartime letters. Without those letters I would never have been able to remember enough details to reconstruct so many of my military experiences.

My wife of nearly fifty years, Alda J. Huff, provided me with the encouragement and confidence to start this project. After her tragic death in 1998 I wanted to finish this project as a tribute to Alda.

My three children, David S. Huff, Sandra Huff Waldrop, and Nancy E. Sholl, have all been a source of immense support and guidance throughout this endeavor. In 1995, Dave met Alda and me in Germany to help gather material and to relive some of the experiences I lived through in 1945. He also made some very helpful suggestions throughout the entire time the book was taking shape. Sandy and I work together, so I was able to consult with her regularly. She was especially helpful in the early difficult days of writing this manuscript. Nancy was filled with enthusiasm from the beginning. Her encouragement kept me focused during the times when I found it easy to become disengaged from the project.

My special thanks to Ed Moritz, who teaches research writing at Indiana University-Purdue University at Fort Wayne, Indiana. Ed's writing talent and suggestions were greatly appreciated. Besides being a professor of research writing, Ed has led a varied life, including organic farming, raising purebred sheep and serving as headmaster at a Summerhill-style school.

It was important to Alda that these memories be preserved for future generations. Someday, my grandchildren, Adam Sholl, Kristi Huff, Nikki Huff, and Emily Sholl—all of whom have brought great joy to Alda and me—will be able to share some of their grandfather's experiences during World War II with their own children and grandchildren.

# PROLOGUE

# MERTEN, GERMANY – 1945

It was April 6, 1945. I was sitting in a foxhole on a ridge overlooking the Sieg River, across from the picturesque little village of Merten, Germany. I was a nineteen-year-old combat infantryman serving with the 97th Infantry Division, U.S. Army.

The German Army was still very dangerous, although reeling from the pincer movement of the Allies from the West and the Russians from the East. The American and British armies had encircled 350,000 of Germany's finest troops in the Ruhr, the country's industrial heartland.

This Battle of the Ruhr Pocket was to be one of the last great engagements of the war. The Germans were trying desperately to protect their remaining military production capability. Losing the Ruhr would make continuation of the war impossible; thus, Hitler and his generals were determined to fight to the end to protect the giant Krupp and other war factories.

Although it was in its final stages, we had no way of knowing how long the war would last, nor, more important to us, how many thousands of American soldiers were still to die before the end came.

My only other contact with humanity that night was my foxhole buddy—another nineteen-year-old, Joe Vonksky from New York. This was our first night on the front lines. We had relieved units of the 311th Regiment of the 78th Infantry Division, which had been occupying these positions for two weeks. At night they had sent patrols across the Sieg River, probing German defenses and trying to capture soldiers for interrogation.

They warned us that the German patrols knew the location of every American foxhole. They would attempt to engage us in hand-to-hand combat or throw grenades into our holes, so we had to be extremely alert if we wanted to live to see dawn. It was raining steadily and our foxhole had several inches of water in the bottom. It was cold and very dark. We were miserable and scared. We sat there listening to our artillery shells swooshing overhead as they delivered their deadly cargo to the enemy-held side of the river. Incoming German 88s crashed into the ridge on which we were dug in.

In our hole-in-the-ground we felt reasonably safe except from a direct hit, and we wanted to believe that such a hit was not likely. Our plan was to alternate sleeping so one of us would be awake at all times. On this lonely, frightening first night in combat, we fully expected to be visited by a German patrol.

For a while, Joe and I whispered softly about our situation. Then both of us became silent. My mind drifted back to Fort Wayne . . .

*Sweet corn in July. We used to pick it and run into the house just before dinner. My mom would put it directly into the boiling water and serve it a few minutes later. Loaded with butter, it tasted so fresh and sweet you couldn't eat it fast enough. "Chew before you swallow," Dad would say. There would be green beans from the garden, too, and tomatoes dead ripe, sweet and acid at the same time, still a little warm from the sun.*

*But the main course was chicken, fried as only Mom could. My older brother, Bob, or I would catch the bird and hold it while she expertly removed its head with a butcher knife. But she alone plucked and transformed it into a meal no French chef could top. And for dessert, Mom's incredible pie made with apples she had picked herself that morning. It smelled like cinnamon and nutmeg, and the crust was firm and flaky, almost crunchy. I loved the feel of the crust between my teeth, along with the burst of apple flavor.*

"What was that?" Joe jolted me back to reality. I strained my ears and looked into the blackness. Everything was deathly still. It was eerie. Suddenly, I did hear something. Was it someone walking? Both of us listened intently. Another noise. We pointed our rifles and waited. A large tree branch rustled to the ground and we realized the noises were falling leaves and branches, loosened by the steady rain and the constant artillery bombardment.

My rapid pulse started to slow a little as I relaxed from my near-panic state of readiness. I now understood why we had been told, "Don't move around outside your foxhole at night." The trigger-happy GI in the next hole doesn't know who is walking around in the darkness. His first impulse is to shoot—later he might try to decide what he is shooting. No one was safe walking outside his fox-hole. This was one of the first lessons I learned as I struggled to survive in this very unnatural situation.

Suddenly, an 88 shell rained dirt and debris on us when it crashed into the nearby hillside. We were unhurt, but the German artillery was getting more active. Was this a prelude to an all-out counter-attack? My anxiety rose as I listened intently for the sound of a German patrol. Then, just as surprisingly, it again got quiet.

Sleep was impossible. As I dozed from time to time, my thoughts drifted back and forth . . .

*Riding my bicycle to school wearing the handsome new shirt mom had just made for me.* A crack that made Joe and me both jump, wide awake and alert, but turned out to be nothing. *Dad coming home from the paint store, quiet and tired.* The big guns opening up again, lights flashing in the sky. *The smell of bacon and coffee as I dressed to gather the eggs for breakfast.* Rainwater running down the backs of my legs, my pants soaked and cold, my toes squishing in wet socks. Only my head was dry under my helmet. This was worse than those rainy foxhole nights at Ft. Eustis. *Talking to girls in the din of Manochio's, (the local high school after-game hangout), sipping cokes and milkshakes, all the kids joking and laughing.* It was oddly silent again. Joe's breathing seemed awfully loud. Could the Germans hear it? Maybe he's getting some real sleep. More power to him. *The solid feel of my shoulder against the runner's hip as I make a perfect tackle.*

We survived that first night—and many more—but I was never certain how long my luck would last. During the previous three years much had made me doubt my survival, and the next month did little to reassure me. If I had a rendezvous with death, it would waste a happy Indiana boyhood and destroy my parents' dreams. But I was no different from many other inexperienced nineteen-year-old Americans trying to survive in a faraway land, in a war we had not caused.

Although I hadn't realized it on that crisp cold Sunday afternoon, my ordeal began on December 7, 1941, the day the Imperial Japanese Air Force bombed Pearl Harbor.

# PART I

## THE HOME FRONT

# PEARL HARBOR

SUNDAY, DECEMBER 7, 1941, STARTED JUST LIKE MANY OTHER cool, late fall days in Indiana. After one of Mom's patented Sunday dinners, topped off with hot apple pie, the family often sat in the living room and read the papers and listened to the radio. Since it was still football weather, that afternoon, as we often did, a bunch of guys from our neighborhood, including me, met at Lakeside Park to play a group from that area.

We didn't have any equipment but the ball, and by the end of the game it was never clear which was more beat up—that heavy, old leather ball (it was really pigskin in those days) or us. Nevertheless, we played tackle, and we had to bring the runner down, too.

I remember this particular game very well. Carrying the football, for what I thought would be a touchdown, I was unexpectedly hit from behind, which slowed me down just enough so that another fellow could slam me from the side.

As I crashed to the ground, a third player accidentally kicked me in the head. Intense pain exploded from temple to temple. I feared I had received a concussion. However, being a sixteen-year-old boy, I recovered and played the rest of the game, just as any of the others would have.

Shortly after returning home, nursing a large, painful lump on the top of my head, I was sitting in the living room feeling a little sorry for myself when a special news bulletin boomed from the radio: THE JAPANESE AIR FORCE HAD BOMBED PEARL HAR-

3

BOR, CAUSING A LARGE LOSS OF LIFE AND EXTENSIVE DAM-
AGE TO OUR PACIFIC FLEET.

My first thought was, "*Where* is Pearl Harbor?" In 1941, people
didn't travel as extensively as today, especially outside of the conti-
nental United States. Flying was very expensive, so only the well-off
could afford it. Hawaii was a distant territory of the United States,
and in the days before TV, if people knew anything at all about
Hawaii they thought of it as rather exotic islands where people still
wore grass skirts. So I was not alone in having no idea where Pearl
Harbor was.

I do know that my painful head laceration was quickly forgotten.
The Japanese had kicked America in the head on purpose. The
excitement and unbelievability of the situation took over all aspects
of our Sunday afternoon thoughts. We were in a state of shock.
Americans my parents' age and older could still remember World
War I, and there was strong sentiment for not getting involved in
foreign wars again. During my brief lifetime, wars had always been
somewhere else and never seemed relevant to me. Now, suddenly,
another country had attacked America, killing Americans and
destroying American ships.

Shortly after the announcement, Don Robinson, our nineteen-
year-old neighbor and friend, dropped in to talk about the bombing.
Finally he said, "Well, I guess I am going to have to get my boots on
and go to war." That was the beginning of the realization that all the
*boys*—and that's what we called them—would probably have to go.

At school on Monday, war was the only topic of conversation.
While I was in class, President Roosevelt delivered his famous
speech to Congress beginning, "Yesterday, December 7, 1941—a
date which will live in infamy—the United States of America was
suddenly and deliberately attacked by naval and air forces of the
Empire of Japan." Then, with but one dissenting vote (for trivia
buffs: she was Jeanette Rankin(R) of Montana), Congress declared
war on Japan. A few days later, Germany, with Hitler's usual
bravado, declared war on the United States, and our involvement
was complete.

It didn't take long for me to find out that Pearl Harbor was the home of our Pacific fleet in the Hawaiian Islands. The Japanese attack was a total surprise and the damage was extensive. Launching 353 planes in two waves, they had killed or wounded over 3,000 servicemen, destroyed nearly 200 aircraft, sunk five battleships and three destroyers, and damaged others.

But these numbers did little to prepare me for the tragedies to come.

Pearl Harbor had set in motion changes in our way of life that continue to this day.

# PATRIOTISM
## REPLACES ISOLATIONISM

W E WERE ALL STUNNED BY THE PEARL HARBOR ATTACK. HOWEVER, had we known the history of Japanese-American relations over the previous few years we probably wouldn't have been so surprised. Clearly, the two countries were on a collision course. Had our leaders and military commanders studied the recent history of Japan, they would have been aware of the Japanese propensity to strike first and declare war afterward.

In the early 1900s, Japan and Russia were also having serious disputes. In 1904, suddenly and without warning, the Japanese initiated military action against the Russians. At the time it was considered a "sneak attack." Only 37 years later the United States was the victim of another surprise attack that took place even while Japanese diplomats were in Washington, supposedly to negotiate a peaceful solution to problems between the two countries.

Japan had become very aggressive in the years prior to Pearl Harbor. She had invaded Manchuria in 1931 and carried on a war with China for most of the 1930s. She had occupied Indo-China and dominated Thailand in 1940. President Roosevelt had frozen Japan's assets in the United States in July of 1941. He had announced that the United States would send a military mission to China, which was at war with Japan at the time. He had cut the flow of American oil to Japan to a trickle and had announced an embargo to keep American scrap metal from being sent to Japan.

American historians have said Pearl Harbor was a tactical victory for Japan but a huge strategic error. The attack galvanized public opinion to support all-out war in a way that nothing else could possibly have done. Prior to the Japanese attack, a very strong anti-war feeling was prevalent throughout the country. This isolationism almost totally dissipated after the Japanese attack, and the American people strongly supported the war. The surprise attack, under cover of peace negotiations, actually reinforced widely held American views that the Japanese were unscrupulous and cunning.

The American public's attitude toward war changed completely. Prior to Pearl Harbor, the German-American Bund (a fraternity of Americans of German descent with still-strong German ties) openly supported the Nazi regime as it increasingly committed acts of aggression in Europe. Most other Americans opposed Hitler's actions, but according to the polls, over 80 percent were against entering the war in Europe. After Pearl Harbor and Germany's war declaration, isolationist sentiment changed almost overnight. The new American patriotism was based on anger as well as fear. We were enraged about being double-crossed and attacked. But, we also heard rumors that Hawaii was going to be invaded, and; from Alaska to California residents of the Pacific coast worried about direct bombing attacks or even an invasion. Japanese submarines were detected off the coast. For the first time since perhaps the Civil War, average American civilians were vulnerable and they did not like the feeling.

Isolationism was certainly dead as newspapers all across the country showed pictures of young men waiting in long lines at recruiting stations to enlist in the military. Our neighbor, Don Robinson, was typical of those boys. Shortly after that Pearl Harbor Sunday afternoon gathering he enlisted in the Army, and was assigned to the 94th Infantry Division. Brought up during the Great Depression, he was very familiar with hard times. Jobs were neither plentiful nor well-paid in 1941, and twelve years after the great crash it was not clear if or when they would be. He and most of my friends knew guns well, having hunted rabbits and squirrels for food. Hunger, they say, tends to make a crack shot. The Germans and Japanese would face him and thousands of similar tough, resourceful American kids.

Incidentally, Don saw extensive combat in Europe as a front line infantryman, survived, and returned home in 1945. He had done what was asked of him, and I never heard him talk about it after the war. In that respect, too, he was typical. Although it may seem strange in the post-Vietnam era, the same patriotism that led Don and millions like him to risk their lives motivated the folks back home to give their best, too.

# ECONOMIC 3 MIRACLE

D URING THE GREAT DEPRESSION JOBS WERE SCARCE. THE PRIMARY focus of most families was just getting enough to eat, be clothed, and have a place to live. After his 1932 election, Roosevelt spent the rest of the 1930s trying to jump-start the economy with various governmental programs such as the WPA, CCC, and NRA. By 1938 the country was still struggling with unemployment problems, despite all the new government programs. Many suffered, with 25 to 40 percent unemployment rates in some areas.

My family was pretty typical. Dad worked for a small retail paint store. In 1933 the owner, Mr. Rhoads, called his little group of eleven employees together for a very important meeting. "No one will be laid off," he said, "we're all in this together. Each week, we will pay our bills first and divide whatever is left. Some weeks you may get little or no pay. If anyone wants to quit, you can do so now and I will certainly understand."

No one quit. Dad worked there for the remainder of the depressed thirties. In 1940, when Mr. Rhoads retired, Dad and the other employees purchased the store. They still were not making the comfortable incomes which would become standard after the war, but we lived frugally, thankful that we were better off than many less fortunate people whom we knew and saw every day.

Although we had little money in those days, I never felt deprived or poor. In fact, we probably ate a much more nutritious diet than the kids of today. We didn't have fast food. We ate lots of vegetables that we raised in our garden, and fruit from our orchards. My mom cooked three wonderful meals a day, so we had little desire to eat out. She also made clothes for everyone in the family. We never thought of that as a sign of poverty. We saw it as good luck.

Like millions of other children, I had a happy, carefree childhood. I never thought about economic problems and just accepted it as a fact of life that sometimes there wasn't enough money do something we wanted to do.

I was only a sixteen-year-old high school junior when the war began. It would be nearly two years before I would be old enough for the military. During that time, when the entire nation was consumed with an all-out war effort, I saw and experienced tremendous changes in our American way of life.

The war gave Americans a new unity of purpose as industry geared up for the massive challenge of defeating the Axis powers— Germany, Italy, and Japan. Automobile assembly lines were converted to the manufacture of airplanes, tanks, and Army trucks. Other industries switched to war production, too, and every aspect of the economy was managed to facilitate the war effort. Even food priority went to the military, and farmers were urged to produce more wheat, corn, and hogs for the first time since the 1920s. The result of this frenzied activity was a permanent increase in American productivity.

The production from this collective effort was staggering. The United States industrial machine spewed out nearly 300,000 airplanes, 85,000 tanks, 320,000 artillery pieces, and 12,000 warships. The enemy couldn't possibly match this industrial output. In fact, Germany did not reach its peak military production until mid-1943, when it had already begun to lose the war.

After it entered the war, the country was almost instantly faced with a labor shortage. The military was skimming more and more young men and women from the workforce; our shipyards expanded and our war plants went to double and triple shifts. Most Americans wanted to be part of this gigantic effort to win the war. Women learned to weld and high school kids learned to run lathes after school. When I was stationed in California, some of the guys in my outfit were actually making good money by working at factories when they could get a pass.

Families from the depressed areas of the midwest and the south rushed to industrial cities and the east and west coasts to take advantage of the big money being offered in the new shipyards, war factories, and military bases. Housing was extremely scarce, and trailer camps appeared almost overnight to house the new defense workers. Many of these people never returned to their pre-war homes.

Women left traditional jobs as "housewives" and entered the war factories to help make tanks, airplanes, uniforms, and other war materials. In many cases, they were hired in jobs formerly reserved for males and they got the same pay as men, which was very unusual. Before the war, only clerical or secretarial jobs had been considered "women's work," and were poorly paid. "Rosie the Riveter" became a well-known poster girl and the heroine of a popular song. After the war, women never completely returned to their pre-war roles.

Teenagers like me found it easy to get jobs working summers and Saturdays during the school year. I worked at Sears, at a shoe store, and finally at International Harvester Company, before I enlisted in the Army. For the first time in my life, I had plenty of money. I felt rich making 30 cents an hour! And it seemed incredible that I could spend more than $5 apiece on Christmas presents for Mom and Dad.

In fact, people were making far more money than they could spend, because production of consumer goods was declining. Almost overnight, huge shortages developed. Gasoline, shoes, meat, sugar, coffee, and even whiskey were rationed. People felt patriotic when they planted "victory gardens" to supplement the nation's food supply and produce food they couldn't buy anyway. No new cars were manufactured and few new houses were built. Gasoline rationing was so tight that cars were driven only when absolutely necessary. People walked or took public transportation everywhere. I would estimate that 75 percent of the students at North Side rode their bicycles to school and the rest walked. There was a huge room for the bikes and everyone just left theirs there, unlocked. I never heard of one being stolen!

When the Japanese invaded the East Indies and cut off our supply of rubber, what little we had went to the military and it became nearly impossible to buy new tires. As the shortage deepened, prices climbed and some people put their cars up on blocks and sold the tires, sometimes for more than the whole car had cost a few years earlier.

One enterprising young man invented and offered for sale wooden tires. They didn't provide a very soft ride, and it certainly was not a good idea to drive very fast with them, but people bought them. At least they were a way to keep the family car running. Since the average family only received three gallons of gas each week, they weren't going very far anyway.

However, in spite of shortages and inconvenience, the standard of living actually reached new highs. Absenteeism was at an all-time low and people worked harder because they wanted to support the people in uniform. The civilian labor force remained constant, even with the large number of men drafted for the armed forces. America learned to increase productivity by improved techniques that spilled over into the post-war economy and helped to push our country into a level of prosperity never before attained.

One would expect that an economy with so much excess money chasing too few goods would be highly inflationary. However, it didn't happen. The primary reason, in addition to price controls, was that the excess cash was sopped up by the purchase of war bonds. It was considered patriotic to purchase war bonds, and the public responded by purchasing over $50 billion worth of them during the war. These savings then provided fuel for the post-war expansion.

But before we get too far ahead of ourselves, let me tell you about my last years of high school.

# WAITIN4 TO GO

I WAS ONLY SIXTEEN YEARS OLD, BUT I BECAME FASCINATED WITH THE war. With no television to report the news, we learned what was going on primarily from print, radio, and the newsreels at the theater. I devoured magazines and newspapers for stories of the battles. Every evening the whole family gathered around the radio to hear the most recent stories, often with static-filled, crackling reports broadcast from Europe or the Pacific, sounding mysterious, distant, and authoritative.

Most of us went to the movies every week, and before the feature show there was always a ten- or fifteen-minute newsreel dramatically narrated by well-known news reporters of that era, such as Edward R. Murrow and Walter Winchell. They showed actual battle scenes with bombings and anti-aircraft fire, infantrymen charging across shell-pocked fields, and ships hit by torpedoes. They conveyed a sense of excitement and action but did not dwell on the death or mutilated bodies. Sometimes, the newsreels would end with popular movie stars of the day, such as Carole Lombard (a Fort Wayne native) and Clark Gable, making a plea for the American public to purchase war bonds.

In June 1943, my school friends started enlisting and leaving for Indianapolis, sometimes alone, sometimes in groups of buddies. We really looked at it as an adventure. Join the Army and see the world! But I was just a spectator at those departures for the next five months.

Stan, age 17, prior to entering the Army, with friend Don, who was home on leave, 1942.

During my senior year of high school I worked in the paint department of Sears. Working after school and Saturdays, I made the princely sum of 30 cents an hour, but it was more money than I had ever had before and it would buy a lot. Cokes were five cents, hamburgers 10.

My first work experience did not start auspiciously. Because of the metal shortage, paint was packaged in one-gallon glass jars. On my first day, my job was to stock shelves. I carried the heavy case of four gallons of paint up the ladder and carefully balanced it at the top. When I put the third jar on the shelf, however, the fourth plunged to the floor, splattering paint all over as it smashed. I spent the rest of my work time that day cleaning up the mess, but fortunately they didn't fire me.

After I graduated from high school in the summer of 1943, I was determined to get the highest paying job I could, so I went to the big employers—Magnavox, Zollner Pistons, and International Harvester—on the same day. All three offered me jobs starting immediately, but Harvester had the best pay—$30 per week—so I started there. In fact, there was so much overtime available at time-and-a-half or double-time that I always made $50 to $60 per week. My job in Material Handling and Parts was not difficult. We simply took whatever was needed from the warehouse to the assembly line. Harvester had long since switched to war production, and the factory was turning out military trucks as fast as it could. I probably rode in some of those I helped build.

I had decided to join the Army when I turned 18 in October, so I just wanted to enjoy myself. Of course the dream of every teenage boy was to have his own car. The classifieds were full of cars for sale because many who left for the service were selling theirs. Besides, there was very little demand because gasoline was rationed and it was hard to find tires or parts. Prices were plunging and I had more money than I had ever had in my life.

When I told my parents I was going to buy a car, Dad didn't say much but Mom panicked. It wasn't enough that her baby was going to go to war, now he was going to risk his life in a car. "Why did a 17-year-old need a car, anyway?" she asked. She reminded me of high school kids who had been killed in accidents and appealed to my loyalty to her. When she saw that the safety arguments were going nowhere, she tried a practical approach. Why would I waste money on a car when I would be leaving for the army in a few months? She reminded me that repairs would be expensive and that all cars broke down. The economic line played right into my hands, though. I pointed out that, if the United States won this war, as it already appeared it was doing, millions of servicemen would be coming home someday. Since no new cars were being built, I figured we were surely headed for a huge shortage of cars. Therefore, I concluded triumphantly, the car would be a good investment, not just a toy.

A few days later, I saw an ad for a yellow 1937 Ford four-door convertible. Just what I wanted! I could see myself driving my friends around with the top down, or taking a little trip on a fine day—with the top down, of course. It was a steal at $225, and I almost felt guilty because the seller was a guy going into the Army. Mom, of course, was devastated. Not only had I bought a car, but I had gotten the most unsafe kind of all. "What if it rolls?" she'd ask. "You'll have no protection whatsoever!"

But I was more excited about and proud of that car than any other I have ever owned. For a few months, I drove it everywhere. I was in paradise. I never even considered selling it when I left, not

My sister, Eldena, and my 1937 yellow, four-door Ford convertible.

just because I was convinced it would appreciate in value, but mainly because I couldn't get enough of driving it. My sister and father drove it occasionally during the war, but when I was on leave, my favorite activity was driving the convertible.

After I came home in 1946, I was astonished to find out that my car was worth $950. This was my first great capitalist success and I never forgot that lesson—buy when most are selling and sell when most are buying. This buy-low, sell-high concept has been the cornerstone of my investment philosophy ever since. I have used it successfully many times, and it has helped me attain a financial success that I could only dream about as a young man.

At any rate, I was anxious to do my part to help my country. On October 29, 1943—my eighteenth birthday—I registered for the draft as was mandated by law. Normally, one might have a few months' reprieve while the Selective Service went through the process. First, the draftee was sent to Indianapolis for a physical examination. Then, they put him in one of various classifications, ranging from 1A (immediately eligible) through various deferment categories (occupational, educational, familial) to 4F (physically or mentally unfit). Finally, they sent him the dreaded induction notice if he qualified.

When I went to Indianapolis for the physical, I was told at the end of the day that I had passed and should go home to wait for the letter ordering me to report for active duty. "Go ahead and schedule me now," I said, "I'm ready to go."

The sergeant looked at me as if I was crazy (and now I see he may have been right). "Why would you want to go before you're called?" he asked, as though he could hardly believe his ears.

"I know I have to go anyway," I said. "Most of my friends are already in the military, so I might as well go now. Go ahead and put me on your call-up list."

The experiences I had over the next 30 months are still vivid in my memory over 50 years later. I came close to death many times during those months, and traveled to both Europe and Japan. I certainly had an unforgettable journey.

# PART II

## THE ARMY STATESIDE

# ARMY IN5OCENCE

Since I was one of the younger boys in my class, it was over four months after graduation before I was able to join my friends and former schoolmates in the long parade into the Army. Everyone from Ft. Wayne had to report to Fort Benjamin Harrison, near Indianapolis. As there was no train service to Indy, we took the bus. By the time it was my turn, I had been to a bunch of farewell gatherings at the bus station. They were upbeat; full of jokes and good wishes. No one, boy or family or friends, wanted to think that this could be the last time they would see each other. Besides, no one really knew what the Army was going to be like anyway.

It was a clear, cold November morning when my turn at the bus station came. Most of my friends had already gone. It was a weekday, when most people had to work, so mine was a small party—Mom, Dad, and my kid sister, Eldena. I didn't feel quite so tough facing the reality of leaving home for the first time. My mother was miserable, of course. This was far worse than watching me drive off in that dangerous convertible. Bob, her oldest, had gone, and now her youngest son might never come back either.

I choked back the emotion of the moment and tried to be relaxed and funny. I forced a big smile, shook hands with Dad, hugged Mom as hard as I could, threw a final wisecrack to my sister and boarded the bus.

As the bus pulled out, I waved and smiled. But we were barely down the street when I felt absolutely alone and the big question hit me: What had I done? I began to realize what was happening. No longer would I be allowed to decide where I would live, what I would eat, or even what time to go to bed or get up. I would not be able to drive my magnificent car. Instead of a private bedroom, I would live in a barracks with strangers who were different from me in both background and standards of conduct. Why hadn't I at least waited until they forced me to go? At least I could have had a couple of extra months at home. The reality that it was too late sank in. For better or for worse, I was about to become part of the U.S. Army in the midst of the largest war in history. As I drifted off to troubled sleep in the rhythmically rocking bus, I decided to accept it and make the best of it.

Because so many of my friends had gone into the service before me, and I had talked with them about military life when they were home on leave, I felt like I had a good idea of what to expect. Boy was I wrong! I knew it was not going to be much fun—I didn't expect it to be. But it took a sergeant yelling in my ear to show me what the real world of a soldier was like. I was not used to being shouted at and I was surprised that demeaning bellows seemed to be the only way sergeants knew how to talk.

The drill sergeant barked, "The Army can't make you do something, but it sure as hell can make you wish you had!" And that was close to the truth. After all, one couldn't just quit. Soldiers soon found out that life could be quite miserable if they didn't obey orders.

When we were told to "fall out with gloves on," there would inevitably be someone without gloves. The drill sergeant delighted in singling out this hapless guy (it was Korpinay in our platoon) who was "out of uniform." After screaming at him for what seemed like an eternity, he might order him to do pushups in front of everyone before telling him he would get no weekend pass for a month and, instead, would spend that time doing KP (Kitchen Patrol: the generic name for every food-related duty, from washing dishes and scrubbing floors to peeling potatoes and hauling garbage). It didn't take long for most of us to get the picture that it was in our best interests to just follow orders; but, a few guys like Korpinay seemed to have a hard time learning. He was the one who would be out of step and couldn't get back in. Korpinay forgot to take his canteen on bivouac and lost a part of his rifle while cleaning it. On the bayonet course, he missed the dummy. In fact, it got to the point that when something went wrong, Sarge would automatically shout, "Korpinay!" There seemed to be a Korpinay in every platoon in the Army—the misfit who couldn't get it right.

But the biggest challenge was getting used to the lack of privacy. We did everything in groups: squads, platoons, companies, or battalions. We marched everywhere in a group. We got up together, dressed and shaved together, ate together, exercised together, showered together, and went to bed at the same time. It was pretty strange to be standing around naked with a bunch of men in the showers.

Most barracks had two rows of 15 double-deck beds. We slept head-to-toe so we didn't have to breathe on each other. This was good, especially if the other person coughed or had a cold. All undressing, sleeping, reading mail, and talking took place in front of everyone else. If you wanted to say something without everyone hearing it, you had to take a walk or whisper or go into the latrine.

At the front of each bed was its occupant's footlocker for his personal articles. I can't remember the footlockers ever being locked, and I can only recall one incident when a watch was supposedly stolen. In the 1940s theft was not a problem, even in the crowded Army conditions. Of course, if anyone had stolen anything he wouldn't have had a place to conceal it. So, I guess there were some advantages to the lack of privacy.

Even though we were often partially naked around each other and slept in very close quarters, homosexuality was a non-issue during World War II. Admitted homosexuals were not accepted for military service, so if any did get in they must have kept it quiet. Neither myself nor anyone else I knew was ever approached or had anyone even suggest such a thing. There was the occasional anti-homosexual joke, but nobody seemed obsessed with it.

The high point of the day was the moment the company clerk

yelled, "Mail call!" Whether he was in the mess hall or, in good weather, in the middle of the company area, everyone dropped everything and gathered around the clerk while he called out the names of the lucky recipients.

Some guys seldom got mail, but they waited patiently for every name to be called before they walked back to the barracks with their heads down. I was a major mail recipient. My doting mother wrote nearly every other day, plus I was also corresponding with several girlfriends who wrote very regularly. Besides them, twelve to fifteen friends from high school and my neighborhood, who were scattered around the world in the service, wrote to me. My high school homeroom teacher and several people I knew from International Harvester rounded out my list of correspondents. I'm certain I was the envy of many, though it just seemed natural at the time.

The first couple of days, we went from one building to another, from one line to another. We filled out forms; then we filled out more forms. When we had a little spare time, we filled out yet more forms. We were issued uniforms. We all stood, with only a towel around us, in long lines as doctors poked, probed, and stuck us. This was not how I had envisioned the Army.

Finally, with administrative matters out of the way, I was told to report to M Company at 4:00 the next morning for KP. Immediately, someone told me that M Company was filled with draftees who had venereal diseases that required medical treatment. Having no knowledge about venereal diseases, I readily believed the frightening tales about catching one from a door handle or dishes. I hardly wanted to breathe all day, and I certainly didn't want to touch anyone. In fact, I must have been acting a little strange, because finally one of the cooks asked me if I was worried about catching VD. When I admitted I was, he broke into a belly laugh and assured me that my fears were completely unfounded. I had to agree with him that neither he nor anyone else would work there if VD were so communicable. I relaxed a little then, but it was a hard, unpleasant day anyway. It didn't help that when, exhausted, I got back to my barracks that night, guys asked me if I had caught anything that day while working with all of the VD patients. Fortunately, I never again had to go back to M Company to work KP.

That night the sergeant asked if anyone could type. Eager to escape M Company, I raised my hand.

"How fast?"

"I have an 80-word-per-minute ribbon from high school."

"Huff," he bellowed, "report to Building X at 0700 hours tomorrow."

When he left, the other guys broke out laughing and said, "You are crazy, man! You should never volunteer for anything in the Army. You are probably going to be M Company's clerk and be typing on all the forms those guys have been handling and writing on and sneezing on."

The next morning, however, I found myself processing all of the new inductees. Every day for a week I typed. As often happens in minor bureaucratic jobs, mine gave me a certain power—I knew the names of everyone who was on a shipping list. Therefore, I became a popular person in my barracks. Each night everyone crowded around me to find out where they were going to be sent.

My typing must have been satisfactory—or they were desperate. After only a week I was given a permanent typist job at Fort Benjamin Harrison. I was disappointed, even though this was a tremendous break for me. Staying in Indianapolis, I got lots of weekend passes to go home to Fort Wayne. I was able to see my family and friends, as well as drive my convertible. It was really an easy life. Eventually, I would be in a much better position to put myself on a list for Officer Candidate School (OCS). At that time, they were not taking OCS candidates until age 19.

Nevertheless, I wanted action, so I told the Master Sergeant I didn't want to stay in Indianapolis. I had joined the Army to see the world. I wanted to do something more exciting than type. He (and, I must admit, everyone else) thought I was making a big mistake, but he agreed to let me ship out.

Of course, everyone was right—it was a big mistake. It almost cost me my life.

# THE REAL A6MY AT LAST

I WAS SENT TO TAKE BASIC TRAINING WITH AN ANTI-AIRCRAFT OUTFIT IN Fort Eustis, Virginia. It was the middle of winter—cold and miserable, not much different from Indianapolis.

In basic training, we spent probably 80 percent of our days in physical activity of some kind. This included running an obstacle course, bayonet practice, rifle range, hand grenade practice, gas attack training, 10- and 25-mile marches with full packs, and just plain PT (Physical Training, the Army term for calisthenics). We also trained for hand-to-hand combat, including learning various lethal Judo chops. We learned about the most sensitive places on the body and how to immobilize our enemy. (I still remember the Judo and, to this day, could use it if the need arose; but hopefully those days are over.) On our long marches we walked 55 minutes and rested five minutes each hour.

We did have the opportunity to go into town on weekend passes. The drugs of choice were alcohol and tobacco. Illegal drugs were unheard of during the war. I never knew of anyone who was taking them nor did we talk about them. Only in Japan did I see old men sitting around smoking something that was supposedly opium or marijuana. Most of the guys did smoke tobacco, however. It seemed that someone was always bumming a cigarette from someone else. The health hazards of smoking were neither known nor stressed. No warnings appeared on cigarette packages at that time. C and K rations (K rations and C rations were prepackaged food soldiers received to eat under combat conditions when mass feeding was impractical) had free cigarettes in them and cigarettes were very cheap at the PX (Post Exchange). Smoking was so common that policing (cleaning up) cigarette butts was a typical occupation during general cleanups or when sergeants were mad at you. I resisted smoking for a long time, but finally gave in on the way to Japan 18 months later.

Alcohol was also extremely cheap and readily available. Beer (3.2% alcohol maximum) cost almost nothing in the PX and harder stuff was easily obtained. Some of the guys did drink a great deal, usually on weekends. Not surprisingly, they tended to hang out together. I drank very little, though, and never came back to the barracks falling-down drunk and nasty. When guys did return that way, they soon learned to get into bed and not bother anyone. The rest of us were very hard on obnoxious drunks. They would either shut up and get into bed, or we would take them to the showers and hold them under ice cold water. They sobered up pretty fast.

There were occasional fights, some alcohol-fueled. We would usually let the participants finish, unless someone was getting beaten up pretty badly—then we would stop it. They did not happen often, though, because we were usually dead tired by evening and eager to sleep when lights went out at 10:00 P.M. We wrestled quite a bit, but it was just for fun, sometimes to blow off a little steam when a couple of guys were mildly irritated with each other. I had wrestled a lot at home with neighbor kids, so I had no trouble holding my own. Two guys would wrestle until one could no longer move. He would then signal and the other would relax his hold and it was all over. It was fun.

Since I could no longer go home on the weekends, I started writing my family fairly often. The first letter we found in my mother's collection, however, was written in late March when the Virginia spring was already much warmer than Indiana's. I don't know if I just didn't write before this time or if some letters were lost. I kind of think Mom wouldn't have thrown any away.

Postmark: March 24, 1944

*Dear Folks,*

*Well, it's stopped raining again and starting to get hot so every-one is changing back to their summer underwear again. They've changed back & forth a dozen times the last month.*

*Jack is here trying to press his pants and shirts. I've been trying to talk him into doing mine too, but as much trouble as he's having with his own I don't think he's going to do it.*

*Mom, you could put a searchlight on the Lincoln Tower* [the tallest building in Fort Wayne at the time; approximately three miles from our house] *and turn it toward our house and read a newspaper in our front yard if nothing obstructed the beam.*

*Well, since our school is over tomorrow I'll tell you exactly what I've been doing the past eight weeks. I've been going to searchlight school for five hours a day and studying Army Administration for 3 hrs per day.*

*See, during our first 8 wks we had general instructions in searchlights. At the end of the 8 wks we had a qualifying test and the ones who got the highest grades got to go to searchlight school for specialized training. Well, I passed that but searchlight school was only 5 hrs a day so I picked clerical administration for the other 3 periods. The reason for 2 schools is that they can train you for two jobs and use you where you're most needed. I liked search-lights swell and am going to try to stay with them.*

*I never did like administrative work anyway. I passed in both schools though. In fact I had 94 average in searchlights. We learned all the little parts and how to set up a whole section which consists of the light, control station, sound locator, and power plant, and learned to take any job in the section in case one of the other guys gets sick. Also, if anything goes wrong, we're supposed to be able to take it apart and fix it.*

*I got another medal today for qualifying on a gunnery exam (machine guns).*

*I guess its settled what we're going to do. We go on bivouac Friday, the 31st and live very comfortably in a foxhole in the hills of Virginia. Then we ship out after the 2 wks.*

*They're going to feed us "K" rations for 3 days out there, so I see where there's going to be some hungry guys unless we can sneak up to the PX if we don't go too far from camp.*
*Bye for now,*
*Love,*
*Stan*

The next letter and many others are addressed to my parents and my younger sister, Eldena. She was named after my mother's sister (she hated the name). I usually just called her Al. Today, she lives in California and goes by the nickname, Paddy, which she likes much better.

Postmark: March 1944
Saturday Afternoon
*Dear Mom, Dad & Eldena,*
*I'm sitting here on my footlocker right now, all dressed up. I just took a shower and I've got on a clean pressed uniform. In fact, I've even got the corporal's shoes on. One pair of mine are in the repair shop getting heels put on and the others are a sad sight. See, this morning we marched 3 miles through some of the worst swamps in Virginia. Some guys went in up to their belt. In fact some guys got stuck in the mud and couldn't hardly get out. We were really sad sacks when we got through and we had to work out there all morning in those wet, muddy clothes. But it wasn't so bad. Anyhow, I didn't have any dry shoes so the corporal gave me a pair of new ones he just got to wear this weekend.*
*This is our last weekend pass from Fort Eustis because we'll be on bivouac next weekend and we'll ship out after that.*
*We're going to town in about an hour so if I have time I'll drop you a line from up there.*
*Bye now,*
*"Huffy"*

My brother, Bob, was in the service long before I enlisted. First he was a paratrooper and transferred to the Air Force. Later, though, Air Force personnel still in pre-flight were transferred back to the infantry. So, Bob fought with the 103rd Infantry Division in Europe. He didn't write nearly as often as I did, and I was constantly concerned about him. Today he lives in Colorado.

Postmark: March 28, 1944
Monday Night
*Dear Mom & Dad & Al,*

*Well, I'll write a letter tonight even if I did talk to you. I'm really worried about Bob. It'll be awfully hard on him if he gets transferred. I'm almost positive he'll get transferred because they're transferring everyone who was in the Ground Forces who haven't started flying yet.*

*I paid for that call, Mom. I don't like to keep calling and reversing the charges. Anyway I've got lots of money.*

*Boy, it makes me mad the way the stinkin' Army works. A guy never knows what he's doing. One minute you might be a commando and the next minute a cook.*

*Our administration school this afternoon asked our hometown newspaper and a bunch of other stuff to have put in the paper saying we graduated. One of our instructors in searchlight school said they (searchlights) were going to do the same thing but I don't know when.*

*I just positively can't wait until Friday. It sure will be fun to lay out there in the woods for 2 weeks.*

*Love,*
*Huff*

# COMBAT 7 RAINING: RAIN, MUD, SNAFUS

AFTER COMPLETING SEARCHLIGHT SCHOOL, WE WENT ON BIVOUAC for two weeks. Out in the field, we lived in the woods and slept in small two-man pup tents or in sleeping bags on the ground. We ran obstacle courses, learned to fire and disassemble various weapons, and participated in several field exercises. In general, our training was boring and we looked forward to completing it. I was still looking for something more satisfying, but I never found it.

Army food was adequate (except in combat), if not exactly tasty. When we went through the chow line, the first server would throw the meat into our mess kits, the next one would drop in some vegetables, the next some fruit, and, finally, someone would scoop in some pudding or dessert. This was usually all mixed together by the time we were able to eat it. It was good to remind yourself that it all ended up in the stomach together anyway.

Conditions were generally miserable, and as a result, the vast majority of the guys looked forward with keen anticipation to only one thing—discharge.

But let the letters speak for themselves.

Postmark: April 1, 1944

Friday, 6:30 P.M.

"Somewhere" ????

*Dear Mother, Dad & Eldena,*

*Well, I'm somewhere but I don't know where. All I know is "it's one hell of a place." I've never been so mad in my life as I was today. Here's what happened.*

*We were very rudely awakened this morning at 4:30. At 6:30 we started marching (loaded to the brim). After marching about ?? miles we finally stopped and they told us to pitch our tents. Well I was O.K. up to that point. We got some boards to lay in the bottom of our tent to soak up the water (it was pouring down rain) and put our tent up and got all fixed. Then we all had to dig foxholes 6 ft. deep. That took us until noon. Then the sad part came. They called us up and said 16 of us had to be moved to the 5th Battalion to operate their searchlights, as they didn't have any searchlight men. Naturally I was picked. So we had to take down our tents, pack all the stuff and they loaded us into a truck. We rode and rode and finally got here. Then we walked a long ways. Then they took 4 of the 16 for A Battery, 4 each for B, C, and D.*

*Well, after all that mess up, I finally got here. We had to pitch our tents, dig another foxhole and just got finished. I'm in a tent with a guy I never saw before 5 hrs ago. In fact, I don't know a soul in this outfit. This is Shorty's outfit but I'll never be able to find him. But all I have to do (I hope) is operate the searchlight for the guys. Then after the bivouac I'll be taken back to my outfit. It's really a screwed up mess.*

*It's cold out here too—and rainy.*

*I don't think my mail ever will find me. I don't even know where I am myself. You may get this and you may not. I hope so. It's almost dark so I'll have to close.*

*Love,*

*Huff*

*WRITE TO MY SAME ADDRESS. They'll have to forward it (I hope).*

ᔆ     ᔆ

Postmark: April 3, 1944
Saturday (I think)
*Dear Mother, Dad & Eldena,*

*Well, I'm OK but very uncomfortable. I thought I'd freeze to death this morning but I didn't. It really gets cold out here at night.*

*I haven't received any mail since I've been out here yet & don't suppose I will, but 2 weeks isn't so long, is it?*

*We have to wash out of our helmets. It's a mess.*

*Well, I better* [sentence left unfinished]

*Well, I'm back again. I was sitting here writing when the Sergeant came over & told me I had to be at the classification building in 10 minutes. So I hopped in a jeep & away I went. I had my final physical up there & they put me in Class A which is perfect, so I'm all ready to ship now. I hope my orders come through quick because I'm sure tired of living like a mole.*

*I had my first good laugh since we got out here today. My tent mate & I were walking along when all of a sudden he wasn't there. Then his head came up. He had fallen into a camouflaged foxhole. I thought he'd broken his leg at first but he didn't.*

*Well, I'll have to close so*
*Bye,*
*"Huffy"*

෴ ෴

Postmark: April 7, 1944
Thursday Night
*Dear Folks,*

*Well, they took all the searchlights in and shipped them to Georgia so they had to find me another job. Now I'm doing intelligence work at the Command Post. Leave it to Huff to find an easy job. I don't know how long it will last, though. I was sent over here as a searchlight specialist and as long as they had searchlights these guys couldn't make me do anything else, but now they can make me do anything and my outfit can't do anything to help me until the bivouac is over and I go back to my regular outfit. But so far these guys have given me a good job (if you can call any job in the Army "good").*

*I got 5 letters tonight. I got one from that lady at the Harvester. She said Johnny Achenbach is the only boy left from our old gang out there, "but she said all the girls ask about me all the time."* AHEM. . .MOST OF THE "GIRLS" ARE OLD WOMEN.

*One week from today this bivouac will be over and I'll be shipped out. I don't have any idea where I'll go but just for the fun of it—I'll guess. I'll say I'm going to the 2nd Army Replacement Depot at Camp Forrest, Tennessee. We'll see how close I come to it.*

*There's an 'alert' tonight so I may have to stay up all night. We're expecting an attack upon the camp by another battery. We had one at 2:00 a.m. last night and I came running out of my tent and fell smack into my own foxhole and it was half full of water. I was really a "sad sack."*

*Well, bye folks—I better get to work. I'll have to keep on the ball or I'm liable to find myself in the kitchen.*

*Bye, Stan*

ᔄ    ᔄ

Postmark: April 10, 1944
Saturday, 2:00 P.M.
*Dear Mother, Dad & Eldena,*
*Well, another week is gone and only 5 more days.*

*If you'll promise not to disown me, I'll tell you something. I've had the same clothes on now for 9 days without taking them off. It can't be helped, though.*

*I wish you could see our tent. I suppose you've seen pictures of an Army pup tent. Well, they're just big enough for a pup, too. And with two big long-legged guys like me & Hohler in here it's slightly crowded. I wake up every morning with my feet sticking out the end. One end doesn't have anything covering it so when it rains we just hang our raincoats up there.*

*Incidentally, I was sorta paid a compliment this afternoon. About 20 minutes ago, I was called to the switchboard, as someone wanted to talk to me. Here's what they wanted: Over in my regular outfit (C-14) the 4th platoon had challenged the 2nd platoon to a game of basketball. And with 60 men to pick 10 players from they asked the sergeant if they could get me to play. So Sarge*

*Bowler called over here and got me off duty and said he would send a jeep over to pick me up if I'd play. Well, you know how I like to play basketball so naturally I was tickled. It starts at 4:00.*

*It's getting cloudy and will probably rain tonight (maybe sooner). That's the trouble with Virginia . . . In 2 hours a sunny day can cloud up, rain, sleet, snow and get sunny again . . .*

*We had a gas attack last night at 12:45 a.m. I had just got in bed from work when someone (guard) started hollering "gas." I had a heck of a time finding my mask and getting it on in the dark. Hohler put his on and went to sleep with it on. You have to lay down in these tents because they're not high enough to even sit up in. So Hohler just struggled into his gas mask and while waiting for the gas to go away he went to sleep . . .*

*Bob will soon be 20 years old won't he? Then he'll be 2 years older than me again.*

*How's the war coming? I haven't seen a paper since we came out here.*

*This bed gets softer every day. I can even get to sleep on it now. I guess I'm just getting used to it. It's not so bad. We've got a comforter and 2 blankets next to the ground. Then 2 blankets and a comforter on top of us.*

*Well, folks, if you don't mind I'd better wash my face and hands and get ready to show these Southerners and Easterners some Midwestern basketball. AHEM!!!*

*Bye now,*
*Stan "Huff"*
*Most everyone down here calls me either "Huff" or "Huffy"!!*

As I neared the end of basic training, I could see that it had been a mistake to go to an anti-aircraft unit. American air power was now controlling the skies over Europe, and more anti-aircraft units were not needed. Instead, infantry was in demand because of heavy casualties in both the European and Pacific Theatres. Rumors were that we would all be sent to the infantry.

I applied for the Army Specialized Training Program (ASTP). Anyone accepted into ASTP would be sent to college for an accelerated two-year program, which would culminate in a bachelor's degree and a commission as an officer.

This was an excellent program, and over 75,000 such students were already studying at various colleges around the country. Unfortunately, someone in Washington decided these kids would make excellent infantry replacements, which were desperately needed. The ASTP program was canceled, and most of the students were sent to infantry units. Only the Army would ask young men to take a scholastic exam and then send the ones with the highest scores to the infantry as cannon fodder. Many ASTP kids were killed or captured.

This is my last letter from Virginia:

Postmark: April 17, 1944
Saturday Afternoon
*Dear Folks,*

*Well, you'll probably talk to me before you read this but as I don't have anything to do I'll scribble a letter to you. I'm going to try to call you tonight.*

*We're restricted to the barracks all day tomorrow so I guess some of us will ship.*

*I really saw a swell show last night. It was "You Can't Ration Love." We get all the shows long before you poor civilians.*

*I'm going to get a new pr of shoes (GI). I turned in my shoes to get the heels fixed but they lost them and are giving me new ones. I also have an extra pair of gloves . . .*

*They say all shipping orders have been changed so none of us know where we're going. But I think it's a pretty good bet that I'll end up in Georgia.*

*We had a big physical training course to cover Friday morning to see what "stage" of physical condition the battery has reached. About 3 or 4 guys fainted and one guy fell and hit his head on a stake and was knocked out. That was when everyone was carrying another guy on his back. He was too exhausted to stand up so when he fell, the guy on his back fell on his head and knocked it against the stake. Here was the course.*

*Run 300 yards in 45 seconds.*
*Run 10 yards, then crawl 10 yards for 200 yards.*
*March 4 miles in 47 minutes with full pack.*

     *Carry a man on your back for 150 yds (running)*
     *15 pull-ups*
     *35 push-ups*
     *The battery commander got exhausted and passed out and had to be carried away on a stretcher. A lot of the guys got real white. That old saying about the Army building you up is a "thing of the past" around here. Personally, I think it wears you down. It really tired me out and everyone else, too.*

     *Well, I'm going to quit as there isn't anything else to talk about. I'll put Bob's picture in. He looks just like he always did. Swell picture.*

     *Bye now,*
     *Stan*

# THE 97TH INFANTRY DIVISION

MY POWERS OF PREDICTION TURNED OUT TO BE PRETTY POOR. Instead of Tennessee or Georgia, May of 1944 found me on a troop train heading for Fort Leonard Wood, Missouri. Those trains were fun, but they were also exhausting. Every seat in every car was full. These weren't Pullmans, so you had to eat, sleep, read, and do anything else right there in your seat. Of course, everyone was in high spirits and there was a lot of fooling around as well as card games and animated arguments. But, there was no privacy or time to yourself either, and sleeping sitting up just never got to be very restful, even if the other guys quieted down for a while.

My new outfit, the 97th Infantry Division, had participated in the Louisiana Maneuvers, which consisted of actual combat conditions for over 250,000 men. Afterwards, the Army sent all of the privates overseas as infantry replacements and kept the officers and NCOs at Wood to train the newly arrived replacements, consisting of mostly ex-ASTP kids and ex-Air Force cadets who hadn't entered flight training yet.

From the train, I went directly to L Company and fell immediately into bed, exhausted. I was feeling quite depressed and alone in the world. My dream of going to college with the ASTP program was shattered. I was now an infantryman, and it appeared I would soon be in combat. For the first time I realized that I had a high probability of not surviving the war. Sleep seemed the only way to forget the situation confronting me.

"FALL OUT FOR REVEILLE!!" ended my escape at 5 o'clock the next morning.

I didn't know one person in the barracks. While I was eating breakfast, I searched the room for a familiar face. There were none. The thought entered my mind: No one here knows me. I think I could disappear today and not even be missed.

The more I thought about it, the more it seemed like a good idea. After breakfast, instead of returning to my barracks, I went directly to the base service club. I didn't know anyone there, either, but the club was full of magazines and books. I spent the entire day reading and writing letters, and occasionally I would buy a chocolate sundae. Just before 5 o'clock, when the rest of the guys would be coming in from the field, I went back to the barracks. A few people looked at me as though they were wondering where I had been all day, but no one said anything. New replacements were arriving daily, so it wasn't too unusual that I wasn't recognized.

The next morning I went to reveille and breakfast, where I decided I would take another day off. Back to the service club I went. That evening, when I returned to the barracks, the platoon sergeant looked at me and it appeared he was going to say something, but he continued on his way, saying nothing. I know he was thinking that he couldn't remember seeing me all day. He had that right, because he hadn't. I decided that maybe I shouldn't push my luck any further. The next day, I went out with my platoon. My little vacation was over.

I soon found out that the infantry was much tougher than my basic training. For two months, we did a lot of physical training, ran obstacle courses, learned hand-to-hand combat, took 25-mile forced marches up and down the Ozark Mountains, lived in the field for weeks at a time, and ran gas warfare training drills.

Sometimes we tied our tent between two trees so we were off the ground because of the large number of copperhead snakes, lizards, and wild boar. One night I was awakened by a herd of wild boar, some grazing right under my makeshift hammock. The training was supposed to prepare us to withstand both the emotional and physical rigors of front-line combat. It succeeded in doing two things—

putting us in superb physical condition and making our lives perfectly miserable.

It seemed that almost everyone had a nickname and I picked up my first ones in Missouri. One day before we were to go on a 25-mile hike with full packs, I got stiff, new combat boots. Instead of taking the usual two weeks to break them in, I wore them on the long march. After a few miles, I knew I was in big trouble. Painful blisters were developing. At about eight miles, I actually started limping. Walking directly behind me, Bob Derosier seemed to take particular pleasure in my anguish and started chanting, "Hippity-hop, hippity-hop." We walked 55 minutes and rested 5 minutes each hour. In our rest period around the 15-mile mark, Bob said, "Hey, Hippy, are you going to make it the rest of the way?" From that time on, some of the guys started calling me "Hippy" or "Hip," and these nicknames stuck until we got to Europe.

Although it was one of the best-trained divisions in the Army, instead of being transferred as a unit, the 97th had had 5,000 soldiers "stripped" from it in 1944. Some were sent to the China-Burma-India Theatre, where they were infantry replacements to Merrill's Marauders, an American unit that fought the Japanese under very difficult conditions in the jungles of Burma. Others were sent to Europe, where many were killed in action. The "stripping" process had a negative effect on strength levels, morale, and military effectiveness; however, morale problems were overcome to a certain extent by the high quality ASTP and Air Corps replacements, even though they were initially angry and depressed at their re-assignments.

I was fortunate to be able to serve with some really great guys in L Company. We were together throughout training in Missouri and California, combat in Europe, and occupation duty in Japan. Len Babcock, Bob Derosier, Warren Hammond, and Bill Hill were all ex-ASTP-ers; George White came from the Air Corps. I also spent a lot of time with Joe Vonksky, Eldon Schlesselman, Bill Nichols, Al Slade, Don Bevelacqua, and others whose names have escaped me after 50-plus years. Bones Bartig was in a different platoon so I didn't know him well at the time, but have enjoyed seeing him regularly at reunions since the war. All of these guys were a joy to know and serve with.

We were able to get away from Army life occasionally by taking weekend passes to St. Louis or Jefferson City. I got a ten-day leave in June and went back to Indiana just as the weather was getting nice. A buddy who worked at the local airport got me some extra gasoline, and I all too briefly became a real party animal as I cruised the house parties at the lakes in my magnificent Ford convertible. It was so great that I hated the idea of going back to camp.

But I had to and I did. As soon as I arrived at 8 P.M., I was told to report for close order drill at 9. I asked the Sergeant why. He explained that a week before someone had a watch stolen from his footlocker, and the orders were that the entire platoon would do two hours of close-order drill every night until someone confessed to taking the watch. I explained that I shouldn't be punished because I wasn't even in camp when the watch was stolen, but that didn't impress anyone. The orders were that everyone would do close-order drill. So, after working all day, I still had to fall out every evening for close-order drill—until the watch finally reappeared and was returned to its owner.

In July, we were sent to California for amphibious training with the Marines. I was happy to escape the Missouri heat. My letters from Fort Leonard Wood show the mood of the day as I struggled to get used to life in a unit that was preparing itself for front-line combat duty.

I am aware that terms like *Jerry, Jap,* and *Kraut* are offensive to many people, and I certainly would not use them today. However, those were the terms (along with others that were worse) most Americans actually used during the war. Of course enemies will denigrate each other. Therefore, rather than falsify the letters by changing them to some more acceptable late-twentieth-century vocabulary, I chose to leave them as they were.

Postmark: April 23, 1944
Saturday Night
*Dear Folks,*

*I just got through taking my red braid (Anti-Aircraft colors) off my overseas cap to put a blue one on for Infantry. I also took my collar insignia for AA off my blouse to put on the crossed rifles for Infantry, so I'll send them home for a souvenir. I sure hated to take them off, but it couldn't be helped.*

*The average age in this outfit is 21 years old, and it's supposed to be a crack division. It was rated first in the Louisiana maneuvers, but half of the division has been sent over to Italy since then. We're the replacements.*

*These infantry packs are about another time as big as AA packs. We're carrying enough clothes and equipment to last 2 weeks, so you can imagine how big it is. It consists of tent, tent poles, blanket, overcoat, toilet articles, towels, washcloths, gas mask, cartridge belt, bayonet, shovel, raincoat, besides mess kit, canteen, etc. The bivouac area is way back in the Ozark Mountains.*

*All these infantry guys are glad we got put here and they really rub it in. So we and the Air Corps guys stick together and try to avoid those guys who have always been in the infantry. I'll close for now. I may not be able to write much in the next 2 weeks, so don't worry.*

*Bye with love, Stan*

*P.S. I'll probably get a furlough in about 4 or 5 weeks. One thing's sure—the longer it takes for them to give me a furlough, the longer it'll be before they can send me overseas.*

*Bye again.*

∽      ∽

Postmark: May 4, 1944
The Ozarks
*Dear Folks,*

*Am O.K. and still out in the Mountains. It has really been rough out here.*

*Cold and rainy. We're going in Saturday (21-mile hike with full pack) and stay Saturday night and come back out Sunday. It's very discouraging.*

*Night before last, I got bit by either a rat or lizard. It really hurt and woke me up. I scared it away, but it was dark and although I could hear it run out of the tent, I couldn't tell whether it was a rat or one of these lizards that are thick around here. My buddy didn't believe me until last night when he got bit in the ear by probably the same thing. He said he raised his head up and it hung right on, but he made it leave go and it ran out the tent. It really scared him. I had to laugh. A guy in a tent near ours said something ate all his candy up last night. I wonder what'll happen tonight.*

*If we fall out of that 21-mile hike Saturday, we'll have KP on Sunday. But I don't think I'll fall out. I never have had to yet.*

*One of my best buddies is a kid from Idaho (a former Air Cadet). He's a pretty swell guy.* [This is the first of many references to George White, who became one of my closest friends. He was injured a few days after we went into combat in Germany, and I didn't see or speak with him again until 1998!]

*Eldena—Mom said you got to drive my (I STILL LIKE TO SAY "MY") Ford after milk. How was it? I'd certainly like to buzz around in it. Did you have any trouble? (Besides forgetting to turn it off.)*

*When I get home on furlough, I'm going to put on my civilian suit and take off my dog tags and pretend like I'm a civilian again and go uptown in it. I'm also going to wear my civilian shoes. I haven't had on anything but these big heavy clodhoppers since I got in the Army.*

*Don't mind me. I'm just talking to fill up space. I better close and wash before dark. I hate to wash, though, because it's so dad-blasted cold.*

*Well, so long and cheerio and all that sort of thing.*

*Love, Stan*

*P.S. You don't have to worry about the war lasting long because we're all so mad at the Japs and Germans that we decided to go over and beat he— out of 'em.*

ᔐ   ᔐ

Postmark: May 13, 1944
Wednesday Night
*Dear Folks,*

*Well, we got back in again. What a time we had out there for 3 days. I made expert again.*

*We killed a copperhead snake about 20 feet from my tent. It almost bit a guy but he was lucky. It would have killed him in a few hours after it bit.*

*I really should be cleaning my rifle and my tent, etc., etc., and etc., but I thought I better write.*

*I got a letter from Bob tonight. He's still disgusted. He said he was broke. Write and ask him if he needs any furlough money. If he does, send him some of mine. If I have any left after my furlough, I'm going to leave it home, but I'll keep it here until I get the furlough because I may need it. I've got over $100 in my pocket.*

*Monday afternoon we fired for 4 hours in a driving rainstorm and quit firing at 7:00 p.m. and ate chow and went up to our tents (wet, tired and disgusted) and cleaned our rifles in that wet, cramped tent, then went to "sleep."*

*It isn't so bad, though. I have to laugh at some of these guys, though. They just can't seem to adjust themselves to this life and it almost drives them crazy. (bivouac)*

*Well, I better close and clean my rifle or I'll be cleaning pots and pans Sunday (maybe I will, anyway).*

*Adios, hasta la vista, adieu and all that there stuff,*
*Stan*
*P.S. We're going to be inspected Sat. by the Undersecretary of State. The big shots decided to come and see me off before my long trip.*

$\backsim$    $\backsim$

Postmark: May 18, 1944
Tuesday
*Dear Folks,*

*Wow is it ever hot here! We went through the infiltration course this morning and the ground was hard as a brick and sharp stone and glass was all over it and they set off smoke screens and land mines until you couldn't see 3 ft. in front of you. We almost smothered before we got through. I was so miserable that the bullets whizzing over my head didn't bother me a bit.*

*I'm still waiting for my furlough, as are all the other fellows. I'll get it some of these days and then—watch out!*

*I had fun in Jeff. City. Had my first date since I've been in Missouri and these Missouri gals are O.K. The girl I was with is a senior in high school. She's only got 2 more weeks, then she's going to a sorority camp (PHI BETA CHI).*

*Al, you know how everyone in Fort Wayne always goes to Lake James for house parties? Well, everyone in Jeff. City goes to the Lake of the Ozarks. I saw pictures of it, and it's really beautiful. Evelyn said there would be 200 girls there. She wants me to come up there as soon as she gets there, but we're going to the field the 28th and may be out there for 6 weeks. I sure hope not. It's too darn hot to be out there. And the snakes, lizards, mosquitoes, flies and everything else are thick. But if we have to, we have to.*

*Well, I better close now and drop kid brother a line.*

*Bye folks, Stan*

*P.S. Mother, I started to call you on Mother's Day but they said the lines through St. Louis were all tied up.*

つ      つ

Postmark: May 29, 1944

Monday Night

*Dear Mom and Dad,*

*Is it raining back thar in Indiana? It is pouring here. We're laying here in our "cozy" pup tent listening to the rain on the tent and watching it seep through. I'll probably be laying in 2" of water by morning.*

*Only 4 more days out here, then we march in. . . . I've lost weight since I got here, though. You could understand that if you could see us sweat during the day. The sweat just rolls off.*

*How was the Spotlight Band? I personally wouldn't know. The lazy MPs, quartermasters, and medics and field artillery got to see it but the dear old 97th Division was laying out here with the snakes, bugs, mosquitoes, and chiggers. That's the Army. Some get everything—others get nothing . . .*

*I wish you could have seen the big land turtle we saw today. I never saw anything like it. These Ozarks have everything imaginable in them.*

*Well, so long for now.*

*Love, Stan*

෨          ෨

Postmark: May 30, 1944

Tuesday Night

With the 97th Division in the foxholes of Missouri

*Dear Mother and Dad:*

*It's still raining and I'm still huddled in our tent. I haven't been here since last night, though. It started raining just after chow.*

*I talked to "THE DOPE" about my furlough again tonight, and they said it would be sometime within the next month, so just look for me when I get there.*

*I heard a pretty good rumor today. Of course, it was only a rumor but a pretty strong one. I heard we were going on 3 months maneuvers in Tennessee about August. That's not the good part, though. They say after the maneuvers are over we will pull into Camp Breckenridge, KY. The 75th Division is there now and they are supposed to come here after their maneuvers. It may be true and it may not.*

*We killed 4 snakes today. One of them was another copperhead. I can't say I'm particularly fond of them.*

*I think I walked a thousand miles and sweated off 3 bucketsful of sweat today. It was really hot. Incidentally, I didn't get any mail today.*

*Well, goodbye for now, Stan*

෨          ෨

Postmark: June 20, 1944

Monday Night

*Dear Mother, Dad and Eldena,*

*Everything is O.K. here (I guess). It's hotter than heck, though. And I got soft on my furlough. The bottoms of my feet are burning like heck from too much walking.*

*I guess our little trip to California is pretty much the real thing. We're supposed to go to a camp 200 miles from San Francisco.*

*We'll be (forced) to live and train with those lowly, uncouth sailors of the Navy, so you can bet there'll be some real battles between the 97th and the gobs. It's going to be tough training, too. (amphibious assault training) The Navy will take us out to a little island about 10 miles out and we will be lowered into landing barges from the troopships and attack and take the island. The training is supposed to last 3 months. I can't wait until we go. We're supposed to leave about the middle of July.*

*All George, Bill Hill and I talked about today were our furloughs. George got engaged. He only had 6 days home.*

*I haven't pulled KP yet. I figured I'd get it today for sure but someone slipped up.*

*When I get to California I'll have traveled from coast to coast. George has a cute cousin who lives in Los Angeles. We're going to pay her a visit. (If we're there long enough.)*

*I always wanted to see California so here's my chance. I'd just as soon stop right there, though, as to go on to those beautiful tropical islands.*

*Huff*

ு    ு

Postmark: June 26, 1944
Saturday Evening
*Dear MA and PA,*

*I guess I better write you now and tell you not to look for any more letters for awhile because we're leaving tomorrow on a 5-day problem and will not be able to write, but you be sure to keep writing anyway.*

*I got a letter from that babe in St. Louis today, and she wants me and 2 buddies (Bill and George, of course) to come to a party at her house. I don't know whether we'll go or not. She's only 16 and that's sorta young. But I guess we'll end up going.*

*A girl from Rochester wrote Bill and wants to bring a girl with her and come down here over the 4th of July, but he told her not to come because we may not be in the barracks then.*

*The girls must be having it tough these days. If a soldier steps outside the camp, they stand there ready to kidnap him. (A slight exaggeration, of course, but it's pretty bad.)*

*It's still hot here. I'll be glad when we take off for California. It gets cool out there at night anyway—I heard.*

*We are going to wear our winter uniform when we leave here so maybe we'll end up in Alaska, but that isn't likely.*

*Bill & I are table waiters today, so we have to clean up the tables tonight. It makes me very unhappy. . . .*

*I better close now and go take a shower. Bye,*
*Love, Stan*

༄      ༄

Postmark: June 30, 1944
Friday
*Dear Folks,*

*Well, I've finally got a little time to write so I'll take advantage of it.*

*We were on a five-day problem about 50 miles from camp way back in the mountains. It was pretty tough. They would only give us 1 pint of water per day and that was not nearly enough. We walked all night all five nights and had platoon tactics during the day. We got about 3 hrs. sleep a night and all we had to eat out there was "C" rations. The chiggers were thick. And you should have seen the wild hogs. They were really thick. One woke me up one morning trying to root under me. It could have been worse.*

*One day Bill and I sneaked off and went to a farmhouse about 1/2 mile away. The only one home was a cute little hillbilly gal about 15. She gave us some cold water, which really helped. We talked to her about 3/4 of an hour. I thought she was going to talk all night. She started explaining about the cream separator and the well and everything else. The well was a funny contraption. It had a long cylindrical bucket that went in a hole and you had to pull it up with a rope. It really was good water. She said if we would have come about an hour sooner she would have given us some milk but they gave all their extra milk to the hogs and they had already given it to them.*

*Those mountains were really beautiful, but it is really tough walking up them all night.*

*After we got in off the problem, we thought we would get the weekend off but George, Bill and I had all pulled Guard Duty tonight and Saturday and probably KP Sunday. It's a great life.*

*I got another big letter from Doris.* [A sweet and pretty young woman I dated and corresponded with during the war. I will always be indebted to the friends who were so faithful in writing to me. Letters and boxes of cookies and candy, especially from girls, was a great morale booster for a soldier. I dated several hometown girls while I was on leave, though no one seriously until I met my future wife, Alda, a year after my military discharge.] *I sometimes think she's never going to run down. The first was 7 pages and the next was 6-1/2 . . .*

*Bill got a letter from those 2 girls in Rochester. They said they were coming Sat. night. He called and told them not to come because he wouldn't be able to see them anyway.*

*Well, folks, I better close now so goodbye for now.*

*Love, Stan*

ᔕ ᔕ


Postmark: July 7, 1944

Thursday Evening

*Dear Folks,*

*I can finally give you a little information. But remember—you don't know anything about it. We're leaving Tuesday for San Luis Obispo, California, for amphibious training. I'll be glad to get out of here. I don't see how it could be much worse there. I never saw such hot weather in my life. After this war is over—I won't say anything about good old Indiana weather.*

*George and I went down to bowl, but there was too big a crowd.*

*From coast to coast in 8 months. How about that?*

*Hey—tell that big, rugged infantryman brother of mine to write me just one or two little bitty lines sometime—will you? I haven't heard from him since I got back from furlough and I've written him 2 or 3 times. He can't tell me he's just absolutely too busy because I do the same thing he does and I manage to find time to write.*

*Incidentally, Eldena, I thought you said you were going to write me when you were at the lake. You wrote Aunt Ruth. It seems like I'm just a poor little orphan. No one will write to me. Don't you feel sorry for me. I didn't even get a letter from Mom today. If it wasn't for Doris, Pat and that babe in St. Louis, I wouldn't get any mail.*

*Bill is on KP today. He dished out the dessert tonight and I got more dessert (chocolate pudding) than anyone else in the company. George was on the day before and then he gave me double help-ings. It's about my time. I haven't had KP since I came back from furlough. But I had table waiter once.*

*Here's an example of the 97th Division. They don't want us to sit down for 4 days just looking at scenery so they're going to make us have classes on the train. Besides that, they are going to stop in Kansas, New Mexico and Yuma, Arizona for calisthenics. How do you like that stuff? My first look at a cactus—and desert.*

*There are 2 big beaches near this camp so we can at least go swimming.*

*Well, folks, I'll have to close now so write but don't write after Saturday as I won't get them.*

*Love, Stan*

ᔇ     ᔇ

Postmark: July 9, 1944
Sunday
*Dear Folks,*

*Bill, George and I have been running around all over camp and as there is nothing to do we decided to come here to the ser-vice club and write a letter or two (the stationery is free). This will be my last letter from MISSOURI.*

*Last night, Bill and I went to Lebanon. There wasn't much going on there, although there was a carnival going on. Bill and I had our fortune told. You don't have to worry about me in this war because she said I was going to live to be 81 yrs. old (ha, ha).*

*We have our barracks bags all packed and everything is ready to go. We scrubbed the barracks this morning and boarded them up and are going to sleep outside on the ground tonight and tomorrow night so as to not get them dirty.*

*We are going to take the southern route to California. That is through Kansas, Oklahoma, Texas, New Mexico, Arizona and California. San Luis Obispo is in between Los Angeles and San Francisco so we can make either of them on a weekend pass.*

*We are supposed to have an hour of swimming every day, but it won't be just regular swimming. It will be with packs on our back, etc.*

*It certainly is hot here today. This sure is a screwy state. It hasn't rained for weeks here. They say it is like this every summer. I feel sorry for these poor hillbillys.*

*Well, I guess I better close this and go down stairs and get a luscious banana split. Or should I get a chocolate malted? They're only 15 cents and you know sundaes are a dime . . . .*

*Well, so long until you hear from California.*

*Bye,*

*Love, Stan*

# Fun in the Sun—
# Camp San Luis Obispo

O̲n̲ ̲J̲u̲l̲y̲ ̲1̲1̲,̲ ̲1̲9̲4̲4̲ ̲w̲e̲ ̲a̲g̲a̲i̲n̲ ̲p̲i̲l̲e̲d̲ ̲i̲n̲t̲o̲ ̲a̲ ̲t̲r̲o̲o̲p̲ ̲t̲r̲a̲i̲n̲—t̲h̲i̲s̲ time bound for California—land of palm trees, beautiful white beaches, and movie stars. At least that is what we expected—and we were not disappointed. The Missouri heat was stifling and the cars were not air-conditioned. Luckily, we could open the windows and hang out for a breath of air. When the train finally started moving it felt better than any cooling system we could imagine. Surprisingly to us, when we hit the desert, it got so cool at night that we had to close the windows. Missouri was behind us for good!

We were to be trained for initial beach landings in the Pacific. We would learn to climb down large cargo nets into small landing craft, which would disgorge us on the invasion beach to the accompaniment of entrenched enemy fire and our own naval guns. So, there I was, an eighteen-year-old Indiana boy, in that paradise of mountains, beaches, and ocean, preparing for the grisly prospect of mixing my blood with the surf on some obscure island.

The guys in L Company came from all over the country, and many varied backgrounds. My two best friends came from Idaho and upper New York State. At Camp San Luis Obispo, we lived in five-man huts, so we became well acquainted with at least four guys. Our hut, or L Company as a whole for that matter, could have come right out of any of the popular war movies. There was a guy from

Stan with buddy George White at Camp San Luis
Obispo, California, 1944.

"Joisy;" a Jew; a Mormon from Utah; an older, more mature man;
and, of course, the kid from the Midwest—me. And—just like the
movie characters—we tended to stereotype each other. But we did
so out of innocence and a desire to have fun, never with malice.

Marshak was the colorful character from New Jersey. He had a
heavy "Joisy" accent, which none of us had ever heard before and
which made his quips sound even funnier. He could make you
laugh at anything and he always had a little different, humorous
slant on whatever was going on. We called him "the mad Russian"
because of his name and his antics. We were in the same squad for
about two years, but he was not a close friend and I never saw him
again after the War.

Friedman was the Jewish kid from New York. The guys were
constantly teasing him about what the Germans would do to him if
he got captured. He never found out if the guys were right because

he didn't get captured. He was a big tough guy—quite capable of taking care of himself. (One time we captured about a dozen German soldiers. With Friedman prominently displayed, a fellow told the prisoners, in rather broken and garbled German, that they were unlucky enough to have been captured by the 97th Division, which was made up entirely of New York Jews. A rustle went through the captives as they looked around nervously, not quite certain if they had heard correctly. He then told the Germans that they would be taken to the rear by one of the all-Jewish platoons. He concluded by warning them to be careful, because prisoners sent to the rear seemed to be having a lot of mysterious accidents. The Germans, who looked glum anyway, were clearly stunned by their unexpected ill fortune as they left for a rear echelon POW camp under heavy guard. Nothing actually happened to them, but they were definitely frightened as they left our company area. We were barely able to keep straight faces until they got out of sight—and earshot.)

Although his name sounded like he came right out of northeast Indiana with me, Liechty was a Mormon from Utah. Of course, we didn't know any more about Mormonism than we did about Judaism, so we went for the stereotype. We constantly kidded him about how many wives he had. Liechty, however, didn't think this was funny at all. He was married, but I always assumed it was to one wife. Despite his irritation at our ribbing, he was always a nice kid who got along with everyone.

Number five in the hut was a Pennsylvanian. Hovis was a little older than the rest of us and was quite shy. He was also extremely religious. Regularly each night, after lights out, he would get out of bed, kneel beside his bunk and commence praying out loud. Although all of us heard him, to my knowledge no one ever mentioned it to him. There was an unspoken willingness to accept individual preferences and eccentricities.

This was my first trip to California, and I loved the beautiful beaches, the mountains, and the warm climate. Also, celebrities were eager to entertain the troops. Since we were close to Hollywood we saw big name entertainers of the early 1940s, such as Bob Hope and Dorothy Lamour.

We were able to get to Los Angeles nearly every weekend. We enjoyed going to the Hollywood Canteen, where the big bands played for the troops, and we could go to dances and get free food and lodging at USOs and at some of the high schools where they set up cots in the gyms for us.

At these places there were plenty of girls to dance with, but I never developed a relationship with any of them, partly because we moved around so much. We were in three camps in five months and also spent a lot of time at sea practicing amphibious landings. But it was also because girlfriends at home were writing to me, and, anyway, I was a little suspicious of the girls who spent so much time at the USOs entertaining the troops.

One day at the Hollywood Canteen a popular radio personality of that era came to our table and interviewed my buddy, Bill Hill. Back in Fort Wayne, Mom happened to be listening and she recognized his name and knew he was one of my closest buddies. She was hoping it wasn't just someone else with the same name, when the interviewer asked me my name and outfit. Mom was so surprised and happy that she just kind of shrieked. This was her boy on national radio. What incredible luck!

The MC asked where I was from. "Fort Wayne, Indiana," I said quite proudly.

"Tell me about Fort Wayne," he said.

"We don't have mountains. We don't have palm trees. We don't have ocean beaches; but we do have lots of humidity in the summer and extreme cold in the winter, and it is the most wonderful place in the world. I can't wait to get back there again," I said enthusiastically. "I have a wonderful family there waiting for me to return, and we have the most beautiful girls in the world."

He talked to me several minutes more and Mom couldn't believe her ears. The second I was off the air she started getting phone calls from both friends and strangers who had heard the interview. It seemed that all of Fort Wayne had been tuned in.

Although we had no cars, on a weekend pass we could travel anyplace in California almost as easily as if we had one. All we had to do was go to the base entrance and hitchhike. We would usually get picked up by one of the first few cars that came along. Just like the entertainers, average people wanted to do whatever they could for the troops. During the war, they were never afraid to pick up servicemen. Even older women traveling alone would pick up three soldiers and take them to Los Angeles without fear of being harmed. We really appreciated it, too. We got a chance to meet a lot of interesting, nice people who often reminded us of folks back home. It was as if all Americans—civilians and soldiers—were in this thing together.

The very difficult training was also dangerous; we suffered casualties while engaging in very realistic combat training, but you wouldn't be able to tell it from these letters, although there is certainly a note of disenchantment creeping in.

> Postmark: July 16, 1944
> Saturday
> *Dear Mother, Dad and Eldena,*
> *We finally got here after 5 days and 4 nights on the train. We went about 600 miles out of the way. I'll tell you the cities that we went through and you can trace our trip. We went through Springfield, Missouri, Oklahoma City, Oklahoma, Austin, Texas, San Antonio, Texas, El Paso, Texas, New Mexico, Tucson, Arizona, Phoenix, Arizona, Yuma, Arizona, Los Angeles, and here. We could see over into Mexico. . . .*
> *As for California—AHEM.*
> *The climate is swell. We wear our winter uniforms, and the state is very pretty —(palm trees, etc.) but this camp isn't so swell. And this amphibious training is going to be the roughest thing I ever went through.*
> *There are sailors and Marines on this same camp. The sailors say they thank their lucky stars that they got the Navy after seeing the soldiers and Marines training.*
> *We will be going to sea before very long and will be to sea for about a month training. Then we will come back to Obispo for more training or else take the rest overseas.*
> *I got your letter when I got here and was never more happy to see anything as that letter. I am really one heck of a long ways from dear old Fort Wayne.*

*Coming across the Arizona desert, I got something in my eye and I went to the dispensary when I got here and the doc worked for about a half hour and said he thought he had it out but he put a patch over my one eye and told me to come back in the morning to be sure. It keeps watering all the time and still hurts but will probably be OK tomorrow. I'm going to bed early tonight. It is awfully hard to see out of one eye. I look like a pirate with my patch. We sleep in 5-man huts out here.*

*I don't mind saying that I'm plenty disgusted but I always am when I move, so I'll be OK in a day or two. We passed right by Camp Swift, Texas. It is really hot there, but Austin is a beautiful city (lot of cute girls, too). Phoenix, Arizona is sure a swell place. It sets in a place with big mountains all around it.*

*Did you get my card from Phoenix? I got a porter to put it under his hat and mail it. We weren't supposed to mail any. I also wrote Eldena one but I think the Captain took it away from the girl I gave it to. Maybe he didn't, though. Tell me if you got it.*

*That trip out here was something I'll never forget. I wish you could see El Paso, Texas. It's full of Mexicans and about the wildest town I've seen outside of Norfolk. I'll tell you about it when I get home. I'll be home soon, too. The Germans are practically licked and it won't take us long to lick the Japs. (I keep telling myself.)*

*There is a beautiful beach a few miles from here.*

*I saw some blimps today. The first ones I ever saw. Funny-looking creatures.*

*We saw jack rabbits on the desert as big as medium dogs.*

*California is full of palm trees and they sure are pretty. I'll get a bunch of postcards of this place tomorrow and send them to you. Right now, I'm going to quit and go to bed so you be sure to write me every day because I'm very much in the mood for mail.*

*Bye,*
*All my love, Stan*

ဢ     ဢ

Postmark: July 16, 1944
Sunday
*Dear Mother & Dad,*
*'Tis Sunday morning and a nice peaceful breeze is blowing in*

*off the Pacific. Salt air smells swell. The weather out here is per-*
*fect so far except that the sun doesn't get up until about noon and*
*goes down at about 6:00 PM. Last night I slept with 2 wool blan-*
*kets over me and was just right. But it gets pretty warm in the day.*
*There are absolutely no flies or mosquitoes out here.*

*Pismo Beach is just a few miles from here and is supposed to be*
*a swell place. It has one of the largest beaches in the world and a*
*big dance hall and skating rink.*

*My eye is OK today. I slept for 11 hours last night. There are*
*mountains all around this camp and much bigger than the*
*Ozarks.*

*The girls in California are cute but are hard to get acquainted*
*with (so the other guys say). Of course, they haven't seen me yet,*
*though, ahem.*

*Maybe you think I've changed quite a bit because I used to talk*
*of wanting to go overseas and fight. Well—that was when I was*
*too innocent of world affairs to know what I was talking about.*
*I'll go when they send me but I can't say I'll be happy about it. I've*
*seen enough already. I'm lucky though, because I've already had 8*
*months of training and will get a couple more. That's more than*
*a lot of guys get.*

*One good thing I've noticed about California is the abundance*
*of fresh fruit. I think we've had an orange every meal since I got*
*here. And they are really good.*

*We saw cactus plants in Arizona about 25 feet tall.* I saw the
*place where Bob Putt* [see "Farewell for Fifty Years" for the story
of my lifelong friend] *was stationed at Yuma, Arizona and it*
*was right on the desert and hot as heck. I don't see why people live*
*in a place like that desert. It is so hot you can't hardly stand it. But*
*there are people living there. Personally—I'm ready to settle down*
*in Indiana. I'll have to admit that this weather is much better*
*than in Indiana, though.*

*Santa Barbara is a nice city. It is about 100 miles from here.*
*We stopped there awhile coming here. It is where a lot of big shots*
*and movie stars have summer homes.*

*We brought Rusty, our little dog, from Va. with us. He has gone*
*from coast to coast now. He seems to like California just fine but*
*got sick on the train. . . .*

*Well, I better close now and write Bob a letter.*
*Bye now, Stan*

ᔕ     ᔕ

Postmark: July 17, 1944
Monday, Station Hospital
*Dear Mom & Dad,*

*Now listen—don't get excited just because you see "Station Hospital" up there. I'm not sick. I've just got a skin rash caused by the change of climate. It is just red pimples on my chest. They thought it was measles, at first, but it is pityriasis rosea.*

*Boy, it is really swell here. Nice soft beds, swell food, movies at night. Besides that, a buddy of mine from Washington, DC is in the next room.*

*Just keep on writing to my regular address because I won't be here long.*

*I was just informed that my chow will be served in bed in a few minutes (ahem).*

*George and Bill are still in our company. Bill put in his application for Officers Candidate School but he said he didn't expect to make it. If I was 3 months older I would put my application in, too. (You have to be 19.)*

*Well, I fell asleep last night before I finished this letter so I'll finish it now.*

*There isn't much to say as nothing has happened.*

*But I found out one thing. I don't like hospitals as well as I thought I would. I remember when Bob wanted out and I couldn't understand why he wouldn't rather lay in bed than work but I understand it now. These hospitals give me the creeps. An army hospital and a civilian hospital are two different things.*

*Bye with love, Stan*

ᔕ     ᔕ

Postmark: July 24, 1944
Saturday Evening, Station Hospital
*Dear Folks,*

*Well, a good bit has happened today to talk about so maybe I can make this a few pages long anyway.*

*First of all, I'm still here as you probably noticed, but I don't know why. My pityriasis rosea has almost cleared up except for a couple little pimples and they won't let me go until it's all cleared up.*

*George and Bill came up to see me this afternoon and brought me 9 things. 8 of them were letters and the 9th was a slip of paper showing that I had been promoted to a Pfc. Maybe I should have come to the hospital long ago and maybe I'd have been a general by now. They've really been having it rough back at the company according to Bill & George. They have to start working an hour earlier and quit later.*

*Bill and George are both brown as Indians from this California sun. This sun isn't really bright but it burns or tans you easily.*

*I was sure glad to get my mail. I hadn't had any since I got here. George & Bill are both swell guys and no one could ask for better buddies to fight beside. Bill turned my clothes in (the ones that were worn out) for new ones Wed. when they had salvage day. He also turned in my name as needing a bayonet as I broke mine back at Leonard Wood.*

*Our outfit is really about ready for its little journey across the seas. But we probably won't see action for awhile. I think Germany is on its last legs. I sure hope so. I think if I ever get home I'll never gripe about anything again.*

*Guess what! I was sitting here looking out the window today when I saw 3 soldiers walking out in front. One of them was too short to be anyone but one guy—Shorty. And it was. I opened the window & hollered at him and he came running up and we talked for about 30 minutes. He said he'd come over tomorrow and see me. He's still a medic. Lucky guy.*

*Well, I better close now so keep writing every day.*
*Love, Stan*

            ↄ     ↄ

Postmark: July 24, 1944
Monday, Station Hospital
*Dear folks,*
*Everything here is OK and by the sound of the radio, it's not so*

bad in Europe, either. Those Russians are either so darn dumb that they don't know when they're tired or else just awfully good fighters. As you see, I'm still in the hospital and feeling fine. The food here is really good.

I've still got a few pimples under my arms yet. I hope they stay there a couple of days yet. I'm beginning to like this place. But I can just see myself the first day back in Co. L. when we have physical training, close order drill, bayonet practice, squad & platoon tactics, etc. I'll really be tired the first night or two, but it won't take long to get back in my "old form" (ahem).

Got a letter from Roy Peters telling me of Homer's death in the invasion of Saipan [see "War and Its Myths"]. Boy, he sure got a dirty deal. You know, he never even had a furlough.

Keith Harter also got a rotten deal. He went in the Army just a little before I did. I remember talking to him just before he left. We were at a football game. He was on one of my intramural teams when we were juniors at North Side and also in my homeroom. Miss Huffman told me he was in Italy when I was home on furlough (wonderful furlough). She'll take it hard when she hears about it.

I suppose George & Bill will be up to see me tonight. Bill said, "Isn't there some way you could give that [pityriasis rosea] to me so I could come in with you?" He & George acted like little kids when they came Saturday. Both tried to tell me all the things that have happened at once.

Boy, oh boy! Oh boy! You should see my nurse. Every time she takes my pulse my heart must jump a mile. She must be one of the California movie stars. But it'll have to end right here.

Bye,

Love, Stan

 train    train

Postmark: August 3, 1944

Tuesday

Dear folks,

Another day—another dollar (almost).

I went over and got some Mentholatum for my face and neck. It sure feels good. I've really got a sunburn but it's starting to turn to tan. It doesn't hurt much. I just got the Mentholatum to keep it from getting so bad. You know—a stitch in time saves nine. I never had so much of a sunburn before in my life. Everyone else is in the same fix only some of the guys with light complexions are a lot worse off. Mine doesn't really hurt but it's just annoying.

After a while here we'll really be in good physical condition. We've got a lot scheduled and we don't sweat away our energy like we did in Missouri. This is swell weather. Only it gets pretty cold at night. (We have to have a fire every evening in the stove.) And I sleep under 3 blankets. We don't have any sheets here.

George is still laid up. They've got him in an old shack across the road. The hospital is all filled up with that poison or whatever it is and they didn't have any more beds. We have a 25-mile hike every week here. Our schedule for today was:

Articles of War – 1 HR
Hand grenade range – 2 HRS
Obstacle course (twice) – 2 HRS
First aid & Field Sanitation – 1/2 HR
Bayonet course – 1 HR
Extended order drill – 1 1/2 HR
PT (physical training) – 1 HR
PRETTY DARN ROUGH!!

I've got guard duty tomorrow night. I'll be a man if I stay around this stinkin outfit long.

I got a letter from Sally today. She sent me one of those invitations to Eldena's & her birthday party. Guess I'll come. HA

They are going to give the expert infantryman test in a couple of weeks and I'm going to try for it. It's really tough but if I pass it I'll get the expert infantrymen badge and $5 extra a month.

I mailed a bond home today. Tell me when you get it.

Well, I'll close for tonight.

Love, Stan

ᔕ          ᔕ

Postmark: August 9, 1944
Tuesday Evening
*Dear Folks,*

*My first day with the Marines. And what a day. I thought I had a good deal but I'm beginning to wonder. Marine officers were teaching us and they tried to make it rough as heck just because we were Army men. But the Marines certainly aren't as tough as people think.*

*We were practicing coming off the ships into LCVPs (Landing Craft for Vehicles & Personnel). They are those small landing boats. The training isn't so bad. It's pretty interesting, in fact. Tomorrow we go out into the Ocean and practice coming down with the boat swaying and the ropes all wet.*

*I think after my first day with Marines that the infantry is as tough as any Marine. In fact, one of our S/Sgts got in a fight with a Marine Sunday and beat the heck out of him.*

*Jimmy Roosevelt* [son of President Franklin Roosevelt] *(Stinkin' Marine) was there and a bunch just back from Saipan were also there.*

*Guess what! Kay Kyser, Phil Harris, and a bunch of other jokers are coming here Aug. 16.*

*Got 2 letters from Mom today, 1 from Dad & 1 from Stonebreaker.*

*I wish you could see me now. I never was so dark in the face in my life before. This sun is ideal if you want a suntan and it reflects on the Ocean and in no time you're either burned up or tanned. My face finally decided to tan . . .*

*I guess rumor has it that they finally caught up with "Hangman Himmler." I wish they'd hurry and kill off the whole bunch so I can come home.*

*We sure have fun out there with Soldiers, Sailors & Marines all on the same ship. We've been getting along pretty good so far.*

*Is Bob there yet? If you are, Bob, I hope you're having fun. I know you are, though. I could have fun at home if I did nothing but sit in the front room and rock.*

*Well, guess I'll close now.*
*Love, Stan "The Sailormarine"*

 formats∽ ∽

Postmark: August 14, 1944
Saturday
*Dear folks,*

*Another stinkin' week gone. But this week wasn't bad. We had fun running around in those LCVPs. Boy, they'll really go. You know we've been attacking small islands off the coast and just as we get almost to the beach of one of those islands the Navy man driving the LCVP gives her all it's got and when it hits the beach it really stops in a hurry. Then the front ramp comes down and we come barrelin' out. Then the stinkin' Navy gets out of there.*

*You can imagine how brown I am after running around on that ocean all week. I look more like a Cherokee Indian than Stan Huff.*

*I don't guess I'll go anywhere this weekend. I've got a pass & may go over to Pismo for a swim tomorrow, but I'm just going to a show here in camp tonight.*

*Hey, wouldn't it be the cat's meow if I could get a furlough in October and maybe be home when Germany gives up? I like to think about a furlough in October even though it is but a very remote possibility. Our amphibious training will be over in mid-September and it's hard telling what'll happen.*

*I suppose Bob's home this very minute. I can just see you all setting down to eat supper. Sure would like to see Bob now. Remember when he used to be able to beat the heck out of me. Well........ PROBABLY STILL COULD!!*

*Did I ever tell you we've got a palm tree outside our hut? It's pretty. I like these 5-man huts. In our hut, one guy is in the hospital and our corporal went to the Paratroops so there's only 2 others & me in this hut. Right now one's on pass and the other is asleep so I've got the place all to myself. George, Bill & I just got back from the show about 15 minutes ago. It's about 10:00 PM.*

*I've got a swell little fire going in our oil heater so it's pretty warm in here now. But it's pretty cold outside this time of night. I sleep with 3 wool blankets over me.*

*Well, I'm going to go to sleep as it's getting late.*

*Love, Stan*

෨     ෨

Postmark: August 16, 1944
Tuesday Night
*Dear Folks,*

*I guess I better take a little time & write a little bit. I've been so busy lately I haven't had much time. I have to go on a night problem at 9:00 PM tonight so I'll write now.*

*That big Kay Kyser show with Phil Harris, The King Sisters, etc. is going to be here tomorrow night. It should be pretty good.*

*I got a good letter from Sieling yesterday. Also one from Stonebreaker, one from Sally, and one from Clark. I owe about a million letters.*

*RESTRICTED INFORMATION: After our training is over (Oct. 8) we'll either get furloughs or go right on over, but it's certain we'll be overseas by Dec. 1. We were issued all new rubber clothes today and rubber barracks bags. Also a rubber cover for our weapons.*

*We are going to be attached to the 5th Marine Division after we get overseas and form a combat team. Half Marines and half Infantry. The 5th Marines are in Hawaii now but some of them moved to Saipan so when we leave the States we'll go either to Hawaii or directly to Saipan for 6 to 8 weeks jungle training— then we'll be ready for combat.*

*George & I were uptown Sunday and got some of those cheap pictures taken together. These are even cheaper than the others and aren't much good but you can at least tell what George looks like.*

*Well, I guess I'll close for now.*
*Love, Stan*

ॐ    ॐ

Postmark: August 17, 1944
Wednesday Night
*Dear folks,*

*Boy, oh boy! I can't begin to tell you about the fun we had tonight. I was sitting in the 2nd row and it was about the best 2 hrs. of entertainment I ever had. I sure hope you heard it. Phil Harris really gave the 97th a good bit of publicity.*

*There were 10,000 soldiers turned down at the gate. I would have been way back at the back of the field house but Huber (that*

*Long girl's boyfriend) is a Sgt. in the MP's and he took me &*
*White around to the back and took us in and put us in the 2nd*
*row. What a deal.*

*Tell me if you heard it.*

*Phil is a pretty good-looking guy with that usual suntan that*
*all Californians have and the classy sport coat he had on. And you*
*should see the King sisters. And Ish Kibbible* [a popular come-
dian] *is a sad looking sack.*

*Well, it's late so I guess I better go to bed, but I can honestly say*
*this has been the most entertaining day of my military career.*

*Bye, Love, Huff*

*They gave me 2 packages of Luckies and I could have gotten*
*10 more if I would have wanted them. Classy band, too!!*

ᔕ    ᔕ

Postmark: August 20, 1944
Sunday
*Dear folks,*

*Another week gone by. The weeks seem to go by pretty fast but*
*we don't seem to be accomplishing anything. Germany is still*
*plenty tough and the Japs tougher.*

*Well, things around here have sorta settled down a little now.*
*No one really knows what the score is. But we are leaving this*
*camp a week from tomorrow for Camp Callan. At Camp Callan*
*we are supposed to get some replacements from IRTC's. IRTC's are*
*where they give them 13 wks. basic—then bingo like Bruick. I feel*
*sorry for those guys who have to come to this outfit with only 13*
*wks. training.*

*The division was issued our new infantry combat shoes last*
*week. You remember me talking about them. They look like para-*
*troop boots only they buckle instead of lace. The supply Sgt. still*
*has them but he'll probably issue them out next week.*

*There was a dance at the service club last night but there were*
*about 12 old bags to 150 soldiers. I left right away. They weren't*
*even cute. I might be hard up but not that hard up.*

*Well, I guess I'll close & read the paper.*

*Bye, Stan*

# SAN DIEGO 10 INTERLUDE—
# CAMP CALLAN

AFTER SIX WEEKS IN SAN LUIS OBISPO, WE TOOK ANOTHER TRAIN RIDE, this time to Camp Callan near San Diego. The climate was as close to perfect as any I had ever seen—warm with low humidity during the day and pleasantly cool at night. The sky, the ocean, and the beaches (even when we were "attacking" them) were beautiful. San Diego itself was a sleepy Navy town with wide palm-lined boulevards, Spanish architecture, and manicured public parks.

We made amphibious landings under battle conditions on both San Clemente Island and San Nicholas Island. We also engaged in realistic amphibious training at both Camps Callan and Pendleton. Because of the intensity of this training, I was not able to write very often.

> Postmark: August 29, 1944
> Tuesday, Camp Callan
> *Dear folks,*
> *Well, we got here today and everything is still all screwed up but the camp is swell. Nice barracks, beautiful service club, swell PX and only 11 miles from San Diego and 100 miles from Los Angeles. We're only about 35 miles from Mexico and I'm going to try to see a bullfight before I leave. We'll only be here about 6 weeks. On the train coming up here was the full combat team.*

Al and Bill, L Company buddies, at the San Diego Zoo, 1944.

*Infantrymen, Sailors, Air Corps and Marines. We are going to join the 5th Marines when we get through. Boy, we laughed at those poor sailors till we were sick. The day before we left we had to eat in the field out of mess kits. That was all new to them & they had a heck of a mess. One of them was sitting there with his food full of sand and ants crawling all over him and he said, "Oh, if my mother would see me now she never would stop crying." He said it so funny and was such a screwy looking guy anyway that he had everyone laughing.*

*Well, it's time for lights out so I'd better quit for now.*

*Love, Stan*

      ᔕ     ᔕ

Postmark: August 30, 1944
Thursday
*Dear folks,*

*Well, the situation is still normal—all screwed up. I'll try to tell you a little of what's happened in the past few days.*

*I'm not with Co. "L" anymore, although my mail will still be addressed to it. My mail has to go to San Luis Obispo, then down here to Co. "L," then over here so it's really screwed up.*

*I told you before that I'm on the Shore Party Team. The Shore Party Team is the men who land first to get the beach cleared up and ready for the main body of troops. The Shore Party is made up of Infantrymen, Engineers, a few MPs, some Sailors, and Marines. Each has its special job. The Marines & Infantry chase the enemy back away from the beach and hold them back. The engineers build roads, etc. on the beach to move supplies across, the Sailors clear the water of all obstructions, and the MPs who come in with the main body of troops keep them moving to the front. All of us in the Shore Party are living together. Sailors, Engineers, MPs and everything else live in our barracks.*

*I saw Fred Huber yesterday. He's an MP, you know, and he sleeps just two barracks from here! We were supposed to come down here by truck but at the last minute they changed it and we came by train.*

*Sgt. Nichols, Slade & I are going to San Diego tonight. Nichols is my squad leader. Swell guy. He keeps me off of details. Every time someone puts me on something he comes and gets me off. He's only 20 yrs. old and real good looking.*

*Bill & George aren't in the Shore Party. They both tried to get in so we could be together when we went into combat but they couldn't get in.*

*Boy, oranges sure are thick around here. I ate 4 of them yesterday afternoon and we can get them anytime we want them from the mess hall.*

*Slade is the guy who was in the hospital when I was. He sleeps right beside me here.*

*Well, I'll close for now.*

෨    ෨

Postmark: September 22, 1944

Thursday

*Dear folks,*

*We went swimming today in the Del Mar Hotel pool. It is a big resort hotel used now only by military personnel, but it used to be a really ritzy place. We were practicing jumping off a big 15-foot diving board like we would have to jump off a sinking ship.*

*We're going aboard an LC1 next Tuesday and stay at sea a couple days, then go aboard the transport for the 10 days. They say we won't come back to this camp at the end of the 10-day cruise. They are going to leave us off at the Marine base at Camp Pendleton. We're going to stay with the Marines a couple days, then move on up to Camp Cooke. At Camp Cooke, we're supposed to get a month of tank & infantry co-ordination training.*

*So you see I'll be pretty busy starting next week, so my letters will start dropping off in a few days and you won't hear from me at all for 10 or 12 days, but don't worry cause I'll be OK.*

*Well, we have to get up at 4:00 tomorrow so I better go to sleep.*

*Bye, Stan*

# CAMP COOKE

11

OUR SIX-WEEK AMPHIBIOUS TRAINING ENDED WITH YET ANOTHER transfer, this time to Camp Cooke, near Santa Maria, California. There we concentrated on combined armor and infantry maneuvers. This was the first time we had worked extensively with tanks. Several soldiers were killed during this training phase, but my letters sound almost blasé as they report it. I think that is how we protected ourselves from both fear and morbid thoughts.

> Postmark: Monday, October 16, 1944
> Camp Cooke, California
> *Dear folks,*
> *I was going up to the Service Club and write letters and get a few super-deluxe sundaes but we're restricted tonight. We have to stay here and sign the Pay Roll and also get our new issue of Infantry boots. There's going to be a foot specialist here to examine our feet and give us a lecture on how to take care of our feet in combat, then we'll get the boots. . . .*
> *We had a field problem today attacking a fortified pillbox like the Japs use. We really fired the ammunition. First they peppered it with mortar shells, then we moved in and slammed a few bazooka rockets & rifle grenades into it. Then one guy snuck around the flank and threw a phosphorus grenade at it which made a smoke screen. Under cover of the smoke screen we moved up close and gave it a few doses with a flamethrower and auto-*

*matic rifles. By that time anything in it would have been slightly dead.*

*Dad I'm sending that carton of cigarettes tomorrow. I told them to put in a couple Phillip Morris's because I didn't know what you're smoking now.*

*I'll tell you something. I doubt if you'll believe it but this is the honest truth. I DON'T SMOKE. I've started it once or twice but hate it. I haven't smoked a cigarette for months.*

*Have you heard from Bob lately? Let me know every time you hear from him. It takes so long for a letter to get way out here. I know he'll be O.K. but I just like to know how he likes those French gals.*

*I saw in this morning's paper where there's a big naval battle going on. It's about time they made those lazy sailors do something.*

*You should have seen the big rattlesnake a guy killed today. It had 7 rattles on it.*

*I talked to an Italian prisoner yesterday who used to be an American prisoner and now he's in the American Army. He's got ITALY written on his cap and I could hardly understand him.*

*Bye til tomorrow.*

*Love, Stan*

ب‍‍‍‍‍‍            ب‍‍‍‍‍‍

Postmark: Thursday, October 19, 1944

Camp Cooke, California

*Dear folks,*

*Boy, have I got a good deal today! I'm Barracks Orderly. (Just another name for Goldbrick.) All I have to do is stay in the barracks and see that nothing is stolen. One man stays in every day as barracks orderly. This is only the 2nd time I've had it since my triumphant entry into the Army so I think it's about time I had it.*

*We trained with tanks all day yesterday, then had to clear a minefield last night. We all had to get in a foxhole and let a tank run over us.*

*I get my pictures back today. Mom, what size film does that camera at home take? We can get 3 or 4 different kinds here. If I can get the size it takes I'll get them and send them home.*

*We're going back down to the Marine base at Pendleton to visit our buddies—the 5th Marines—a week from today. We'll be down there about 4 days. Its seems silly to go 100 miles just to run a problem but that's what we're going to do anyway.*

*It's pretty certain that I won't go overseas until the last of November anyway. Even then we'll probably train for 6 months over there before seeing action. I never saw an outfit that likes to train as well as this one.*

*I'm almost sure I'll get Guard Duty this weekend. I haven't pulled Guard for at least 2 or 3 months. I don't really care if I do get it because I wasn't going anywhere anyway.*

*We've got another problem tomorrow night. We'll be out all day tomorrow, tomorrow night and Saturday morning.*

*Well, George White is a happy boy today. He left on furlough last night. He had his last furlough on May 29. Bill & I don't get any because we had ours in June. Bill's was June 1. But if there are any more furlough periods, we'll be next. They won't let anyone go now though because we're supposed to leave this camp sometime in November. If we're lucky, we'll get one from our staging area. If not—that's why they thought up that old Army expression—T.S.*

*Well, this is the 5th page, so I better close.*

*Bye for now, Stan*

෧    ෧

Postmark: October 23, 1944

Sunday Morning

*Dear Mother & Dad,*

*Here goes that big letter I promised to write today. I'll start by telling you about that battalion combat problem we had Friday and Saturday. I never saw anything like it in my life. Every man had all the ammunition he could carry. They had dummies resembling Japs all through the hills and around certain objectives we had to take. My platoon went after one objective up the right flank while the 1st platoon took the left and the 2nd covered our advance by firing over our heads. Boy the bullets were landing all around us but no one was hit. I never saw so much firing in my life. At one time there were over 70 rockets in the air and artillery shells were going over our heads all the time. Everything worked perfectly. I don't think I could find a better outfit to go into combat with. General Lear was out there and you should have heard his praise for the 97th.*

*Incidentally, it was our sister division (the 96th) who made the initial landings in the Philippines. They left San Luis Obispo for overseas just a week before we got there. We know practically for sure now that it won't be too long. They're working 24 hrs a day building waterproof boxes for our equipment. But, honestly I'm ready to go. I've had a lot better training than lots of the guys who are over there and besides we'll never win the war setting over here. Anyway it won't last long when the Trident Division gets there.*

*There are a few guys getting hurt over there but there is a heck of a lot more who aren't getting scratched. So there's really not much to worry about. I doubt if I'll see any action before February or March because we'll get a couple of months of jungle training before we see action. Anyway, we won't leave the states for a month yet. . . .*

*Well I better close for now and go downstairs (I'm at the Service Club) and get myself a sundae.*

*Love, Stan*

᧝     ᧝

Postmark: Tuesday, October 31, 1944
Camp Cooke, California
*Dear folks,*
*Here I am back again. We were gone 5 days. I still can't figure out whether we went down there for a sightseeing trip or to better our relations with the Navy and Marines. All we did was run a little problem at Pendleton and 250 miles is a long way just for that. We stayed with the Bellhops* [derogatory Army term for Marines because their dress uniforms resembled a bellhop's] *3 days and on the way back we stayed over night at a Naval Base near Ventura, Calif. The sailors turned over one of their theatres to us and we all went to the show free. The show wasn't much good though. The sailors don't get their shows as quick as the Army does.*

*The best part was getting back and getting my mail. I got 3 packages and about a dozen letters. Thanks a lot for everything. The bracelet was neat. And thanks for the candy, Al. After 5 days without sweets, it tastes swell. (Everyone else in the barracks thinks so too.)*

*I also got a swell box of cookies from Doris. I don't know why but she seems to be counting on my furlough pretty heavy. But I'm afraid she won't see me for a long time. It's a sure bet that we won't get furloughs. This outfit is red hot and won't sit still much longer. Tomorrow we have equipment inspections all day. And tonight they called everyone over to check on the one to notify in case of emergency.*

*Boy this is a bad looking bunch of boys in this outfit this last week. At least 50 per cent of the outfit has poison oak all over them. Bill has had it bad. He's been putting that calamine lotion of mine on it. Remember when you told me to get it when I was on furlough, Mom? It's a wonder I haven't got poison oak too. I slept in the stuff just like the other guys but it just doesn't take on me.*

*I worked all day Sunday — my birthday. But my mind was home. That's where my body should be too.*

*I'll tell you what I think will happen to this outfit. It's purely a guess but I think it's a good one. We'll go overseas about Dec. 1. We'll stay in Hawaii about 2 or 3 months taking jungle training and about March 1, we and a couple Marine Divisions will invade Formosa. When Formosa is invaded, see if the 97th isn't there.*

*A bunch of combat dogs came to the outfit last week. They've been training to fight and they're the meanest things that ever walked. Poor Japs.*

*Bill got 3 Christmas boxes today. When we were at sea, all his relations thought he went overseas so they sent his Christmas presents.*

*You should have seen the people line the streets of every city when we went through on that trip. They waved and cheered and held up V for Victory signs and everything. I guess they thought we were on our way over.*

*Everyone in Calif. knows the 97th Division because we've been all over the state. They all know we're ready to go and I guess they thought that was it. Anyway it was fun waving at the girls.*

*Eldena, just for waking up and letting me know you are still alive, I'll see that you get a Jap souvenir of some kind.*

*In case you're still wondering what I want for Christmas, I'll give you a little "hint." (Ha). I'd like to have a hunting knife about as long as our scout knives used to be only sharpened on both sides and coming to a point. It might come in handy.*

*So Miss Huffman called up* [my high school homeroom teacher]. *I can just see her. Probably worrying her head off about every kid in the homeroom. Its silly but she's always worrying about something.*

*Well Bill and I are going to get a couple sundaes and go to the show so bye until tomorrow.*

*Love, Stan*

ᔦ    ᔦ

Postmark: Wednesday, November 1, 1944
Camp Cooke, California
*Dear folks,*

*I just got a haircut and look plenty sharp too (Ha!). We've got a guy in our company that used to be a barber and he cuts all of our hair. He's about the best barber I ever saw.*

*Well, we made out our cards today like you got when Bob went over but they aren't going to send them until we leave.*

*Guess what! This division is really on the ball. They bought $5,000 worth of recreational equipment such as baseballs, footballs, basketballs, cards, magazines, books, stationery and a fishing kit for every man. I can't figure it out. Are we going over to fight the Japs or beat them at a game of basketball? I'll let you know when I catch my first fish over 5 ft. long. Sorry you folks can't go with us on our vacation to the beautiful South Sea Islands but I guess we can't all be lucky. But I'll tell you all about it.*

*I'm sending home a bunch of stuff. One box has a sailor hat which I got from a sailor on that cruise. It also has a rifle sling, shoe dubbing and an armband I used to wear in the Shore Party.*

*Well I'm going to the show so I better close until tomorrow.*

*Love, Stan*

*P.S. Would appreciate it if you would send my Christmas present early — namely that hunting knife. Almost everyone in the outfit is trying to get one and I'd like to have it before I go overseas.*

*Bye, Stan*

෨          ෨

Postmark: Thursday, November 2, 1944
Camp Cooke, California
*Dear folks,*
*Well it's a beautiful day in California. Hope it's the same at home.*

*This outfit has gone work crazy. We're on a 7-day, 10 hrs a day schedule for the next two weeks. After that I don't know what happens. I guess they're trying to make us want to go overseas. I don't know why it makes any difference though. We're going whether we want to or not.*

*I've got 3 packages of clothes and stuff ready to send but have to wait til I can get to the post office.*

*I'm laying here on my bed writing this. The radio is playing "San Fernando Valley" again. Incidentally I was through the San Fernando Valley. It's an awfully nice place.*

*Did I tell you that the division is buying a short wave radio for every company in the division? You'll probably be at home worrying about me and I'll be out there in the Philippines or somewhere listening to Bob Hope and having a heck of a good time. That's why it seems so foolish to worry about the guys overseas. All a guy has to do is be careful and he'll be O.K.*

*They're also buying $75 worth of those pocket sized books of all kinds. The TRIDENT DIVISION is on the ball, huh?*

*Rusty will probably get eaten up by a panther or something about the first day over. He's always nosing around for something to fight. He almost killed the Colonel's pedigreed dog the other day. Boy was the Colonel mad. Rusty hates sailors too. He barks and growls every time he sees one.*

*Everyone's been going through their footlockers and barracks bag and getting rid of all the excess stuff they've accumulated in the last 6 months.*

*I sure wish I had one of those Kodak cameras to take with me. I'd like to get a picture of a Jap.*

*Slade, White, & Nichols will be back tomorrow. Bill & I got hooked in a way. But actually I didn't because those guys were all in the Army 5 or 6 months longer than me so I had a lot more time home in the long run.*

*Bye for now, Stan*

છ છ

Postmark: Friday Night, November 3, 1944
Camp Cooke, California
*Dear folks,*
*I'm on Guard Duty tonight so I haven't much time to write.*

*The outfit has been running a combat course this past week, which is really rugged. There's been one company taking it each day. There's already been 3 men killed running it. One was killed in K Company today. He was one of the kids that came into this outfit from ASTP. L Company takes it tomorrow but I don't have to take it because I'm on Guard.*

*We've got a 25-mile hike coming up next Saturday, Nov. 11 (Armistice Day). I hope it will be the end of this war too like it was the last.*

*I got a letter from Sally today. She writes like we have been going steady for 2 years. She talked a whole page on my furlough that I'm not going to get.*

*Boy it's hard to get out of this camp. The bus service is terrible. We waited an hour last night to get to Santa Maria.*

*Well there's nothing to say. I feel swell.*

*Love, Stan*

છ છ

Postmark: Thursday, November 9, 1944
Camp Cooke, California
*Dear folks,*
*I finally got an evening off so I'm going to write and read. We've been pretty busy lately. I got two shots last night.*

*We had another combat squad problem today. We've really*

been using a lot of ammunition since we came to this camp. We're
getting pretty darn good too if I do have to say so myself.

Is it cold back home? It gets cool here at night but warm in the
daytime.

I'm also going to send home a bazooka rocket. It's harmless now
so don't be scared of it. I've taken it apart so it'll be in 3 pieces
when you get it but it is easy to put together. Just screw that long
piece into the other two and it will be together. I may not send it
for a few days.

Well there's nothing else to say except I feel perfect.

Bye, Stan

ᔰ          ᔰ

Postmark: Tuesday, November 14, 1944
Camp Cooke, California
*Dear folks,*

*I finally got around to writing a couple letters. This is the first
chance I've had since I got back from L.A.*

*Boy, Bill & I really had fun in Los Angeles and Hollywood. We
saw the Hanly Stafford and Fanny Brice (Baby Snooks) program.
We went to the Hollywood Canteen, the Palladium* [a huge
dance hall featuring top bands]. *and Earl Carroll's* [a popular
music hall famous for its chorus line] *Saturday night.*

*I never saw so many girls in my life as there are in Hollywood.*

*Once—Bill & I were walking down the street when a girl
grabbed my arm and almost dragged me the opposite way begging
me to come to a dance but we didn't go because we already had
dates. We stayed at Hollywood High School Sat. night and high
school girls fed us Sunday morning. Are the Ft. Wayne girls as hard
up as these out here?*

*Sardi's (an upscale Hollywood restaurant frequented by movie
people) is really a swell place. I had one of the best meals since I've
been in the Army there. It cost $2.75 but was worth it. We started
it off with a champagne cocktail.*

*Boy this outfit's days in the states are really numbered. We'll
leave here about Nov. 26 or 27. It's rumored that we may leave
the states from Seattle, Washington. I hope so because I've never
been up in that part of the country.*

*Let me know when you get that bazooka rocket. It's illegal to send that through the mail so I'm sorta anxious to know when you get it.*

*There's a convoy of 800 Merchant ships massing in the ports along the coast here waiting to take supplies & troops aboard for the next big invasion. We're the ones who'll make that invasion and I'd sure like to know where it'll be. . . .*

*Bob Hope was at the Hollywood Canteen Sat. night.*

*Well I'll close for now.*

*Bye, Stan*

෪        ෪

Postmark: Sunday, November 19, 1944

Service Club, Camp Cooke, California

*Dear Mother, Dad & Eldena,*

*Boy, this is a beautiful day here in California. The sun is shining real bright and the grass has all turned green and it almost makes me wish I could stay here for the duration. But that wouldn't do. Just think of all the exciting adventures of far-off lands that I'd miss. (Yeh)*

*Don't forget to let me know when you get all that stuff. I sent the jacket yesterday. You can take a razor blade and take the Trident insignia off the sleeve if you want to. It's dirty anyway and I won't need it on there now. I took the stripes off before I sent it. I don't know how you guys like it but I think it's really a classy looking jacket when it's adjusted right. But it doesn't look quite as good as our new jungle jacket.*

*Bill and I were going to go to L.A. again this weekend but Bill pulled Guard Duty today. George got it too. I don't know how I was lucky enough to stay off but I was.*

*George, Bill & I went to Lompoc for dinner last night and had a swell meal. Then we went to the show and came back to camp. The show was pretty good but I think we get a lot better shows on the post than in town although the theatre isn't as nice here.*

*Bill and I went down to get our pictures taken yesterday but decided to get them taken in field jackets which we didn't have with us so we didn't get them. We may go Monday evening but haven't decided yet.*

*We were told yesterday what we could say and what we couldn't say when we get overseas. The things we couldn't say greatly outnumbered the ones we could say but you'll be able to tell how I'm getting along which is sufficient I guess.*

*They told us we could send home souvenirs which we capture from the Japs so you'll probably get some after I go into action (which won't be for awhile). I'm going to try to get one of those hari-kari swords which the Jap officers carry. But don't worry, the only thing I'm really interested in bringing back is myself — in one piece, and that's going to be my primary objective.*

*Boy I'd hate to be the Jap that gets in the way of one of these man-eating dogs we've got. They're the meanest animals that ever walked.*

*Well, I guess I'll close for now.*

*Love, Stan*

ᔕ    ᔕ


Postmark: Friday Afternoon, November 24, 1944
Service Club, Camp Cooke, California

*Dear folks,*

*I suppose you're wondering what I'm doing at the Service Club in the afternoon. Well I had guard duty last night so I get this afternoon off. Rough.*

*No, Mom, it won't take all 800 ships to take the 97th but the 86th is here ready to go too and a lot of the ships will be needed for supplies, ammunition, equipment, gas, etc.*

*Mom, you said you wish you knew where I was going. So do I. But I've got a good idea. It seems to be the general idea that we're going to Hawaii for jungle training (about 6 wks) then on to the Philippines. It'll take 8 months or more to liberate all of the Philippines and I'm afraid it'll be a rugged 8 months. One soldier in the 96th Div on Leyte sat down on a stump and it was a 30 foot snake. . . .*

*As I said before, forget the knife if you haven't found one.*

*Have you found out how that compass works yet, Mom? Bet you haven't.*

*One year ago today I made my fateful entry into the Army. TS . . .*

*I wish we'd hurry and ship out. It's hard to just stay and wait when we know we have to go.*

*I feel that I've got as good a chance to come back as the next guy and we know that everyone won't be killed. They put all new parts in my rifle so it's really swell now. They also took in our bayonets to sharpen them. They're going to put razor sharp edges on them.*

*Well I'll close for now,*
*Stan*

ᔥ        ᔥ

Postmark: Sunday, November 26, 1944
Camp Cooke, California
*Dear Mother, Dad & Eldena,*
*Well, it's been two hours since I called you and it seems like a month. As soon as I hung up I went over to an artillery mess hall near here and ate breakfast, then came back here.*

*Boy it sure was swell to get to talk to you. All of you sounded just like you always did, but it was sorta hard to hear you. I had a lot of stuff to talk about when I called but as soon as I started to talk I forgot it all. I'll send a money order home in a few days and you can take out the cost of the call. I would have paid for it here but didn't have any change to put in the phone so I just reversed the charges. I just wanted to talk to you before I shoved off.*

*I hate to think of Bob in the front lines but I think he can take care of himself as well as anyone. We got some letters from the guys who shipped out of this outfit back in San Luis Obispo that went to Europe. They're all in the front lines too now. Most of them were real young kids (18 and 19). If they don't watch out there won't be any young guys left except for the 4-F's and the Sailors.*

*There is really going to be a swell show here this afternoon. It's "Meet Me in St. Louis"* [Judy Garland starred in this hit movie about the 1900 World Fair] *and just about everyone is going. We're all wishing we were back in Missouri now. I'd give anything to be there. It gives one a sense of security to be close to home. (650 miles seems pretty darn close now.) We never do anything anymore except go to the show because the transportation out of this camp is terrible now that there are two divisions here.*

*We were talking to a guy last night that spent a year in the South Pacific and he told us all about it. He said at night you couldn't walk without squashing a toad or lizard at every step. I still want to go though. It'll be a unique experience to go through. And how.*

*Well I'll close for now and read the paper.*

*Love, 'Huff'*

∽ ∽

Postmark: Sunday, December 1, 1944
USO, Los Angeles, California
*Dear folks,*

*Well it's all over—our 3-day pass. In about an hour we have to catch our bus back to camp. Boy, I'm sure tired. We've been on the go almost continually since we got here.*

*Did you hear us this morning from Sardi's Restaurant? Boy we really had fun. Mom, some day I'll bring you to Hollywood and let you go to breakfast at Sardi's because you would really like it.*

*The people here are swell to servicemen. They'll do anything for us. Last night a woman stood in line for 45 minutes to get some cigarettes and as soon as she got them she turned around and saw Bill & me standing there so she came up and wanted to give them to us. We had been standing there but we didn't want any cigarettes. We were just talking about how crazy people were to stand in line that long for a pack of cigarettes.*

*Boy we had some swell dates last night. My date looked just like Pat. (Wish it would have been Pat!) It seemed like old times almost when I used to date Pat all the time because this girl sure looked & acted like her. . . .*

*Mother, some big department store here took my picture for nothing and they're going to send it to you when they get it ready. They took it and the girl said she'd pick out the best proof and have it made and send it home all free. Let me know if it's any good.*

*We went out to Chinatown today and also went to the radio program "Glamour Manor." Did you ever hear it? . . .*

*Well, I guess I better close. This has been a pretty swell pass but I'd rather have one day at home than 2 months anywhere else.*

*Bye with love, Stan*

*P.S. I bought a pr of those real good sunglasses like General MacArthur wears.*

∽　　∽

Postmark: December 2, 1944

Service Club, Camp Cooke, California

*Dear folks,*

*Well, I'm back to the ole' hole again. I thought I'd just get back and go right on the train but I was wrong. In fact they say we may not leave for a week.*

*As you know we were scheduled to leave Nov 27 but are being held back for the investigation of some artillery officers. A few weeks ago in a combat firing problem, as we (the infantry) were advancing on a position, the artillery was supposed to be giving us overhead fire and they "goofed up" and put a shell right in the middle of a platoon of infantrymen. It killed a lot of them and injured some. So now they're trying to find out why it happened and get rid of the responsible people before we go.*

*I got the box of candy you sent. Thanks! I've been eating it all afternoon.*

*We sure had fun in L.A. & Hollywood. You know, I'd sorta like to live in Hollywood if all of my family were out here. But I'd rather have snow on the ground in the winter, and lakes rather than an ocean to swim in so I'll still take Indiana.*

*We saw Warner Bros. studio and had passes to go through Walt Disney's studio but we didn't have time.*

*Hollywood sure has its share of pretty girls. Bill and I had 4 dates on Thursday night but of course we couldn't keep them all. They weren't old rips either. The girl I went with had a date with a Marine but she broke it. That doesn't sound logical but it's the honest truth. Boy he sure was mad. . . .*

*Well I'll close and go get a sundae.*

*Bye, Stan*

*P.S. Got a letter from Bob which he wrote Nov 19. Said not to worry but he'd been in action about a week.*

∽　　∽

Postmark: Sunday, December 3, 1944
Service Club, Camp Cooke, California
*Dear folks,*

*Well, I've got 3 letters to write so I guess I'll start with yours. I'm going to write Bob and Doris too.*

*Things around here are sure screwed up. The 86th Division, which just got here from amphibious training, is going back to San Luis Obispo and do it all over. They really messed up in amphibious and they also flunked their I.G. (overseas) tests. . . .*

*As for us, they're still raising heck with the artillery officers so I don't know what they'll do with them.*

*Now I'll try to answer a few of your questions, Mom.*

*No, you don't have to try for a knife because I think I can get one in Hawaii. Don't worry about me going to Alaska because I'm pretty sure we won't, even though we leave from Seattle. I wish we were though. It's a lot more healthful climate than the Philippines. We were talking to a Spanish-American War Veteran in L.A. who spent 30 months in the Philippines and he said it was a living hell. Of course that was 40 yrs. ago.*

*I wish you could see the picture Doris sent me of herself. It sure is cute. Bill had a little frame, which just fit it so it's setting in my footlocker. I guess I should send her a picture of myself. She said "Now, listen, Stan, I've hinted, pleaded, begged and now I'm demanding—send me your picture." So I'll try to send her one.*

*Well I've talked about everything I could think of so I'll close.*

*Love, Stan*

ೋ      ೋ

Postmark: Monday, December 4, 1944
Service Club, Camp Cooke, California
*Dear folks,*

*Well, the "fighting 97th" is still fighting it out in the U.S. I've seen a lot of screwy messes since I've been in the Army but wait til you hear this one.*

*We shipped out 75% of the division trucks and jeeps, all of our bayonets, turned in all our clothes except 1 pr of OD's* [olive drab winter uniforms] *and 2 pr of fatigues, made out allotments & bonds so that we'll only draw $5 or $10 next month, and now we* *don't know whether we're going now or a month from now. General Halsey (Div Commander) was called to Washington 2 wks ago and since he came back rumors are getting strong that we may not go for another month.*

*No one knows exactly which the deal is but there are 3 so-called answers to the situation. One is that they have decided to keep us in the states until they see what's going to happen in Europe, one is that we can't go til the 86th gets ready and they have to take amphibious over and the third is that the U.S. Divisions that they pulled out of Burma are going to do the job we were supposed to do so we'll stay in the states a couple more months.*

*I don't know what the deal is but they better either send us over or give me some clothes. Did you ever hear of such a mess? I don't care though—the longer they leave me in Calif. the better I'll like it. Maybe I can see that cute little chick in L.A. again.*

*I got a Christmas box from the Harvester and guess what was in it. I'll make a list of it:*

> *A cigarette lighter*
> *Fruitcake*
> *Candy*
> *Toothbrush*
> *Comb*
> *2 handkerchiefs*
> *Deck of Cards*
> *Eversharp pencil & box of lead*
> *2 cakes of soap*
> *A wreath of holly or something*

*It was really swell.*

*I can't think of anything I want, Mom. I've got just about everything I need. The best Christmas I could have (next to being home) is being in the states and I've got a good chance to be now.*

*You should see this outfit now. They're the happiest bunch of guys you ever saw now that there's a chance to stay awhile. They're not afraid but none of them have any ambitions of being a hero.*

*Now don't get me wrong. I'm not positive we're staying. We're all packed and could pull out overnight. It may just be to get the guys off the track so the move will be more secret. We just don't know so you'll just have to wait & see and we will too.*

*It was a swell day here—nice and warm.*

*Well I guess I better close and write Robinson* [see Pearl Harbor, December 7, 1941] *a letter. I have to keep those combat troops' morale up you know.*

*Love, Stan*

ᔥ    ᔥ

Postmark: Tuesday, December 5, 1944

*Dear folks,*

*I was going to the show tonight but Hill got table waiter and can't get off til about 7:30 so I guess we won't go.*

*Well it looks like we are going to stay awhile. But we still haven't any clothes except for 1 pr and no jeeps except a few. If we stay much longer though, we'll probably get our duffel bags. See, they have a duffel bag for each man with all brand new clothes & shoes in it (also a new field jacket and jungle jacket). That was the funniest deal I've seen yet. Some guys are even starting to talk about furloughs for the guys who had their last one in June. I'm not going to count on one but if any are given, I'll be one of the first to get one.*

*This was really a pretty day here. But when winter comes, I want snow not sun. We really give these California boys a bad time when they start bragging about their lovely climate. We gripe about it just to make them mad.*

*About 75% of the guys got crew cuts because they didn't want to monkey with long hair overseas but now they're madder than heck because it looks like we may stay awhile.*

*How would you like to have some fruitcake? I've got one here. That package must have cost the Harvester quite a bit.*

*Well, I'll close as there is nothing to stay.*

*Love, "your non-combatant infantryman" –Stan*

# A Christmas 12 Furlough

By the fall of 1944, the 97th Division was in a high state of readiness, having been in training for two years. We were notified that we would be sent to the Far East in December. We began making preparations for overseas movement. Fortunately for us, the War Department changed the embarkation date to January 1945. In the middle of December, however, these plans, too, were abruptly altered.

On December 16, 1944, in an attempt to cut the Allied Forces in two, the German Army launched a major offensive through the Ardennes Forest—the beginning of what was ultimately to be called the Battle of the Bulge. The American Army suffered massive casualties, and the 97th was suddenly ordered to Europe. Although we had trained to establish beachheads for five months, we were fortunately spared that very dangerous mission.

The reward for our deployment to Europe was a Christmas furlough while our equipment was winterized. I felt lightheaded and almost breathless as I boarded a train to Indiana. It seemed an endless journey, with the train stopping at every small town and water tower. For four nights I could barely sleep, although I spent my waking hours dreaming of home. My folks had no idea when I would arrive. It was 3:00 A.M. when I got off the train in Fort Wayne. My California yearnings had been fulfilled: a thick snow covered the ground and a bitter cold wind slapped my face.

It never entered my mind to call Dad at that hour. I just picked up my duffel bag and started walking home. It was 4:00 before I was greeted by Rocky, our collie, who slept outside—even in the winter. We were so excited to see each other that I just sat down in the snow and played with him. After rolling around with Rocky for awhile, I quietly went into the house (which was never locked in those days) and up to my bedroom, where I fell deeply asleep for the first time since I had left Camp Cooke.

The next morning, when she saw my duffel bag, Mom knew I was home and ran upstairs to see "if it was really her baby boy." When she saw me sound asleep, the worries of the entire previous year lifted from her shoulders.

There was no joyous Christmas for our troops in Europe. It was one of the coldest winters in fifty years. They had to battle the cold, trench foot, poor food (because of overextended supply lines) and, most of all, a very competent and dangerous enemy fighting desperately on its own soil. Also, the SS (Hitler's elite Nazi fanatics) executed 50,000 German soldiers that winter for either desertion or retreating. As a result, most of the rest did what they were told to do, which was to stand their ground and fight.

Back in Fort Wayne, Christmas was a seemingly endless round of dances, parties, and movies. In addition, I had the rare pleasure of being in constant demand because most guys my age were in the military. Besides enjoying my family, I had time to see the girls who had been writing to me, as well as many of my old friends who were not in the service.

I had dated Pat Prange in high school, so I called her. We enjoyed several dates. On December 21, 1944, we saw the popular movie of the 1940s, *Sensations of 1945*. I had known Dorothy Chandler in high school; we had become good friends but had not dated because both of us were going with someone else. But I called Dorothy and she took the next day off work. We went sledding in Franke Park all afternoon. That evening we went back to Franke Park, which was close to her home and easy to get to in those days of gas rationing. It was so peaceful and beautiful in the park, with the newly fallen snow, that it was hard for me to believe I would soon be on a battlefield far across the ocean.

Although I dated several girls, the most memorable evening was with Doris. She invited me to a dance sponsored by her high school sorority. There would be a "big band" and everyone would be there, so I would see a lot of old friends. However, complications set in almost immediately. Although Doris had been writing to me regularly since we had met on my last furlough the previous June, she was also going steady with the son of the high school principal. When she found out I was in Fort Wayne, she told Bob that I was a friend who was home from the service and that I would soon be going overseas. She wanted to show me a good time prior to my going into combat.

On the big night, of course I drove my yellow four-door 1937 Ford convertible. At her house, I was a little surprised to see another car in the driveway, but assumed it belonged to someone visiting her parents.

Inside the house, however, was a scene of panic suitable for a good movie comedy. The car, you see, belonged to Bob. The first time the doorbell rang, Doris had expected to see me. To her horror, it was Bob, who had decided to make his contribution to the war effort by coming over to meet her military friend. Doris calmly invited him in, graciously excused herself, and then ran to her mother in the kitchen in terror.

"Mom? Mom! That was Bob and Stan will be here any minute. What am I going to do?"

Just then, the doorbell rang again, and Doris bolted back through the living room to answer it. "Hi, Stan," she said with great composure. "Come on in. I'd like you to meet Bob. Bob, this is Stan. He just got back from California and he's going overseas after the holidays."

Bob was definitely ill at ease and I wondered what was going on. I was primed to have a good time with Doris and I didn't really care to be especially friendly or talkative to this intruder. I guess it never entered my mind that this pretty, popular girl would be dating others while I was stationed in California. After all, she had been writing seven-page letters to me about three times per week. How could she possibly be seeing someone else? This was perfectly illogical reasoning, of course, but how was I to know?

After a few ominous silences, punctuated with false starts at small talk, Doris and I put on our coats and left. In our mutual agitation, we practically ran to my car. I just barely spun the wheels backing out of the driveway. I don't remember what was said, but Doris recently told me that she was "jabbering like a nervous teenager. I tried to apologize, explain, comfort and scream—all in one breath." According to her, I just laughed.

At the dance I had a wonderful time talking with a lot of friends I hadn't seen since joining the Army. The highlight of the evening, however, was a complete surprise. Although I remember the scene, for obvious reasons, Doris recalls it in much more detail. Here is her version.

"We were dancing, when you twirled me around. I opened my eyes and almost lost it. I couldn't believe I was seeing Bob enter the room. My first thought was 'How did he get another date that soon?' My shock was complete when I saw that his date was my mother. How could they do this to me?

"Mother was wearing my black taffeta formal with aqua inserts and bows down the front. She was also wearing my long string of pearls around her neck, tied in a knot at the waist with the lower end bouncing from the knot (as was the style for teenagers in the 1940s). I was horrified.

"Everyone was greeting her and talking to her. I will say she was behaving herself. But then she saw us and the whole group danced over to say hello.

"You started laughing and I threw up."

What actually happened is she grabbed my hand and pulled me in the direction of a stairway which we took to a balcony where we could watch the crowd. I was laughing and she was crying, "Stan, get me out of here!" What an excuse, she thought, to leave in the yellow convertible.

Later, when I took her home, she found her black onyx ring lying on the piano—a sign that Bob was no longer going steady with her.

The next Monday morning, she was called to the office of the principal, Bob's father. With a stern look on his face he told Doris to have a seat. "I understand you caused my son to go out with a married woman Saturday night." Doris says now, "I was so naive I thought I might not even be able to graduate."

Bob's father then smiled and pulled a bunch of bananas—her favorite fruit and very difficult to get in wartime—from under his desk and gave them to her.

I didn't keep track of the Doris-Bob relationship, but she and I were together a lot for the rest of that furlough. After my return to camp and journey overseas, her letters increased in size and frequency. However, I was careful to not let myself get too emotionally involved with any of these cute girls. I knew I was headed overseas as an infantry scout—a dangerous job with a high mortality rate. I had been with girls who had just found out that their brother or boyfriend had been killed in action and it was not a pretty picture.

A season so glorious always passes too quickly. It was soon time to get on the train for the long trip back to California. I left home knowing I was heading overseas for battle, and I also knew that infantry companies were experiencing horrendous casualties. I wondered if I would ever see my family and Rocky again. I tried to tell my parents not to worry, as I felt capable of taking care of myself. I think it was good that, at that time, I could believe it was possible to take care of myself in battle and that I was innocent about the brutal realities of front-line infantry combat.

Postmark: Wednesday, morning
*Dear Mother and Dad & Eldena,*
*Here I am back in the old rut again. I got here about 1:30 last night. I sorta pulled a few strings here and there and got barracks orderly today so I didn't have to out to the field. Now I've got my stuff all straightened up.*
*Boy what a train trip I had. I was about as sick as you were when you went to Evansville that time, Mom. But I'm getting a lot better now in this California sunshine. Boy it's really shining too. (Ahem) Cough!! Cough!!*
*Everyone has been teasing me about my nightclub tan. I didn't realize how white my face had gotten in 19 days.*
*Well I suppose you're wondering what we're (this fighting outfit ha ha) going to do now so I'll tell you what the latest dope is. We're supposed to go to Northern California for 30 day maneuvers the 21st of January. If so I doubt if we'll leave the states before the last of April. I certainly can't figure this Army out.*

*Coming out here on the train I talked with some 18 year old kids who had only been in 4 1/2 months, had a 5 day furlough and were on their way to a port of embarkation for overseas action as infantrymen. That is what will happen to Jim Field and Wagner.*

*Why do they send them over while we stay out here and "enjoy" California's Golden Sun? Beats the heck out of me.*

*Boy that furlough was the cat's meow. It was really wonderful. Mom thanks a lot for the lunch and for packing my bag and putting in all the handkerchiefs, etc. I didn't even say a thing about it before I left but I didn't think much about that bag and what I was going to bring with me. I sure hated to leave. I was a pretty sad sack when I left wasn't I? I didn't even take a bath and I had on those wrinkled pants but I didn't give a darn then. (I was a sadder sack when I got off the train ha ha.) I thought that train never would get to L.A. I sat with some soldiers who had just returned from 34 months overseas. That's a long time isn't it?*

*George has been working out here at a big defense plant during weekends and 3-day passes. He wants me to go out too. I guess I will after I get rested a few days. But we've got a 25-mile hike Friday so I suppose that will kill me.*

*This outfit seems to have turned over a new leaf. They allow each man a 3-day pass every month.*

*I got a letter from Hench. Oh yes, I got a letter from Bob. I started to tell you that the first thing and forgot. He said he'd seen plenty of action and said he would be willing to go home and play nursemaid to a kindergarten. He said he had enough rough stuff. He was in a barn when he wrote it. It wasn't dated but was postmarked December 21 (I'll send it).*

*I had a seat all the way from Ft. Wayne to camp. I was about the only one that got on at Ft. Wayne that got a seat. They were standing all over the place but some sailor was saving one for some serviceman he said and he gave it to me. Good ole Navy.*

*Well I'll close for now,*
*Love, Stan*

# Hurry Up And Wait

WHEN I RETURNED TO CAMP COOKE, JUST TWO HOURS BEFORE MY leave was up, most of the group that had gone to the western states were already there. Few, if any, were happy campers. Like me, they had had just enough taste of civilian life, family, rest, and relaxation to make it tough to come back. Also, like me, they knew that many of us would not come back from Europe. The only mystery was who the unfortunate ones would be.

In fact, uncertainty about the future was the norm. We actually stayed at Camp Cooke for a month, but we never knew when we would leave. Also, plans had been changed so many times that by now, no one was certain that we would even go to Europe. Then, too, there was always the lingering hope that the war would end before we were sent anywhere.

Prior to the change of orders, we paid close attention to the Pacific war. We followed the progress of our troops as they made their way towards Japan, invading and conquering islands such as Tarawa, Saipan, Tinian, Guam, and the Philippines. Now we were interested in the progress of our troops in Europe.

We read about the atrocity of Malmedy, where the Germans decided to machine gun to death a large group of recently captured Americans. We read about the 106th Division. Most of them surrendered almost as soon as they arrived at the front. They were unlucky enough to be at the place the large German offensive first broke through the American lines. Many of us had made up our minds to make every possible effort not to be taken prisoner.

In early February we finally boarded a troop train for a long, cross-country ride. We came out to California on the Southern Pacific Railroad, but we left on the Santa Fe. We traveled through Los Angeles, Flagstaff, Fort Worth, Memphis, Atlanta, Baltimore, and finally arrived at Camp Kilmer, New Jersey. We were only there about a week, mostly getting shots and orientations.

As the 97th Division prepared to cross the Atlantic, we were well aware of the danger. Under tight security most of the time, we were constantly reminded not to talk to anyone about shipping out. We were told about the German U-boats sitting off the coast, waiting for the next big convoy. We knew we could be torpedoed. Suddenly, the war started to seem more real to us. We certainly didn't need much convincing to refrain from talking about our movements. We went sightseeing in New York City, but we always kept in mind signs at the base that said "Loose Lips Sink Ships."

> Postmark: January 6, 1945, Saturday Afternoon
> Camp Cooke, California
> *Dear folks,*
> *I got your first letter today Mom. Doris beat you—I got one from her yesterday. Hers was air mail though.*
> *I'm at the Service Club now. There are some German PW's about 6 ft. from me washing windows. They're really scrubbing away.*
> *I just got a haircut. It was about time don't you think?*
> *Guess what?! Bud Foote just now came up. We talked about 20 minutes and now we decided to write some more. I've got a million letters to write.*
> *I busted my watch crystal good this morning. I'm going to send it home and let you have it fixed if you will. Nick and I were wrestling when it busted.*
> *Love, Stan*

Postmark: Saturday Afternoon
USO
*Dear Mother, Dad, and Eldena,*

*I'm here in Santa Maria now. It's a city about the size of Angola* [a small town of about 1,000 in northern Indiana] *and about 20 miles from camp. The drive in here is really beautiful. Green grass all over the mountains and the sun shining bright. It's a wonderful day. I'm going to hate to leave California. The people out here are so swell to soldiers.*

*I got my watch crystal fixed this afternoon. I'm going to get Bill a jar of Noxzema (cold cream) before I go back too if I don't forget. He and George have guard duty and couldn't get a pass so he asked me to get him some.*

*Well the situation on the Western Front is looking a little better isn't it? (It'll look a lot better pretty soon.) I figure it should take about 6 weeks for the Trident Division to clean it up (yawn). One thing's pretty sure, I think it'll be over by August at least.* [A pretty good prediction, as it turned out.]

*I don't think we'll leave here for about 2 weeks yet and maybe not till 3 weeks. But we know it's mighty close. In fact, 4 kitchen cars came into camp yesterday so we think they're the cars for our train (purely speculation).*

*Whatever happens or wherever I go, just remember that I'll be O.K. I can't kick about being sent over. I've been in the states for 14 months and a lot of poor guys don't get near that much training.*

*You'll probably get a bond before long. I'm getting a bond a month out now.*

*Well I guess I'll go back to camp and go to the show. (The shows in camp are newer than those in town—cheaper too ha.)*

*Love, Stan*

൭     ൭

Postmark: Sunday Morning, January 14, 1945
Service Club, Camp Cooke, California
*My dear Mother and Dad,*

*Well, this is another beautiful day here. The sun is as bright as a warm day in June back home. I'd just as soon stay here for the duration but I guess we can't fight a war on this side of the pond.*

*I saw a swell show last night. It was Betty Grable in "Pin-Up Girl." Has it been there yet?*

*We were planning on going horseback riding today but Bill and George "goofed up" and got guard. Bill gets so mad. It seems like he gets something every weekend and I've had every weekend off since we got to this camp. That's the breaks of the Army.*

*Remember that ring Stonebraker gave me?? Well it was too big for my little finger and too little for all the others so it kept coming off all the time. I lost it on the train but another soldier found it. I was about ready to throw it away because it didn't fit but I got another idea. I put in on my dog tags and it's been there ever since. Pretty good place for it, isn't it?*

*I've really been writing Bob a lot. I write him about every 3 or 4 days. In fact I'm going to write him as soon as I finish this. I know how it would be to stay in the front lines for 4 or 5 days then come back for a rest and not have any mail. (Ahem—Eldena, have you been writing him?? You better.)*

*We've been having it pretty easy lately. You know—just sorta putting on the finishing touches.*

*We've been having a lot of classes on first-aid. One of the main things is trench foot. That was pretty bad over there but they've got it under control now. And after April it should disappear almost entirely because it won't be so cold.*

*Well I'll have to close now as there's nothing else to write.*

*With love, Stan*

ᔓ    ᔓ

Postmark: Tuesday, January 16, 1945
Service Club, Camp Cooke, California
*Dear Mother, Dad, and Eldena,*

*This is another swell day here. It's about 10:00 AM now and the sun is just starting to get nice and warm. Don't ask me how I can be in a position to write a letter at ten in the morning. It's just 'one of those things.' I figure I might as well rest while I can.*

*I got that picture of myself last night. It was the one Eldena gave Doris. She sent it to me to sign. She even sent the return postage. I haven't mailed it yet.*

*I think the Russians mean business this time. They've thrown 2,000,000 men into their big offensive. Well, I hope they win the darn thing before I find myself over there. It wouldn't be so bad over there if we were fighting dummies like on these combat problems, but according to rumors they shoot back at you.*

*Well I guess I've done enough 'blowing off' for today. There's nothing happening around here that I can write about.*

*Bye, Love, Stan*

*P. S. Happy Birthday, Mom*

ꙮ    ꙮ

Postmark: Friday, January 19, 1945
Service Club, Camp Cooke, California
*Dear folks,*

*All's well here. I'm at the Service Club again as you can see by the stationery. There's a big dance here. We just got here from the show. Saw a swell show. I danced a couple times but decided I better write you a couple pages so you won't think I left or anything. Anyway I didn't like the babe I had so I ditched her.*

*Boy, I love those Russians. After they go about 200 miles farther we'll get there for the parades etc. We've got connections. You don't think we're going over there to fight do you? We've got inside dope that the war'll be over before we get there. (I keep telling myself.)*

*That sure is pretty music down there. I'll have to go down for another fling pretty soon.*

*This afternoon we studied the German "s" mine. It's called "Bouncing Betty" and is what caused the Fifth Army so much trouble in Italy. It's a very ingenious piece of mechanism.*

*Bill got $15 from his girl for his birthday. She really likes him.*

*There's a bunch of WACS here tonight but they have a rough time getting any attention with these civilian girls. No one goes for WACS very much.*

*It turned cooler today. In fact it was almost cold. I don't care how cold it gets out here now.*

*Bye, Stan*

ᔐ    ᔐ

Postmark: Thursday Night, January 25, 1945
*Dear Mother and Dad,*

*Mom, the most terrible thing happened here today. Do you remember me telling you about George's girl (the one who wrote me a letter). Well, George got word that she was killed in an automobile wreck. He sure is taking it hard. I never knew a boy who was so crazy about his girl. I think he's cried continually since he heard about it. He can't wait to get to combat now. The thing, which made it all the worse, was that she was with a 4-F when it happened.*

*I guess that you'll see now Mom that there's no use to worry about Bob and me. You can get killed on the home front too. Eldena you be careful with the darn Ford. It's dangerous if you go too fast and aren't used to it. I don't want to have to worry about you too with everything else I've got to worry about.*

*I'd give anything if they'd hurry and get this darn division over and put us in the 7th Army so we can help Bob.*

*Things are getting about to the boiling point around here. We've got about all of our share of California sunshine.*

*Mom, a G-2 is the intelligence section of an infantry division. It tries to find out all about the enemy and know all about the deployment of our own troops.*

*I'm feeling swell and (as Bob would say) am very contented so just don't worry and I'll be happy.*

*Lots of love, Stan*

ᔐ    ᔐ

Postmark: Saturday, January 27, 1945
Camp Cooke, California
*Dear Mom, Dad & Eldena,*

*I didn't get 1 letter today. But I'll be lenient and attribute it to the fact that the mail system is all screwed up. Before long I'll probably be lucky to get one every 3 weeks so I don't suppose I should holler about 1 day.*

*There sure is a lot I'd like to tell you but I can't. They go through some of the mail and if they find any one who is talking too much—it's T.S. They even listen to telephone conversations and cut you off if you say anything you shouldn't.*

*But I guess I can tell you we're as close as we were last time. Possibly even closer for one of the regiments. We aren't going to be the first regiment to leave.*

*I always wanted to see the Statue of Liberty.* [My way of letting them know I was going to the East Coast.]

*I slept almost all afternoon so I feel pretty good now.*

*I'm glad we're leaving here in a way—3-1/2 months in the same camp. That's against the principles of the 97th. We usually average 6 weeks. I imagine we'll be over there a little longer though. Anyway almost everyone is over there so I might as well go too. When I get to be an old man I can feed my grandsons a lot of bull about how we licked the Germans. I'm beginning to think we're going to be too late to have anything to say about licking the Germans though. The Russ are 90 miles from Berlin this morning.*

*This is going to be a dull weekend. Nothing to do but eat sundaes and go to the show.*

*From all reports, Wednesday of next week won't be very dull though.* [The day we were to depart.]

*Bye for tonight,*

*Love, Stan*

ை      ை

Postmark: Tuesday, January 30, 1945

Camp Cooke, California

*Dear folks,*

*I haven't much time but that's OK because I haven't much to say either. I just want to let you know I'm still here. (For the very present.) Bud Foote left today.*

*It's sorta chilly here tonight. But I guess I better start getting used to cold weather.*

*I didn't write yesterday because I was on guard duty. I had a good deal on guard. I just had to sit in the guardhouse and watch a prisoner they had in there. Then I had to take him to chow at mealtime. I felt kinda funny following a guy around with a gun stuck in his back but that is what I had to do.*

*Well I'm sorta tired so I guess I better close.*
*Bye til tomorrow,*
*Love, Stan*
*P.S. Here's a piece about the 103rd Division. I hope Bob's*
*okay.*

ᔪ　　　ᔪ

Postmark: February 8, 1945
Camp Kilmer, New Jersey
*Dear Mother, Dad & Eldena,*
*This is a slightly different climate than California. When we*
*got off the train we were cordially greeted by snow, sleet and more*
*snow. It's pretty, though. Makes me homesick for Indiana snow.*
*Well, I don't know exactly what to write about. This is my first*
*"censored" letter. But I'll try. If he doesn't like what I say, he can*
*always cut it out.*
*As you probably guessed, we're in a camp on the East Coast.*
*The chow here is swell. Guess George and I will go to the show*
*tonight if we can find it. The PXs here are well stocked with about*
*everything.*
*I got your letter today and 1 from Doris. I sure was glad to get*
*them.*
*Mom, when those pictures come from the May Co., will you*
*let Eldena take one to Doris? She's asked me for a big one every let-*
*ter since I came back from furlough and I said I'd give her one*
*when she gave me hers, so I guess I better.*
*Keep writing every day and don't worry about me. As Bob &*
*Uncle Vernon would say, "I'm fine," and "contented."*
*Bye for now, Love, Stan*

ᔪ　　　ᔪ

Postmark: Saturday, February 10, 1945
*Dear folks,*
*I'll start this now although I don't know when I'll get it fin-*
*ished. We'll probably fall out before long. There isn't much going*
*on worth mentioning. I really like this camp (as well as I could*
*like any Army camp). The PXs, Service Clubs, etc. are a lot bet-*

ter than those at Cooke. George, Slade and I went to a dance last night.

I'm going into New York City as soon as I get the chance. Artie Shaw [a popular big band clarinetist and leader] is at the Strand, so I guess I'll try to see him.

It's not near as cold here as I thought it would be. In fact, it's pretty warm considering the fact that the ground is covered with snow.

There was a basketball game at Gym #2 last night between the post team and some Navy team. The gobs won by 1 point. We just watched a little of it, then left and went to the dance. In the preliminary, some WACS played some civilian girls. But I haven't seen anything yet to compare with Indiana basketball. There's nothing I need, Mom, but don't worry, I'll ask for it when I do.

Some of these days I'll write you a letter in a foreign language. I'm getting pretty good at it. (In a rugged sort of way.) I've been studying the most common words. (I can say about 6 words—ha ha.)

Well, I'll close for now as there's nothing to say anyhow.
Love, Stan

᷍     ᷍

Postmark: Tuesday, February 13, 1945
*Dear folks,*
I went into New York City last night. We really had fun. White was with me and we went all through Rockefeller Center & Radio City. We went to the top of the RCA building (70 floors) and could see all over New York City. Have you ever heard of that skating rink in the middle of Rockefeller Center? Well, George and I went ice skating there, and if you would have wanted a good laugh, you should have been there. There was all of those professionals turning somersaults and everything else, and George and I barely able to stand up. There were about a thousand people watching, and they about died laughing at us.

But I met some cute gal who could skate good and she taught me a lot. There were a million girls there.

We were in Radio City Music Hall and it's really beautiful. It's supposed to be the biggest theatre in the world.

*Mom, you know how I'm always forgetting something. Well, I forgot all about Valentine's Day and didn't send Doris a thing. I couldn't have gotten anything in camp anyway, but I could have gotten something in New York City but forgot. And she sent me two valentines. Oh, well. —Rough war, ain't it?*

*I've got a date with that babe in New York for tomorrow night. I don't think I'll go, though. Her name's Annette.*

*We're going down to the gym and play basketball before long, so I'll close now.*

*Love, Stan*

෨    ෨

Postmark: Friday, February 16, 1945
*Dear folks,*

*Nothing much to write about so this'll be pretty short.*

*Some of us got to go to a show this afternoon and listen to a band. It was really hot. It was made up of former members of Cab Calloway, Count Basie and other top bands. The girl singer was from Tommy Dorsey.*

*We got some wool sweaters today from the Red Cross. Mine was made in Indiana. Maybe someone in Ft. Wayne. You don't have to worry about me getting cold. I've got enough clothes to keep ten men warm.*

*Some guys were at that show with 36th Division patches on. They were wounded & just got back. Maybe Uncle Vernon knew some of them.*

*Well, I'll close for tonight.*

*Love, Stan*

*Sat Morning—I've got to add a little. Still can't say anything except "So long, lots of love, don't worry and be good. I'll be back before you know it."*

*I suppose you have guessed what is happening—this is it!*

# PART III

## THE EUROPEAN WAR

# AN ATLANTIC CRUISE
# TO FRANCE

SHORTLY AFTER PEARL HARBOR, HITLER AND HIS ADMIRALS BECAME convinced that many troop and supply ships could be sunk as they were leaving the United States. Therefore, they deployed large numbers of submarines (called U-boats) off the American east coast. They were shockingly successful. It proved to be easy to sit in the shipping lanes just offshore and torpedo ships. By October of 1942, the German U-boats had sunk more ships and killed more men than we had lost in the Japanese attack on Pearl Harbor.

This was a crisis of the greatest magnitude. We could not carry on a large-scale war effort in Europe if we couldn't get our men and equipment across the Atlantic, and airplanes were still too small and crude to carry the massive amounts necessary. Americans, however, have always been ingenious and, much like the British at Dunkerque, they came up with an idea that, at first, seemed almost laughable in its absurdity. The plan was to recruit men who were 4F (the draft classification for physical deferment from service) but who had peacetime experience as sailboat and racing yacht operators. Many of these boys were sons of wealthy individuals who owned sailing boats, racing yachts, and even fishing schooners. The government recruited these young men and their boats into what became known as "The Hooligan Navy." The vessels were painted black and fitted with underwater listening devices, ship-to-shore radios, and 50-caliber machine guns. Dispersed over the shipping lanes 50 to 100 miles offshore, they were referred to as our "Picket Fence Defense Line." In those days, long-range radar was not effective, so these small vessels became the eyes and ears of the Navy.

This operation was controlled from a hastily put together headquarters in Greensport, Long Island. The German submarines usually could not detect these small craft, especially the sailboats. It was also unlikely that the U-boats would waste a torpedo on one of them. The underwater listening devices could sometimes detect a sub's engines, and when they surfaced at night to recharge their batteries, the Picket Fence Defense forces detected them and radioed the locations to the Navy, which immediately sent destroyers or torpedo planes out.

The Navy also learned that large, well-protected convoys were much more successful at combating the U-boat menace than single ships trying to elude the underwater predators. Because of America's success in dealing with the subs, the German losses mounted. It soon became almost suicidal to operate so close to the coast. They were withdrawn farther out into the Atlantic or moved closer to the European theatre. Their losses were so great that a large percentage of German U-boat crews did not live to see the end of the war.

In 1945, the American public generally did not know how successful our Navy had been at reducing the threat to our troops and supply line. And, in fact, ships were still being sunk. When we departed on that cold winter sea, we were not alone in our anxiety that we might not even get to Europe before the war got to us.

On February 19, 1945, a huge convoy sailed out of New York harbor. There were ships as far as we could see in every direction. On the farthest horizon were sleek, speedy destroyers to protect us from U-boats. Dozens of supply ships of every size and shape made up the next ring. In the very middle of this armada were the troop ships, including ours, the *Marine Devil*. We were packed into its hold like sardines.

This wartime voyage by troop transport in convoy was a unique experience. Groups of us were assigned to windowless compartments equipped with long wooden tables and benches. We ate, wrote letters, played cards, in fact we did everything that required sitting at those tables because there was no other furniture. Each of us was assigned to a white, canvas hammock slung from hooks in the ceiling. I had been surprised at the lack of privacy at Fort Benjamin Harrison, but I hadn't seen anything. There was just enough room to slide into the hammock. The hammock above me was within inches of my face. If I weren't careful when I moved at night, I'd hit the guy above me. You couldn't move quickly or you would bump into someone or something. Since everything was made of steel, it hurt. In those close quarters we wanted to stay clean, but there was no hot water. We got a lukewarm, saltwater shower about every three days.

Mingled with the salty ocean breezes was the smell of seasickness. The Atlantic was quite rough in February and many of the guys were nauseous. Some didn't eat much from the time we left New York until we arrived in France.

The guys spent their time reading, writing letters, and gambling. It seemed that the same ones won most of the money. Some guys lost what they had, borrowed more from their buddies, and then lost that. No one seemed to worry too much about money, though. Actually, it didn't seem very important. We knew that a torpedo could come crashing in at any moment, so winning or losing money was pretty insignificant.

During the daytime we could go on deck. It was cold, but it was still preferable to being down in the crowded hold of the ship. Hour after hour I stood at the rail looking out over that armada gliding through the water. The ships seemed to constantly shift from one pattern to another. Some would speed up and others drop back. At the same time, the entire convoy, as a unit, was zigzagging constantly. The turns were sometimes sudden, and we imagined they were caused by us being in suspicious waters.

One night we were told to put on life jackets because submarines had been detected. We could hear the explosions of depth charges dropped by our destroyer escort. We fully expected a torpedo to come crashing into the ship at anytime. Fortunately it didn't happen. Had the *Marine Devil* taken a torpedo, we probably wouldn't have had a chance to get out of it. Even if we did, the Atlantic was so cold we probably would not have survived very long. As far as we were concerned, though, the new convoy system of transporting men and supplies to Europe worked.

I almost hated to see the trip come to an end because I was sure we would soon experience something far worse than being on board ship. But we were spurred on by one overwhelming obsession—going home. We could only return home after completing the mission we had come over to accomplish—the defeat of Nazi Germany. We were actually anxious to get started so we could get it over with.

Postmark: ?????,??,??

*Dear Mother, Dad & Eldena,*

*You'll probably be mad because I didn't date this because I know you always look for the date first, but we aren't allowed to date them yet. I wrote you a letter about 4 days ago and you'll probably get this and it the same time. We're still on this overgrown bathtub which someone mistakenly called a ship. It's rocking back and forth like a pendulum on a clock. That's my excuse for this poor writing.*

*It's really pretty out here on the ocean but rather windy at times.*

*I hope Bob's OK. You know, I haven't heard from him for an awfully long time. In fact, I haven't heard from anyone for a long time. I guess I expected a shark or something to bring us our mail but they didn't.*

*This is only the second letter I've written since we came aboard. I'm going to write a few tonight, though.*

*I could have written a lot of them as we don't have anything to do, but there isn't anything to say and they won't be mailed til we get there anyway, so what's the use?*

*I'll come back and go to your commencement, Al. I figure the Jerries should last about a month now. If they're lucky.*

*From the news, it seems like the Japs are really pounding the heck out of the Marines on Iwo Jima. Ask Dick if he still thinks they're tough. If he still thinks they are, ask him why they don't hurry up and win this war so I can come home. If you want to know the truth, I don't care if the WACS get the credit, just so someone ends it.*

110

*Mom, if you want to, you can send me some cookies or candy. That's all I need, though, and I don't really need that but it might come in handy.*

*Boy, yesterday was about the dullest Sunday I've spent in a long time. You know, I don't know if I'll ever be able to find anything to gripe about when I get home. It would have to be pretty bad.*

*Well, I better quit for now.*

*Love, and "Guten Abend" (Good night), Stan*

↝   ↝

Postmark: [censored], 1945

*Dear folks,*

*It's about 7:30 P.M. now and I'm sitting up here in George's 'sack.' It's the 4th one up, so we're really up in the air. This darn ship keeps rocking back and forth til I feel like I'm in the porch swing on our front porch. (Well, it's almost the same except this is a much more sickening swing.)*

*I'll be glad when I get off this tub. I'm not sick now, but I was a little woozy this morning. A few of the guys were pretty sick, but most everyone is OK now.*

*This won't be mailed til we get where we're going, but I decided to write at least one on the ship.*

*The only bad part of this overseas business (so far) is the irregular way we'll get mail.*

*This stinkin'* [censored] *Ocean is a lot rougher than the* [censored]. *When we were on* [censored], *it was nice and calm, but this son-of-a-gun is just the opposite. Oh, well, that's life.* [In retrospect, this censorship is pretty funny. Presumably, the fear was that the letter would fall into the hands of the Germans. If that were the case, it would have been pretty obvious that the writer was referring to the Atlantic since that is the only ocean near Europe. Also, Pacific would have been just as obvious.]

*Guess I better hit the sack. I've done enough sleeping on this trip to last me six months (more or less).*

*Love, Stan*

# 15
## EUROPE AT LAST:
## A BRIEF TOUR OF FRANCE

O N MARCH 1, 1945, THE 14,000 MEN OF THE 97TH DIVISION landed at Le Havre, France, the scene of heavy fighting just a few months earlier. Only a handful of buildings were left standing and none were undamaged. Everything else was rubble, punctuated by bomb and artillery craters. Many streets were still blocked by holes or the remnants of collapsed buildings.

We were taken to Camp Lucky Strike, a tent city erected by the Army Engineers, where we lived for almost four weeks before leaving for the front. On March 27, we boarded French "40 and 8s," box cars with straw on the floor that theoretically could carry 40 men or 8 horses each. They had been such a staple in World War I that the American Legion still names one of its organizational units a "40 and 8." As the train was pulling out, Pfc. Manny ran and tried to jump on, but he fell under the wheels and became our first European casualty.

The ride through Belgium was bone rattling. There were no shocks on those boxcars, so we felt every rail joint as the steel wheels hit it. If we sat down, we got sore from bouncing, but if we stood up, we were thrown around by the swaying of the car. It was cold, noisy, and we couldn't see much because the windows were at shoulder height. Nevertheless, it beat walking, as we were soon to find out.

Not far from Liege in eastern Belgium, the tracks ended unceremoniously. They had been bombed out as far as we could see. Sore and tired, we piled out, lined up, and began marching east through the devastated countryside. We walked about 15 miles before crossing the border west of Aachen, Germany, and entering the city. The site of a major battle in October 1944, when the U.S. First Army breached the Siegfried line, it was more battered than Le Havre. Block after block of burned-out buildings, piles of rubble, partial walls, bomb craters. To add to the eeriness, this large city was virtually abandoned, or else the civilian population was staying out of sight. We seemed to be alone in a wasteland.

As we rounded the corner of a cobbled street I glimpsed a young, pale, blonde woman glaring at us through the rubble of what had probably been her home. Like a trapped animal, her look combined fear and hatred in a way that still haunts me today. As we picked our way through the debris, which had once been a great city, I became aware of what a horrible thing war is for all concerned. This pretty young German lady could have been my sister. I felt sorry for her.

As we exited Aachen, we began to realize how out of shape we were. The trip from California, the time at sea, and then the long stay at Lucky Strike had taken its toll. Although we had walked 33 miles during training, many of us were dragging after 15 or so miles. A lot of guys were suffering from foot problems, which continued to plague them for the next several weeks. True infantrymen, though, we continued walking through the devastated, ghostly countryside toward the front. Everywhere we looked, trees were shattered, buildings were burnt, and mangled war equipment lay about. Among green signs of spring, there was unrelenting destruction. As darkness closed in we could see yellow-orange flashes on the horizon—silent, distant, and small.

Our steady pace, however, gradually brought the flashes closer. As they filled more and more of the sky, they acquired sounds—low, dull thuds at first, then more explicit cracks and roars, and, finally, the full voice of heavy artillery. Dog-tired, sore-footed, and hungry, we finally arrived in Neuss, on the west bank of the Rhine across from Dusseldorf, the large industrial city still in German hands.

We had marched more than 55 miles while carrying 60-pound packs and rifles. We rested only five minutes per hour, sometimes eating C rations as we walked. The two days spent in Neuss were not enough time for us to rest and recover completely, but we did get used to the constant artillery duels. We soon learned to tell the difference between outgoing and incoming shells, as well as the whistling sound of the smaller shells and the whooshing sound of the larger ones.

So, too, the reality of my situation sank in. Training and practice were behind me. This was war. At Camp Lucky Strike they had told us that some men would not make it to Berlin, but the warning had seemed routine. Ever since Pearl Harbor, I had known in one way or another that some who went to war would die there. My mother's fear as I left had been another reminder. When guys were killed in training, I had known it would be worse in battle. Seeing the destruction since we left Le Havre had shocked me, and the flashes of exploding shells and the ground trembling beneath my feet at last made clear how fragile we humans were—and how quickly we might be gone from the earth.

We were walking into one of the last great battles of the war.

Postmark: March 4, 1945
France
[Note scribbled at the top of the letter] *How about some Air Mail stamps and some cookies?—please. Even a cake if it would last that long——homemade one.*
*Dear Mother, Dad & Eldena,*
*I'll start this now although I'm not sure when it'll get mailed. I suppose you've begun to wonder what the heck happened to me, especially if you don't get this for about a month or so. I can see that from now on my mail will be very few and far between.*
*I told the general that they couldn't ship me over here until it got warm here, but someone must have slipped up because it's far from hot.*
*I'm glad we're fighting this war over here instead of the U.S. because I'd hate to see our cities bashed up like these are.*
*The cities over here are sure screwy looking (what's left of*

*them). The streets are real narrow. They seem to specialize in cathedrals and churches with steeples about as high as the Empire State Building.*

*I wish someone would get on the ball and get our mail over here. We haven't got any yet.*

*They're going to take our American money and change it into francs. I never will get used to this screwy money system.*

*We're in a camp which the Jerries used for 3 years. And for my part, they can have the darn thing back. I can understand why Balboa and Columbus and those guys went looking for a new world.*

*Don't take me serious in all this criticism. It really isn't too bad. In fact, it wouldn't be such a bad place to live in peacetime. Of course, it couldn't near compare with the U.S., but I guess no place could.*

8:30 P.M.

*I'm here again. I had to stop to eat chow. Also, something else real important happened. We had mail call. I got 4 letters from you, mother, 2 from Doris and 1 from Prange. One of Doris's letters cost her 12 cents.* [Standard postage was 3 cents.] *It had 7 pages.*

*I'm a pretty important and popular guy here at the present time. I've got a candle. See we're living in 24-man tents and my little candle is our only light. I thought it might come in handy so I brought it from California.*

*Don't worry about the chow we get over here, Mom. It's quite sufficient. In fact, we eat darn good compared to these poor French people. I wish some of those people back there could come over here for awhile and I don't think they'd gripe about anything.*

*We were issued sleeping bags today and they're really OK. It's cold in this tent but warm in those bags.*

*I'm sorta worried about Bob. I know he can take care of himself OK, but I haven't heard from him for so long I can't keep from wondering. I should be able to hear from him quick over here.*

*I hear a big drone of airplanes. It sounds like the Air Corps is going over for their nightly visit to Germany.*

*Well, get ready to start celebrating. This war will be over soon now.*

*Good night, Love, Stan*

*P.S. Just happened to think. Next week is Rocky's birthday. He'll be 3 years old, won't he? Tell him "hi" for me.*

◈　　◈

Postmark: March 6, 1945

France

*Dear Mother & Dad,*

*Maybe you'll be able to read this better than the last one I wrote. I was too darn cold then, but I'm warm now. (I'm sitting practically on top of the stove.)*

*We turned in our American money today. I guess we'll get the French francs tomorrow. One franc is worth a little over 2 cents, so we'll have to have a suitcase to carry our money in. (Almost.)*

*I guess we're going to be able to turn in our laundry to be washed, and dry cleaning, too, before we leave here. It's a good thing because my clothes are getting a little dirty. My OD's aren't too bad, though, as I just had them cleaned before we left the States.*

*Boy, the 1st Army is really raising hell according to the bulletins. I hope they keep on.*

*I saw a French farmer plowing yesterday. He had one old horse which the Germans probably didn't want but he was getting it done.*

*You should see my haircut. On the ship, I had it cut to about 1/2 inch all over. It's not near as much trouble as it was.*

*Well, there's nothing to say so I better close.*

*Love, Stan*

*P.S. I think our chow is better over here than it was in the States.*

◈　　◈

Postmark: March 18, 1945

France

*Dear Mother and Dad,*

*Guess I better get this written before dark or I won't get it written at all tonight. They're getting a volleyball game up but I'll sit this one out and write. This is Sunday and it has really been a beautiful day. We played volleyball almost all afternoon. I'm afraid our days of playing are almost over for a while though.*

*I just now got a letter from you, Mom. I'll do my darndest to find Bob if I ever get the chance. After the war is over we should be able to get to see each other before one of us gets shipped out. I figure this German war will be over by June 15.*

*I'm getting so I can understand some French and speak a little. Our GI French book really comes in handy though. I'm studying German too and I'll probably be using it.*

*I'm sending a French 2-franc coin home in this letter. I've got a couple little articles here about Bob's 103rd division that I thought you'd like to see so I'll send them.*

*I always thought the Germans had classy uniforms but I've changed my mind. They aren't any good either. As far as that's concerned, there isn't a uniform in the world I like except my civilian clothes.*

*P.S. I'm feeling swell.*

*Love, Stan*

# SPRINGTIME 16 GERMANY

WE WERE WELCOMED TO NEUSS BY GERMAN NIGHT PATROLS. Experienced combat soldiers, with the cunning of cornered ferrets, they stole across the river almost every night, regardless of the weather. They knew the territory well, and if they could not win, they were at least going to make us pay dearly for victory.

When the 101st Airborne Division, fresh from Bastogne, relieved us, we piled into trucks for a change and rode south. But this luxurious transportation ended all too soon at a pontoon bridge over the Rhine near Bad Godesberg. We walked across the bridge and then north about 15 miles to the Sieg River, where we relieved units of the 78th Division in a situation very similar to that at Neuss.

We were now part of the Allied forces preparing to fight the Battle of the Ruhr Pocket. British and American forces had surrounded 350,000 German soldiers in the Ruhr, Germany's industrial heartland. This was an area equivalent to Detroit, Cleveland, Pittsburgh, and Chicago combined—very important to the German war effort. The Germans were determined to hold the region at all costs because, with its giant Krupp factories, this was their only remaining center for producing war material.

Thus, one of the last great battles of World War II shaped up.

In a steady drizzle, we slipped and trudged through the dark, looking for foxholes which, though only 20 to 25 feet apart, were still hard to spot. When we found one, the men from the 78th got out and we jumped in. Having been dug in for about two weeks on a ridge overlooking the river and Merten on the other side, the departing soldiers warned us that the Germans knew where the foxholes were and that the nightly patrols always attempted to throw grenades into them.

Only three months after my wonderful Christmas at home in Indiana, I found myself soaked and shivering, isolated in a foxhole in Germany with Joe Vonksky in the same condition. In the cold, wet blackness we were awake all night, listening to artillery whooshing overhead in unsteady rhythm—outgoing, incoming, incoming, outgoing. But what was worse was the full expectation that at any moment either a hand grenade or a German soldier himself could join us in our muddy burrow.

With the first, thin light of dawn, the rain and some of our misery ended. I heard the happy crowing of a rooster. When I peeked out of the foxhole, below me was one of the most peaceful scenes one can imagine: a beautiful, meandering river, and on the other side, a picturesque German village out of the Middle Ages. A few houses had been demolished by artillery, but 90 percent of the town appeared to be the same as it had been for centuries. It looked so peaceful that it seemed it would be perfectly safe to cross the river, enter the village, and wander down the streets. My fantasy was interrupted by an incoming artillery shell crashing noisily into the hillside, soon answered by one of our own shells exploding on the other side of the river.

After we had lived in the foxholes for a couple of days, early one morning word came down from the next hole that we were to prepare to move across the river at noon.

Despite my misgivings, in broad daylight we abandoned our muddy but safe homes and gathered at the river's edge. I complained loudly, "It really takes a pretty stupid guy to send us across this river at noon. We should have gone early this morning under cover of darkness."

After that, whenever orders came down, someone would ask, "Hey, Ike [nickname for Supreme Commander Eisenhower], what do you think about this order?"

Soon, I had my second nickname of the war: everyone was calling me Ike. Some of the new replacements thought my name really was Ike. Even after the European campaign, while on occupation duty in Japan, many of the guys still called me Ike.

The engineers had rubber assault boats ready. A squad of men jumped into each one and started across the river. It was not deep, but the current was swift because of the spring rains.

Just as the first boats bobbed into the middle of the river, the Germans let go a massive mortar barrage. The term "sitting duck" took on a new meaning for us. The concussion of the shells hitting the water created waves, which threw the little rubber boats around like so many corks. To keep from capsizing we would move in unison from one side of the boat to the other. This was a risky maneuver at best. Finally an explosion caught my boat on one side, just as a trough appeared at the other. Everyone was thrown unceremoniously into the churning water.

Fortunately, we were slightly closer to the Merten side. The water was only up to about our shoulders, so we struggled and sloshed our way slowly to the bank. It seemed that for every three steps forward, the current pushed me back at least one. Mortar shell geysers continued to appear all around us, but, as in familiar dream sequences when you are trying to run but can't, we pushed forward for what seemed an eternity until we finally made shore and climbed out of the water. Cold and wet, I tipped my gun down to let the water run out and then scrambled away from the mortar fire toward the sleepy little village.

Initially, my first morning fantasy seemed to be coming true. As we approached, our platoon encountered no opposition. It appeared that we might simply walk in like tourists. But after about half of us had walked to the edge of the town, the Germans unleashed a savage attack. Vicious house-to-house fighting ensued. The German garrison did not surrender until we had seized a good part of the village. It became clear that we overwhelmingly outnumbered them.

We took 65 prisoners with only six casualties. However the first death in our platoon, S/Sgt David Krull, illustrated how helpless we all ultimately were. He was well trained, in excellent physical condition, and seemed as capable of taking care of himself as anyone. Nevertheless, he took a sniper's bullet through the head. T/Sgt.

Bartig first saw him lying face down. Years later, he told me that he had turned the body over, to see if he could help or at least identify it. As he did so, Dave's finger pulled the rifle trigger firing a shot, which narrowly missed another soldier nearby.

Another casualty, Lt. Jim Darrow, cautiously stuck his head up to look over the stone fence surrounding the southern portion of the town. A German hand grenade exploded in his face. Decades later, at a company reunion, Jim told me that when he woke up in a hospital several days later, he couldn't see. Thinking he was permanently blind, he panicked. When the nurse came around, he asked rather pitifully if there was any hope. The nurse laughed and told him they wouldn't know until they took off the bandages, which were wrapped around his entire head. When they were removed, he found to his great relief that he could still see. His face, however, was extensively marked by the exploding grenade.

There was no time for rest after taking Merten, though. We marched on to Fussholden, another small village just to the north. At last we had the opportunity to put into practice the skills at digging foxholes that we had so painstakingly acquired in training. I was genuinely happy that we had had to dig so many. That night, dog-tired, I slept ever so peacefully in my owner-constructed home.

The next morning, April 9, 1945, soon after moving out, we came upon the fairytale-looking Schloss Hernnstein, a great stone medieval castle. We quickly surrounded it, but, striking a blow for civilization, the German soldiers decided against defending it so that it would not be damaged. After taking them prisoner, we toured the ancient halls. It was in remarkably good shape, with massive furniture, tapestries on the walls, and expensive rugs on the floors. We decided it was good enough for us to stay in that night, so I climbed the stone stairs to one of the upper floors. I threw my sleeping bag down on the rug, crawled in and fell into a deep sleep, secure in the belief that we were safe in this magnificent old castle. [The Epilogue tells of my return in 1995.]

Unfortunately, my sound sleep didn't last long. About 3:00 A.M. we were awakened and told to prepare to move out. Our orders were to clear several little villages before dawn. The first of these,

Hernnstein Castle, as it appeared in 1920.

Broscheid, was a short walk from the castle. We surprised a few German soldiers on guard duty and they surrendered immediately. We then made a major error. We walked through the deserted streets without checking the houses. About a half-mile north of town we stopped and tried to orient ourselves on the map. We couldn't, so Jim (from Texas and a different platoon), who could speak German, was told to go back and find out the name of the village. Because we had walked dozens of miles in the previous week, many had sore feet, but mine were in good shape, so I was sent with him.

As we neared Broscheid, we could see some soldiers in the center of town. Since we had come through less than an hour before, we assumed they were Americans. As we got closer, we recognized the distinctive German helmets. It was our misfortune that they recognized us as American at the same time and raised their rifles. We turned and ran as hard as we could. Bullets whined around us as we ducked behind an old barn.

Neither of us was hit, but we had to make an instant decision: (1) take off across a large open field toward a distant wood, (2) hide in the barn, or (3) lie down in a ditch beside it. If we ran across the

Exterior view of Hernnstein Castle, 1995.

The village of Broscheid, taken in 1995.

field, there was a good chance they would pick us off. If we went into the barn, they would probably find us eventually. In less time than it took to write this, we dropped into the ditch, hugging the ground and hoping they would not see us in the darkest hour before the dawn. It proved to be the right decision.

No sooner had we hit the dirt than about a dozen Germans came running around the barn. When they didn't see us running across the field, they assumed we had gone inside. As we lay in the ditch, listening to the voices from the barn only a few feet away, I pulled the pin and held a hand grenade tightly, ready to toss it the very second we were seen. I tensed as the Germans burst out of the barn. But without even looking in our direction, they ran back to their comrades in the center of town. As they disappeared, we jumped up and started running across the field.

We didn't slow down until the barn was lost in the gloom and we figured they couldn't see us. When we finally stopped, we had no idea where L Company was. We were winded, lost, and disoriented. We didn't know what direction we had run in the field and we could hear machine guns, mortars, and small arms fire all around us. At last I realized I was still clutching the grenade with the pin out. We didn't want to draw attention to ourselves, but I had to get rid of it somehow. So we hit the ground and I tossed it into the darkness. After the explosion, we waited a minute or two to see if we had been noticed. Nothing happened, so we started walking.

Broscheid proved to be a communications center. Every house had been filled with German soldiers. Had our company searched the houses when we first went through, we could have eliminated Jim's and my close encounter with death or capture, and a vicious fight that occurred when my platoon came back to town looking for us. They captured 69 prisoners plus extensive weaponry, including mortars and some large artillery pieces (the fabled 88s, large caliber and highly accurate). L Company then moved on, clearing four more little towns and finally entering Koboch.

Meanwhile, Jim and I went a mile or so without finding a clue as to where we were. Since it was broad daylight we decided it would be safer to hide in some thick bushes until something happened to orient us. After several hours of listening to machine gun and small arms fire on all sides, a large artillery shell exploding right in front of us shocked us. It was followed by a group of Germans retreating to escape the American howitzers. The heavy artillery shells kept coming closer and closer. As it turned dark we began digging as furiously as possible without drawing attention. Even a small foxhole would offer some protection. Then a shell hit so close it showered us with dirt and debris. We knew the next one might land right on top of us, but if we left, especially in the dark, the Germans would likely kill or capture us. We reluctantly stayed, waiting for the near inevitable.

It never came. The shelling had stopped. The night suddenly quieted. We decided to try to get back to American lines. At about 4:00 A.M. we began walking in the direction the Germans had come from, hoping to find the troops who had attacked them. We thought we could move under cover of darkness and by the time we found them, it would be light enough for the Americans to recognize us. We knew from experience that soldiers shoot at anything that moves in a battle situation.

Less than a mile from our bush shelter, someone shouted, "HALT! Who goes there?" We couldn't see him so we quickly yelled, "DON'T SHOOT! We're Americans!" Eight or ten GIs suddenly surrounded us. One said, "Where in the hell did you guys come from?" They had heard us for some time and were ready to cut us down if our answer had not been correct.

They put us into a Jeep and returned us to L Company, which was by then about ten miles away. Had we not gotten back when we did, my parents would have received the dreaded telegram, "Your son is missing in action." My poor mother would have had a heart attack. Instead, I was awarded the Combat Infantryman Badge and the Bronze Star for this and other action in the Battle of the Ruhr Pocket.

We rejoined the Company at Stein, and on April 10, we pulled out at 8:00 A.M., continuing in a northwesterly direction. At the highway Zeit Strasse we were pinned down by machine gun fire. We tried to cross the highway one by one. It was a case of being on the wrong end of a shooting gallery. We were lying single file in a ditch beside the highway. One man would jump up and run as fast as possible to the ditch on the other side. We moved up slowly as each man attempted to cross. Some got safely across and some were cut down. Finally, it was my turn. I waited for a lull in the shooting, took a deep breath, and jumped up. As I lunged forward, my foot caught on the edge of the pavement and I fell flat. A spray of machine gun bullets hit the highway directly in front of me. I bounced up instantly and took off as fast as I could. Another volley raked the pavement where I had lain just a moment before, but I was across the highway and into the safety of the woods. I was spared only because I had fallen at the most opportune time. Others, including my good buddy from Idaho, George White, were not so fortunate. George was wounded and spent seven months in a military hospital. I never saw him again. When we regrouped, a search and destroy squad was sent after the machine gun. It was silenced with a shower of grenades.

Among my many close calls, this one ranks near the top. In the fifty-plus years since, I have replayed that scene over and over again. I was surprised, however, at the contents of a letter from a buddy, Eddie Hull. We were together all through combat and the occupation of Japan.

> January 16, 1996, A.M.
> Hi, Stan,
> Sure was good talking to you last evening. Brought back a lot of old memories . . .
> One of the best memories of over there is the one (I can see it just as clear as the day it happened) of you tripping & falling just as that machine gun went off while I laid in the ditch watching the dirt kick up just above my back. God sure has been (and is) good. I'll stop and get this mailed. Keep in touch.
> Remembering long ago,
> Ed Hull

In combat, I didn't have an opportunity to write many letters. We were moving every day and usually I didn't have time or, in many cases, even paper. Censorship limited what could be said in those we did write; however, I tried hard to let my parents know I was still

126

alive, and to give them the feeling that all was going well, whether it was or not. Note this letter is postmarked after the Merten and Broscheid encounters but there is no mention of any danger or even excitement.

Postmark: Tuesday, April 10, 1945
Somewhere in Germany
*Dear Mother, Dad, & Eldena,*
*Well I've finally got time to write a couple pages. We've been pretty busy the past few weeks and haven't had any time to write.*
*We are across the Rhine as you may know now but can't tell you exactly where. I had a pretty close shave yesterday but didn't get a scratch and I'm feeling fine so don't worry.*
*Mom, don't believe all the stuff you hear about the Jerries being licked. They're deteriorating but still pretty tough.*
*Tell Doris not to expect any letters for awhile as I probably won't be able to write except maybe a line or two to you.*
*I've got a swell .32 caliber pistol and a blackout flashlight from the Jerries. They've got some pretty good equipment but I think ours is better and I think the American is as good a soldier as any Kraut.*
*Haven't heard from Bob for a while. Hope he's O.K.*
*So long for today*
*Love, Stan*

# PICKING THE (RUHR) POCKET

<sup></sup>

A<small>T 6:30 P.M. ON</small> A<small>PRIL</small> 11, <small>AN ENEMY COUNTERATTACK BEGAN.</small> (A<small>S IT</small> turned out, it was a delaying tactic rather than a serious offensive move, but we had no way of knowing that.) We fought to disorganize the attack while we formed defensive positions and set up outposts in three towns.

By the evening of the 12th, our third platoon had dug in outside of Stein. Joe Vonksky and I made our foxhole about five feet by three feet and tried to make ourselves as comfortable as possible, expecting to be there at least 24 hours before going back on the offensive.

We shared some small talk, but we were both exhausted after three days with very little sleep. I won the match to sleep first and had just closed my eyes when Joe nudged me. "Stan, look what's coming towards us!"

Out of the woods a half-mile away, a German soldier was walking towards us. We expected there would be others, but none appeared. Apparently alone, he walked fairly quickly with his rifle slung over his shoulder and his arms swinging naturally. We both drew beads on him as he got larger and larger. What should we do?

We had only been in combat a few days and we were supposed to kill German soldiers, but neither Joe nor I wanted to shoot him. This was an enemy, but he was also another human being. He did not seem threatening, walking out in the open like that. He was someone's son or husband. They were as worried about him as my mother was about me.

128

As he came within one hundred yards, we feared he might throw a grenade or start shooting if he saw us, but he just continued walking. At 40 feet, I shouted, "HALT!" Joe and I stood with our rifles pointed at him. He froze in his tracks and his hands shot up. We jumped out of our foxhole and ran to him. He didn't move. Joe grabbed his rifle, and I noticed a pistol strapped to his belt. Under Joe's cover, I removed the pistol and strapped it onto my own belt. I then searched him and found no other weapons.

The tension eased as he saw we had no intention of shooting him and we realized that he merely wanted to surrender. He slammed his steel helmet to the ground with a grimace. Since he didn't speak English, this was his only way of demonstrating his disdain for the military.

We had another decision to make. What would we do with this man? We realized we were exposing ourselves to enemy fire if his buddies in the woods were watching. Our only immediate refuge was our foxhole. Since we had tempted fate so far, we took our prisoner with us. He was quite cooperative and appeared happy to be in American hands without having been shot on sight. Besides, he was unarmed, and there were two of us. The three of us crowded into the hole in the ground and waited.

Talking proved to be an exercise in futility. After "Joe," "Stan," and "Horst," we couldn't figure out anything. He did not understand English or our pidgin German, and we couldn't make out a thing he said. Finally, we pared the conversation down to one word at a time, and were able to communicate a little. He pointed towards his pocket and said, "Chokolat." Joe could understand that and pulled out several large pieces of German chocolate, which the three of us shared.

Several hours later, a food jeep arrived and we got the driver to take Horst. When we told Horst to get into the jeep, he started towards it, but suddenly turned on his heel, stretched his arms out and embraced me. His eyes glistened as he said, "Danke schoen," thank you. He was extremely grateful that we had spared his life. We felt much better than we would have had we killed him. I often wish I had gotten his full name so I could have met him sometime after the war.

This German was extremely fortunate, and he was well aware of that fact. He had survived one of the most dangerous situations faced by a combat soldier—the moment of surrender. There is never a guarantee that a soldier will be taken prisoner rather than be killed. Soldiers on both sides were just teenagers thrown into an unnatural situation. They were scared, they resented being in that position, and they were trigger-happy. No one could forecast how he would be treated by the enemy—especially one who had just lost his best buddy in combat. Only when they were finally behind the front lines in a POW cage could prisoners feel a little safer.

I never actually saw a prisoner harmed by any of our men. However, I did hear of one such incident involving my outfit. While I was separated from L Company at Broscheid, prisoners were taken. As the Germans surrendered, a sergeant from Kentucky was said to have shot a man as he emerged from a pillbox with his hands up. I heard about the incident after I rejoined the company. I have no doubt that it actually happened. I know this type of thing happened many times—by both sides. Sometimes desperate soldiers figured that they themselves might perish unless they killed their prisoners. I am glad I didn't witness any such atrocities. I don't think any records were kept, and I never heard of anyone being court martialed for shooting prisoners. Unfortunately, it happened all too often.

On April 13 we moved to Post Seelscheid, where we had our first hot meal in two weeks. The meal was great going down, but, unfortunately, not very good coming back up. I was so sick, I just moved back and forth from the latrine to my sleeping bag. It may have been because I had had little to eat but K rations for weeks, or maybe I ate too fast, or the events of the previous two weeks may have been too nerve wracking, or it may simply have been some minor food poisoning. At any rate, I went from overjoyed to miserable in record time. And, I was soon to go on a night patrol.

The only thing worse than living in frontline foxholes is going on night patrols. It is an experience totally unlike anything a person could ever suffer in civilian life. You can't see in the dark, so you are in constant danger. You don't know where you are going or even where you are half the time. Often it is raining or snowing, or so hot your clothes are wet with sweat. Sometimes, your orders are to find the enemy, sometimes to capture a prisoner, sometimes to make an attack. No matter the situation, you are stumbling around in the blackness subject to being shot—by the enemy or your own side— at any moment. I am certain the German soldiers didn't like them any more than we did.

At 9:30 P.M. my squad was sent on night patrol. Though I could hardly stand up, I was told to go anyway. Our orders were to start walking toward German lines until we drew fire, in order to find out how far in front of us they were. We knew they had been retreating, but we didn't know if they were one hundred yards or two miles ahead of us.

It was a night so dark I honestly could not see my hand in front of my face. Only a few hundred yards out, we came to a barbed wire fence. Most of us had crawled under the bottom wire when one guy's knapsack got caught. Trying to free himself, he jerked the fence to which a cowbell was attached. The clanging seemed deafening. We all hit the ground expecting a burst of gunfire. There was none, but the rest of our squad had no patience with someone making noise, as we had no idea how close to the Germans we were.

The tense silence was broken by, "Don't move, you stupid S.O.B.! I'll get you loose from the fence!"

Someone crawled back and untangled the knapsack and we moved on very cautiously.

A few hundred yards further, we stopped to regroup. The sergeant in charge started to give orders as to who would lead, who would bring up the rear, and so forth. At that point, we had a mini-mutiny. Private Coolon, a tough kid who seemed to be afraid of no one, said to the sergeant, "You get to the rear of this damn column. You are no longer in charge, and we don't want to hear another word out of you tonight."

When 12 fully armed men are alone in enemy territory where each forward step can bring immediate death, the rules of conduct can change quite rapidly. The sergeant did as he was told, and the incident was never discussed again.

Using a compass and a map, we walked directly towards the Agger River, expecting to be greeted by enemy guns at any time. During the two hours it took us to find the river, we saw no Germans. The crisp air was deadly silent except for the water lapping against the bank. We found a small footbridge that crossed the river and held a whispered conference. Initially, the question was, Who would be first to try to cross the bridge? Since the autobahn incident, no one was eager to get into another shooting gallery.

Someone said, "The bridge is probably mined. I'm not going to be the first one to find out."

Someone else ventured that even if it weren't mined, the Germans would probably be dug in across the river. Finally, we concluded it would be suicide for our little squad of men to cross that river. The consensus was that we should make our way back to our own lines. None of us would cross the river.

When we returned, we were greeted with, "HALT! Who goes there?" We gave the password for the night and were not shot. We quickly reported and hit the sack. It was 3:00 A.M. An hour later, we were rousted and told to move out. The entire regiment advanced to the Agger. It was daylight and German forces dug in across the river opened up on us. Fortunately, we had overwhelming numbers and firepower, and they soon surrendered.

Had our little squad attempted to cross the river alone that previous night, we would undoubtedly have been killed or captured. Private Coolon may well have saved all of our lives.

The next day, April 14, we occupied Mettlesbach, and then stopped at Highway 1 where we took 75 more prisoners. By a rare bit of luck, we boarded trucks for Bergisch-Gladbach. In the truck, one of my personal friends was standing beside me.

He said, "Stan, I don't know how much more of this I can take."

A few minutes later, he shot himself in the foot, only inches from mine. Screaming in agony, he was removed from the truck. I never saw him again. No one will ever know if his gun went off by accident or on purpose. Regardless, he now had a "million dollar wound"—a ticket away from the front lines.

From Bergisch-Gladbach we moved through Vorswinkel and

Blecher into Burscheid, a little village where we set up guard outposts and arranged to spend the night. In the early evening I was standing guard when a young German soldier came riding down the road on a bicycle. He was relaxed, pedaling smoothly and looking at the countryside. When I shouted "HALT!" he screeched to a stop, jumped off the bicycle, and put his hands up. He was, indeed, surprised and frightened. He spoke a little English and informed me that he had been given permission to visit his parents who lived nearby. He was unaware that Americans had occupied the town held by his German unit only that morning.

I took his rifle and asked if he had any more arms. He motioned for me to come with him. I followed him warily into a barn where he reached under the straw, pulled out a pistol and handed it to me. It was fully loaded. I strapped it on my belt and carried it the rest of the time I was in combat. I eventually brought it home with me. Every time I look at that pistol, I think of the surprised and frightened German soldier who had ridden a bicycle into a village occupied by American soldiers.

Dealing with civilians raised different problems than those we encountered handling prisoners due to a stupid and totally unenforceable order. As the American Army drove into Germany, the Supreme Headquarters of the Allied forces ordered a policy of nonfraternization. That is, we were not to talk to German civilians except on "official business," whatever that was. Here are a couple of examples of the meaninglessness of the edict.

One morning I was sitting in a foxhole in the Ruhr area when a girl of about 17 came walking down the narrow country lane right in front of me. Of course, this was extremely dangerous. I suppose it would have been considered "official business" if I had told her to go back where she came from. I was curious, however, as to why she would be walking in a battle area, so I ordered her to my foxhole. She was terrified and immediately broke into tears. Although I tried to calm her, she clearly could not understand a word I said. She finally burst out with what seemed to be a feverish explanation that she was having her monthly period and hence was unsuitable for victimization. I had no such intentions, but the language barrier proved insurmountable. I finally motioned for her to continue her walk at the same time trying to act out in a kind of desperate charade how dangerous it was in the front lines. With her face contorted with fear and confusion, she hurried down the path and out of sight, possibly to her death. According to the non-fraternization policy, I probably should have either turned her back or let her go without a word, but it would have taken a cold person indeed to not want to help her avoid pointless destruction. Of course, no one else would know what had taken place anyway.

Another time, we set up guard posts and took over most of the homes in a small village. My squad was assigned to one house. We allowed the owner, a middle-aged German lady, to stay in one room while we took over the rest of the house. After she saw that we were not going to hurt her, she came out of her room and tried to talk with us in her limited English. We tried to respond in our equally inadequate German.

She showed me a picture of her son, who was in the army on the Russian front. Except for the uniform, he might have passed for an American. As we talked, one of our guys came in and threw his rifle down on her highly polished dining room table. I saw her anguished look as the rifle slid across the table. I felt sorry for her.

I said, "Get that rifle off that table!" (GIs were pretty direct in the way they talked to each other.)

He turned and stared at me.

"I know you wouldn't do that at home," I said. "Get it off that table."

He looked at me for a moment more, walked over, picked up his rifle, and leaned it against the wall. The incident was never mentioned again.

The German lady looked at me with tears of gratitude. The next morning, as we left her house to do battle with her German Army, she embraced me. How could we possibly have avoided talking to her? How could we have treated her as an object, only to be addressed with "official business"?

On April 17, we entered Solingen, the Pittsburgh of Germany, a sooty city of huge steel mills. We quartered in pleasant apartments, though, and rather enjoyed ourselves. We also captured a German communications truck, and set up an extensive telephone system so we could talk to each other in apartments all over the city. GIs were nothing if not inventive.

Enemy soldiers surrendered by the hundreds. We had to set up a large POW camp to handle them. We also captured large numbers of high-ranking Nazi party leaders, SS troops, and one high-ranking German general. In a small village nearby, Germans were surrendering so fast that we could not handle them properly. They kept coming in from all sides with their hands up. They were all armed, but we only had twelve men, so we just had them wait until we could accept and disarm them. It was really a funny scene, all these soldiers with guns, sort of milling around while the greatly outnumbered Americans slowly processed them one at a time.

One day we captured about 75 Germans and told them to stay in a certain area. All of a sudden they started moving to a different place. A German officer was directing them, and they were so used to unquestioned authority that they were obeying as one.

I decided we had to let them know that they were now American prisoners and they would be taking orders from us rather than from their own officers. I motioned to the officer and said in my very limited German, "Kommen sie hier," come here. He looked at me, but didn't move a muscle. I flicked the safety latch off my rifle and repeated my command. That got his attention. He walked smartly over to me. I barked, "Haende hoch," hands up.

He looked at me for a moment, and then put his hands in the air. When he did so, I noticed a watch on his arm and I reached up and removed it. It was a Russian watch, probably taken when he was serving on the eastern front. I put it in my pocket and told him to rejoin his troops. Some of the German enlisted men smiled when they saw their officer humiliated by a young American. Like Americans, they didn't always like their leaders either, but some of them seemed to be as intimidated by their officers as by their captors.

Except for guns, that was the only thing I ever took from a captured German. In fact, it was the first time I ever took anything that didn't belong to me, and later, I was not proud of doing it. Though I felt bad about it afterwards, at the time I believed it was important for them to know they were our prisoners and should do as we said. A few months later, on Cebu Island in the Philippines, I traded the Russian watch to a Filipino for a pearl. War does not bring out the best in men.

Although we did not realize it at first, the Germans were very anxious to surrender to the Americans rather than the Russians, Poles, French, or Yugoslavs, all of whom treated them badly. The Americans hadn't seen their cities destroyed and their wives and girlfriends raped, like many of these other nationalities had. We hadn't spent years in prison camps or as slave laborers, so we treated them well. I never saw any German prisoners of ours physically mistreated. We also made every effort to feed them and see that they got water. They didn't particularly like our C rations, but they ate them the same as we did. They were not treated with any special kindness, but they were not physically harmed either.

On April 20, 1945, the remainder of the 350,000 German soldiers in the Ruhr pocket surrendered. This was the last large battle of World War II. The Ruhr, with its munitions factories, was now in American hands. The German's war-making capability was so diminished that only a crazy like Hitler would have continued the fight.

My letters from this period are considerably more lighthearted than I was.

> Postmark: April 17, 1945
> Somewhere in Germany
> *Dear Mother, Dad, & Eldena,*
> *Here goes with the letter I've been trying to get off for the last week. Hope I have time to write a little anyhow.*
> *As usual I'm O.K. and am sitting at the kitchen table of the cozy little house our squad took over last night. I slept on a feather bed last night.*
> *I don't know about the rest of the front but if they're taking as many prisoners as we are the war must be over. There were about*

*20 times more Jerries here last night than Americans to guard them. They didn't want to get away though. They gave us a rough time during the day though. Glad they decided to surrender.*

*I got a letter from Bob, 6 letters from Doris and a bunch from you yesterday. Also 1 from Aunt Ruth.*

*This is a pretty spring day here. The apple & cherry trees are all in bloom and the grass is real green. Sure wish I were home.*

*I think that by the time you get this the war over here will be officially over. I hope so anyway . . . .*

*Well guess I'll close and write Bob & Doris.*

*Love, Stan*

ॐ ॐ

Postmark: April 17, 1945
Somewhere in Germany

*Dear Mother, Dad, & Eldena,*

*I'll break tradition and write two letters in one day. I wrote you one this morning but I've got some more time tonight so I'll make up for all the times I didn't write.*

*We moved to a different place this afternoon. We've been having it easy the past day. You should see this joint we're staying in tonight. Running water and everything. And you should see the soft bed I've got.*

*I had 3 eggs for dinner today. We have eggs all the time when we get around a hen house.*

*Mom, you remember that picture I've got of George White and the one of Nichols? Well both of those guys were wounded. George got it in the leg but isn't too bad I don't think. Nick almost got his foot shot off. He'll never have to fight anymore. I think he'll be able to walk sometime but will limp.*

*This is German paper and German ink so don't blame me for it. Can't be choosy over here.*

*Some clean uniforms came in last night. I've got a shirt on that's big enough for 2 guys but it's clean anyway.*

*Well it's time for chow so I better go get ready.*

*Love, Stan*

ॐ ॐ

Postmark: April 20, 1945

Somewhere in Germany

*Dear Mother, Dad, & Eldena,*

*Haven't much to talk about but I'll write anyway. I got 3 letters today. Mom I have to laugh at you trying to find out which Army I'm in. If you find out, let me know will you?? We've already been in just about every American Army on the Western Front and I think we're going to another.*

*Boy these Germans make me mad. They know they're licked and yet they still fight. Talk about hating Germans, though, you should see some of these Russians that Hitler brought over here for slave labor. We even met Russian women who wanted to go to the front with us. They're rough too.*

*Tough about Roosevelt dying. Wish he'd lived til the war was over anyway.*

*This is really a fine mess over here. Germany is full of Russians, Poles, Czechoslovakians, French and everything else that Hitler brought here to work. No one will admit being a Nazi.*

*You should see some of the prisoners we've captured. All the way from 13 to 68. But they all know how to shoot although they aren't such good shots sometimes. A couple of weeks ago another guy and I ran into a whole squad of Jerries and they shot at us from about 25 ft and still missed. It was sorta dark though and I'm glad it was. We got out of there in a hurry and after we got started it would have taken a whole panzer division to catch us. My feet never did move so fast. I'll tell you about it sometime.*

*Mom, tell Aunt Ruth I got her letter but won't have time to answer it for a while. I don't think the war will last much longer and then I'll have time to write all I want. I guess I better close for now so until I write again*

*Love, Stan*

# ONE DOWN, 18 ONE TO GO

AFTER LESS THAN A WEEK OF LUXURY IN SOLINGEN, WE LOADED INTO trucks on April 22, 1945, and started moving east. In a cold, driving rain we traveled day and night, bouncing and slamming around as the stiff-springed vehicles smashed through potholes and various other pitfalls of war. Although our truck often seemed on the brink of rolling over, only one truck did overturn, seriously injuring several of its passengers.

We drove through Meiningen, and then Hof. Forty-eight hours after we had left, just south of town, we alighted from the trucks and began walking stiffly to Thiersheim, seven miles from the Czech border, where our division was attached to Patton's Third Army.

Again, our major activity was taking prisoners. Germans were coming out of the woodwork. Everywhere we went, they appeared individually or in groups, walking out of fields, forests, and buildings. We did not know that the Russians had taken Berlin and met the American Army at the Elbe on April 25. Indeed, as we approached Schwartzenfeld on April 26, we were met by a ferocious German defense. For about 24 hours they held the perimeter, despite our best efforts. Apparently, just before dawn, they slipped out of town and beat a rapid retreat.

When we entered the town we found out why they had wanted to keep us out. There was a huge grave so full of bodies that legs, arms, and even parts of heads were grotesquely sticking out of the ground. The Germans had rounded up large numbers of Polish,

An atrocity uncovered by L Company soon after they arrived in
Schwartzenfeld, Germany, 1945.

Russian, and other nationality slave laborers and murdered them. It
appears that they killed these poor people so they couldn't testify
about their treatment and identify the individuals responsible for
the cruelty inflicted on them.

We immediately rounded up all the adult Germans in town.
From the group, we separated the able-bodied males and made them
dig up the corpses and rebury them in individual properly marked
graves. We made the rest watch, to impress upon them the horrible
atrocity that had been committed by their troops while they stood
by. Some of the people got sick, others cried, and some tried to look
away. We—and they—all knew that none of them was innocent.
They had all known about the slave labor and the butchery. For a
nineteen-year-old kid, seeing these deformed and broken bodies
was shocking and revolting. It was a painful way to learn the meaning of "man's inhumanity to his fellow man."

Later that day, April 27, we liberated a Russian prison camp on
the other side of the town. For years, local civilians had spit at them,
thrown stones at them, and in general harassed them because they
were Russian. The prisoners were so overjoyed to be liberated that
they all wanted to hug and kiss the American troops in the tradi-

tional Russian manner. We found their aggressive displays of affection uncomfortable at the very least, and shocking at worst, and therefore made every effort to discourage them.

One of the Russians motioned for me to follow him back into the camp. Very wary of his intentions, I trailed him down the long rows of bunks with a good grip on my rifle. He stopped, reached up under the straw in a bunk and pulled out an old four-bladed bayonet with blood on it. With a broad smile and a bow, he presented it to me. I have found out since that this bayonet is 500 years old and supposedly will make a wound that will never heal—which is why the Geneva Convention outlaws this type of weapon.

Later that night, the Russians unleashed their long pent-up rage by attacking the German civilians in reprisal for the way they had been treated as prisoners. Beatings and rape were their primary methods of expression. So we had to round them all up again to protect the German civilians, especially the women. They were kept in the camp until the Russian army picked them up.

The grateful Germans showered us with small gifts and cookies. They, too, wanted to hug us, often with tears in their eyes. We quickly moved eastward, however, with the veteran 1st Division on one side and the 2nd Division on the other. As the German army crumbled, mass surrenders were commonplace. In one 14-hour period the 97th Division took in 10,696 prisoners, and during the last two weeks of the war, 7,000,000 surrendered overall.

We were the first American combat division to set up a command post (CP) in Czechoslovakia. Some of the retreating Germans were still fighting (none of us knew that Hitler had blown his brains out on April 30th). The Czechs, however, were glad to see us, not only because we were displacing the Nazis, but also because they feared the Russians. Refugees from the east had already brought tales of rape and pillaging by the Red Army. On May 6, Czechs in Prague begged us to liberate their city before the Russians got there. We were prevented from going any further east, however, because the long, brutal war in Europe came to an end on May 7, when Colonel-General Alfred Jodl signed an unconditional surrender at Reims, France. The 97th Division had fired the last shot of the European conflict of World War II.

The sense of relief is impossible to describe.

May 8, 1945 was a beautiful day in Czechoslovakia. The sky was a robin-egg blue, with tiny patches of white clouds. The spring air was pleasantly warm and the hills were alive with masses of wildflowers. In our sector, picture perfect small lakes dotted the landscape.

But to the men of the 97th Division it was even more beautiful because of something that no longer existed—the war. The lovely hills no longer reverberated with the sound of exploding artillery shells. The rattling sound of the deadly machine gun no longer destroyed the silence of the spring green countryside. We no longer had to dig holes to sleep in, and our dreams were no longer haunted by German night patrols. It was a world we had hoped for and knew how to appreciate.

Unfortunately, when the big war was over, chaos reigned. German soldiers continued to surrender by the thousands. Many simply shed their uniforms and attempted to avoid a prisoner-of-war camp. Thousands of people were trying to go somewhere else. Russians, Poles, and Hungarians were trying to go east, while the French, Dutch, and Belgians wanted to go west to their homes. Mixed in were young men masquerading as anything but German. They didn't want the Europeans to know for fear of retribution, and they didn't want the Americans to know because we were imprisoning all German soldiers. Add to all this confusion the large number of languages spoken.

Some tension and danger persisted. We found isolated groups of Germans who refused to surrender. Some crazies were organized into bands calling themselves "Werewolves." Mostly Hitler Youth and ex-SS men, they operated as guerillas and caused considerable mischief in places even after the surrender. Believers in the Thousand-Year Reich, they found a pitiful twelve years to be too bitter a pill to swallow.

The Russians especially, but not uniquely, attacked and beat Germans, raped the women, and took what they wanted. Czech women, too, were indiscriminately raped. We were the only police force, so it fell to us to prevent as much violence as possible. We had our hands full trying to sort ex-soldiers from the other displaced persons, while protecting the women and trying to keep the various ethnic groups from attacking each other.

Nevertheless, these were wonderful days for us. Organized resistance had ended, and we were only too glad to be dealing with disorganized chaos that did not constantly threaten our lives. This was also truly a liberation and we were the ones who had done it. We had beaten the Germans at their own game and thereby helped millions of people. The number of prisoners, however, and the extent of their misery was a complete surprise to us.

Nearly 100,000 Americans were released from German prisons and would soon be going home. Many of them were in bad shape, both physically and mentally. They had been living in horrible conditions with little food or medical attention. In the closing weeks, the Nazis often left them to starve because there was not even adequate food for the troops. Most had been infested with fleas and lice. (Some still felt lice crawling on them months and years after the war. It often took many trips to psychiatrists to finally rid themselves of this feeling.)

V-E Day was also a great day for the millions of slave laborers brought from all over Europe to work without pay for the German war effort. They could stay alive only by being physically able to work. As soon as they became too weak to work, they were in great danger of death by shooting, starvation, or disease.

But V-E Day was even more meaningful for the concentration camp inmates: Jews, Jehovah's Witnesses, gypsies, and anyone else who had dared to defy the Nazi gangsters. The surviving prisoners were a sight one can never forget: human skeletons in striped uniforms, most within days or hours of death by disease and starvation. Their skin appeared to be plastic stretched over a rib cage. There were no apparent faces—just skulls, often hairless, that could have been either male or female, eyes sunken in blackened sockets.

The revelation of human suffering was overwhelming. Each group I beheld seemed more pathetic than the last. In only six years of war, the Nazis had demonstrated a truly unbelievable capacity for inhuman behavior. The sheer numbers made them unique in the history of man. Millions had already been murdered in German camps when we arrived, and millions more were in a state of physical and mental deterioration beyond imagination. The worst cases, of course, were the concentration camp inmates, but other groups were nearly as bad. These included the prisoners of war and the slave laborers from all over Europe. In the final year, the Nazis had even put elderly Germans who could not work in concentration camps, where most perished from cold and starvation.

Many Germans also welcomed V-E Day. Those who had not supported Hitler and his regime of butchers were joined by many who had realized for a year or two that the war was lost, as well as by those who had come to reject their government's atrocities. Many civilians actually greeted the Americans as liberators from the Nazis and the cruel SS.

Of course, V-E Day was celebrated with parades and parties in New York City, London, Paris, and all the other great cities of the world. Millions were laughing and dancing in the streets. But in our little world in Stribro, Czechoslovakia, we did not do much partying. Admittedly, some of the guys drank more German beer and schnapps than they could handle, and a few were more than friendly with some of the many Czech girls who made themselves available. But most of us did not celebrate yet. We were very happy that the European war was over, but our joy was tempered by the sobering knowledge that American military planners had scheduled an amphibious invasion of Japan for November 1, 1945. We knew we were going to be selected because of our previous training in amphibious warfare. A few days after the great victory, we were notified that we would be re-deployed to the Pacific Theatre of Operations to prepare for the invasion of Japan.

Less than two weeks after the end of the war, in keeping with U.S.–Soviet agreements, we pulled out of Czechoslovakia into southern Germany. We stopped at Bamberg, a little over 25 miles from Nuremberg, where the surviving ringleaders of the Nazi regime would be tried and convicted. There we spent almost two weeks more or less relaxing and getting ready to leave for the United States. I boxed up souvenirs we had "liberated" during our days in combat: German medals, pictures, helmets, bayonets, a rifle, and other mementos. I wondered whether those packages sent from a little village in Czechoslovakia would ever find their way to Fort Wayne, but they all did.

In Bamberg, the suffering of the German civilians was heart-wrenching as we saw them fight for scraps of food from our garbage cans. They had accepted a government without morals, run by butchers who had no respect for anyone else's beliefs. It had cost them dearly. They lost over 4,000,000 soldiers out of a country of fewer than 100,000,000 people. Their entire country was in ruins and they were busy trying to begin the almost impossible task of rebuilding their cities and their lives. They were also dealing out their own brand of revenge to those who had controlled their lives for the previous 12 years. Many took action against neighbors who had been radical Nazis or members of the once-feared SS. Even though they had caused me untold misery and nearly cost me my life, I did admire them during that time.

In the letters from this period, I kept writing, "There isn't anything to say." It would have been more accurate had I written, "I can't think of anything to write about that isn't horrible."

Postmark: April 23, 1945
Somewhere in Germany
*Dear Mother, Dad, & Eldena,*

*Just a few lines this afternoon. This is the only sheet of paper I have and there's nothing much to say anyway.*

*It's sorta cool here today. I don't know whether it's just colder in this part of the country or whether this is just a cold spell.*

*Mom, I could use another box of cookies and candy. I haven't got the first yet but am still looking. The food situation over here isn't too good. We get enough though I guess.*

*Well I'll close for now. Maybe I'll be able to write more letters and longer ones soon.*

*Love, Stan*

*P.S. We went through the Ruhr Valley and now are down in Southeastern Germany.*

*P.S. Here's a 1000 mark note.*

൧   ൧

Postmark: April 27, 1945
Somewhere in Germany
*Dear Mother, Dad,*

*Well, you've successfully raised one member of the family to be a man, haven't you?? If I'm not mistaken this is April 27—Bob's birthday. It seems like he should be a lot older than 21, doesn't it?? He's been through a lot in the last 2 years.*

*You should see me now. We moved into a house last night and all this morning we've been preparing a super-duper meal. We killed 2 chickens, found some noodles, potatoes, and some pudding powder and got some milk.*

*Now we're 'trying' to get it ready. I've wished a hundred times that I could ask you (Mom) how to do this or that. We're getting things pretty well under control now. We've got the chicken boiled, then fried, the noodles done, the pudding made and one of the boys is mashing the potatoes now. We've got cocoa too.*

*There's a radio here too. Here we are sitting right beside the front listening to the war news.*

*We passed a bunch of Russian prisoners yesterday who just got out of a German prison camp and I think they saluted every American they saw.*

*Goering resigned this morning. That son-of-a-gun. I think he might as well have. He didn't have any Luftwaffe to command anyway. The only German planes I've seen were 3 of them shot down.*

*2 hrs. later. (1:00 P.M.)*

*Well we just got through eating. I really feel good now. We had all the chicken and noodles we could eat. The chicken wasn't quite as good as yours, Mom, but it really hit the spot.*

*Getting closer all the time. Well so long for today.*

*Lots of love, Stan*

     ﾟ     ﾟ

Postmark: April 30, 1945
Somewhere in Germany
*Dear Mother, Dad,*
*Guess it's high time I got another letter off to you so here goes.*

As per usual I don't know of anything to say. We haven't had any mail for about 2 weeks. They say it's about 100 miles back and by the time it gets here we'll be up another 100 miles. We always seem to be able to keep well ahead of it. The same goes for the hot chow. All they give us is K rations. But we always manage to dig up something else. The other day we roasted a turkey and it was really good. Four of us ate 3 chickens and a turkey in 2 days.

I haven't written anyone except you for quite awhile. There's never anything to say and I don't have paper half the time. I've seen all of Germany that I want to though. All I want is just to get home as soon as I can.

Well Guten Abend until the next time.

Love, Stan

P.S. Wait til you see all the German medals I've got. I just hope I can hang onto them until I get them home.

〜　　〜

Postmark: May 4, 1945

Dear Mother, Dad,

Mom, here's the letter you've probably been wanting. I know you've been wanting to know where I've been and what I've been doing etc. Here's a little information anyway.

First of all, I saw action in the Ruhr pocket. At that time we were fighting with the 1st Army. The Jerries in the pocket weren't too tough except one day when we ran into Nazi Paratroops (fighting as infantry). They gave us a bad time for awhile. But the SS troops are the ones who are keeping the Nazis in the war. They're too stupid and fanatic to give up.

Also, the 97th captured the airfield at Cheb, Czechoslovakia.

I haven't seen nor heard anything of Bud Foote since we got over here. If you see anything in the paper, let me know. Or, Eldena could ask his brother. He's probably doing O.K.

As for Huber—tell Jen not to worry about him. He's in the division MPs, which puts him well behind the lines. Another thing—If Jen gets a lot of letters from him and you wonder why I don't write, just remember that an MP has slightly a little more *time to himself than an Infantryman. I'll write as often as I can but when you don't hear from me, it's because I don't have the time, not because I'm just neglecting to write.*

*I'll let you know when we get to the Russians. I hope they know we're Americans when they do get here. From most reports they seem darn glad to see the Americans.*

*Mom, when we first went into the attack back in the Ruhr we had to cross the Sieg River and I bet you don't know what happened. The assault boat I was in sank. What a mess. I thought we'd be dead pigeons but as luck would have it, we made it. Of course I had to fish my rifle out of the river and pour the water out of the barrel but when I needed it (and I did) it worked. It was funny after it was over, but man, it wasn't at the time. Some day I'll probably be competing with Bob to see who can tell the biggest tale. I think I could tell some pretty good ones now (true too).*

*Hey, Eldena, what do you mean banging up the fender on that poor Ford? And after that classy paint job too. Guess I'll have to come back quick so ole Bessy will have a nice easy driver in her. You know I was really lucky with that car. Remember the night I got it? Boy I was a happy kid.*

*Well, I guess it's about time I cut this off before the censor comes over here and shoots me for writing such a long letter. Anyway I've got a good soft bed tonight and I guess I better use it.*

*Lots of love, Stan*

*P.S. Incidentally, just in case you're wondering. I'm feeling swell and in perfect condition so you don't have to worry.*

ڪ      ڪ

Postmark: May 8, 1945

V-E Day

*Dear folks,*

*It happened at last. I suppose the guys back in the states are really having a big time today, huh?? Well there's a lot of happy son-of-a-guns over here but so far I haven't noticed much change except there's no fighting—But at the present time I'm on guard.*

*It's really a good feeling to know this ETO [European Theater of Operations] war is over but there's only one thing wrong. There's still the Pacific War. I don't know whether the 97th will go or not but someone's going to have to.*

*I'm going to try to send some boxes of souvenirs home today. I've got two ready to go. I hope they get there.*

*Well I better close now. I just wanted to let you know I'm feeling swell. I just hope Bob is the same.*

*Love, Stan*

෨        ෨

Postmark: May 9, 1945
Somewhere in Europe
*Dear Mother, Dad & Eldena,*

*Well, have things quieted down back there yet?? I was listening to the AEF [Allied Expeditionary Force] program yesterday and they were describing the scenes in all the big cities. Sure wish I would have been there.*

*Boy, I feel good right now. I just washed my hair and took a bath. We've got a swell house. There are ten of us living here (my squad) and there's plenty of room. Every morning the woman who owns the place comes and washes our dishes and cleans the house up. This is one of the cleanest houses I've seen in Europe.*

*Mom, I sent two boxes home yesterday and I've still got one to send. It'll probably take a month of Sundays to get there but just so it does, I don't care how long it takes. In one box are a German helmet, bayonet, pocketknife and a bunch of medals. In the others is a German winter coat and is it a honey. I'm also going to send a Jerry rifle.*

*You should see the screwy looking procession in the street, Polish & Russian refugees going home carrying everything they've got. Going the other way are Frenchmen.*

*Well guess I better close for now.*
*Love, Stan*

෨        ෨

Postmark: May 13, 1945
Mother's Day
*My dear Mother & Dad,*

*Just got back from church services and I think I've got time to write this letter yet before chow. This is a beautiful day and we're bivouacking in a big green pasture. I'm sitting here with my shirt off. You know I have to have a good sun tan when I get home (ha). No kidding, though, there might be a chance to come back through the states before we hit the Pacific. Just don't count on it too strongly but there is still that chance I'm hoping for. If Bob goes to the Pacific (I hope he doesn't) he'll almost surely go back through the states.*

*I'm sending home this picture of this mass burial at Schwartzenfeld. Please keep it someplace. (Your scrapbook would be just the place.) I was there at Schwartzenfeld.*

*I've got 4 boxes on the way home. Hope they get there. I'm keeping some of my souvenirs with me. (My pistol and some other things.) An Air Corps guy offered me $40 for my pistol but I won't sell it. One kid in this company sold his for $75.*

*Right now we're in Czechoslovakia. It's a pretty country with quite a few lakes. We went swimming yesterday and it really felt good. This is a poor country though. 5 years under Nazi control really put the works to them.*

*Well guess I better close for now.*

*"See you soon"?!?!!*

*Love, Stan*

৩        ৩

Postmark: May 17, 1945
Somewhere in Europe
*Dear Mother & Dad,*

*Got your letter of May 9 today and one from Bob. Yours got here 3 days quicker than Bob's.*

*We're still in the dark as to exactly what the score is. We've got a good idea where we're going but we don't know which way we're going.*

*At the present we're just "goofing off." We've been going swimming, playing ball, just passing the time away. Don't expect my letters to come regular though as we may move anytime and I can't write then.*

*I'd like to see Bob but probably won't be able to unless we both go back to the states and both get there at the same time. What a deal that would be.*

*If you can't read this, it's because* Eddie Hull [his letter appears in "Springtime in Germany"] *is sitting here pestering me. He said for me to tell you he sends his regards. Now he's telling me how he's going to come down to my house after the war in his plane. Of course he doesn't even have a plane but he's happy so I won't bother to tell him he probably never will have.*

*Well guess I'll quit blowing my top for awhile and go over to the creek and wash.*

*Love, Stan*

*P.S. This is a pretty country even if it is—(just happened to think—we aren't suppose to tell where we are). You can probably guess though.*

*P.S. I'm disgusted with those packages. I only got 1 from you. Doris & Pat both sent one but I haven't got them.*

∽       ∽

Postmark: May 19, 1945
Germany
*Dear Mother & Dad,*
*Boy it's really hot here today. We went swimming this afternoon at a pretty swell pool. For swimming trunks I used a pair of German Hitler Youth athletic trunks. They're pretty good. I'm really getting a good tan.*

*Mom, I'm just a few miles outside Bamberg. It's in Southeastern Germany. And as you already know we're in the 3rd Army. I haven't seen Don's 94th Div. but they were fighting in the Ruhr pocket when we were there. Haven't seen them since.*

*So Doris called up and asked if I had enough points to come home on? Dizzy girls. She must have forgotten about the thousands of guys who have been over here for 2 or 3 years and I've been here 3 or 4 months.*

*It keeps us busy 24 hrs a day to keep up with the rumors.*

*They're flying thick and heavy. One day we're flying back to the states and the next day we're leaving straight for the Pacific and the next day we're doing something else. So just about anything could happen. But I'm not worrying as long as we're here where there's no fighting.*

*I'd like to see Bob or Vernon or someone and give them my pistol to take home just in case we don't get to. You can't mail them. I had two pistols the 2nd day we were in combat. I was on outpost (foxhole) the 2nd morning and a Jerry walked right up to me without seeing me. I don't know who was the most surprised. He was glad to surrender though and he had a lot of good stuff on him including a new Luger (pistol), flashlight, and I even got a bunch of chocolate from him. I wonder if the Japs carry as much "loot" as the Jerries. I don't suppose we'll take as many prisoners if we do go down there. Boy we really captured the Heinies. The night the Ruhr pocket collapsed we had about 15 times as many prisoners as we could take care of. They were coming in from everywhere.*

*Yowie!! I just saw an American girl. She was a Red Cross girl serving doughnuts and she was better than anything I've seen in France, Belgium, Holland, Germany or Czechoslovakia. She was from New York.*

*I'll sure be glad when we get those stinkin Japs licked so I can get the heck out of this Army and come home. Only one man in my platoon had enough points to get out and he was an old Army man who doesn't really give a damn whether he gets out or not. —That's life.*

*Well guess I'll write Doris. I haven't written her for about 2 wks.*

*Love, Stan*

෴          ෴

Postmark: May 21, 1945
Bamberg, Germany
*Dear Mother & Dad,*
*Got 4 letters from you today and a box of cookies & candy from Pat. I wasn't surprised to hear that you hadn't heard from me since April 10. The mail system is all screwed up anyway and no one's*

*mail has been getting home very good. Hope you're getting them more regularly by now.*

*I guess I told you I got another letter from Hill. But I lost the address so I'll write his mother. I haven't written him at all yet.*

*We had a retreat parade today for all the fellows who were killed in action from this regiment.*

*The other day we went up to an old castle near here. It was built in 915 A.D. There was a church near it built in the 12th century.*

*We still don't know what we're going to do yet but there are really some strong rumors going around. I just hope they're true because I may see you before too long if they are. Don't forget, though, they're just rumors and may be all wrong.*

*Well I'm going to write Pat and Mrs. Hill so I better close.*

*Love, Stan*

ی         ی

Postmark: May 25, 1945
Bamberg, Germany
*Dear Mother & Dad,*

*I'll try to type on this thing but I can't get used to these Jerry typewriters. Some of the letters are in the wrong place. Maybe you'll be able to read it though.*

*I'm sending a clipping from the Stars and Stripes telling about the 97th being alerted for shipment back to the United States. You should have heard the guys when they saw it. We had heard rumors to the effect but that was the first confirmed proof. I just hope no one gets any ideas and changes it before we get started. It's hard to believe that we're going back.*

*I guess a lot of the Service Troops will be griping especially if they have been over here for 2 or 3 years then get shipped straight to the Pacific. But I'd rather spend a year over here in the rear areas than a month on the front lines.*

*I just got two packages. One was from Doris and one from Miss Huffman. Doris really had a swell box fixed up. She even had O Henry and Clark bars. I don't know where she got them but she did.*

*I suppose we'll get to the states in July. That'll be a grand sight to see the Ole Lady in New York harbor. Bob's division wasn't alerted yet so I guess he'll go in August or September, which will be better because he won't be in the Pacific so soon. He may even stay here which would probably be better at least for awhile.*

*It's been raining here for the past three or four days but it may clear up today. It sorta looks like it.*

*Have any of my packages arrived yet? I doubt it. I will probably get there fore they do. I hope. Do you think you can put that German rifle together, Dad? I bet you can't. I had to saw a little of the stock off to get it in the box but I can glue it back on.*

*I hope those Joes in the Pacific get on the ball out there and get that war won before we get there. Of course I know that's practically an impossibility. But we've got one of them over with anyway which always helps.*

*I'd like to get into one of these gasoline dumps around Europe and take about a hundred gallons back with me. I easily use that much in 2 or 3 weeks. Mother, you can send that pair of OD pants to the cleaners if you want to. And if I'm not mistaken, I've got a complete sun tan uniform home, haven't I? Maybe I'm jumping the gun a little but there's nothing like being prepared.*

*Well, I guess I better close as it's nearing chow time.*

*Auf veeder sayn, Stan*

ᔥ　　ᔥ

Postmark: May 27, 1945
Bamberg, Germany
*Dear Mother & Dad,*

*It's Sunday morning and pretty dull around here. We just got back from church services and everyone's just lying around. Some are cleaning their German pistols but I think mine's clean enough. I've got it covered with oil so it shouldn't rust . . .*

*We're supposed to have a division parade next week. That should be something.*

*It said in last night's Stars and Stripes that the 97th would take special training in the states. It also said some of the Pacific-bound troops would train here in Europe and some would train in the*

Pacific. So we may stay in the states 2 or 3 months or maybe more. I don't know how long a furlough we'll get but we're all supposed to get one.

Well we've got to turn some stuff in and do a bunch of stuff so I'll have to close.

Love, Stan

# FAREWELL FOR FIFTY YEARS

$A$T THIS POINT WE WERE HOMESICK, EXTREMELY STRESSED FROM everything we had seen, and physically exhausted. Although we had been in combat only 42 days, it had been 42 straight days without relief. We had walked hundreds of miles with heavy backpacks. We had gone without sleep. Food had often been the minimum—not inadequate nutritionally, but just enough for us to get by. Although we were young, the entire time had been what people today would call extremely stressful. We were ready to relax and go home, if only temporarily.

On May 31, we boarded German trains for the first leg of the trip home. These were the kind you see in old movies, with doors to every compartment on the sides. Although we had nothing but K rations and C rations to eat, we were in good spirits; this was as close as we could come to a lark. We put thoughts of Japan in the background and simply enjoyed ourselves. Since the trains were not very fast, we had an excellent view of the countryside as well as the large cities, including Frankfort, Mainz, Remagen, and finally, Aachen, where we had entered the country less than three months earlier.

The devastation was unbelievable. In the rural areas, amidst the greenery of late spring, there were still the craters, wreckage, and burned out buildings. But the destruction of the great German cities was surreal.

In most of the cities it seemed like the cathedrals were the only buildings left standing. Vacant streets defined by piles of bricks, partial walls, and craters were the main scenery.

I was happy to leave all of this chaos and misery behind as I headed west through France to return to the United States.

In France we were quartered at Camp Old Gold (Like Lucky Strike, a cigarette brand; these names indicate how pervasive smoking had become.), a tent city 29 kilometers from Dieppe. We lived in twelve-man tents where we counted the hours until we could board the troop ship.

Only one letter from this period has survived.

Postmark: June 8, 1945
Rouen, France
*Dear Mother & Dad & Eldena,*
*I don't know whether to write this or not because I may be in the states almost as quick as this but I'll write it anyway. I got a letter from Bob yesterday and wowie—he spent 3 pages just giving me he—. He must have been worried about me but I was just as worried about him so who does he think he is giving me heck? I wrote every chance I got to both him & you. I went for quite awhile without mail myself but I guess he didn't think of that. But I wrote him a nice cheerful 4 page letter back so maybe that'll hold him for awhile. I hope they keep him over here awhile rather than send him to the Pacific. The Army of occupation will be a good deal compared to the bloody fighting which seems inevitable . . . It'll probably take the 97th about 4 months to lick them. It took us two to lick the Jerries but the Japs may give us a little more trouble. (cough cough)*

*Hope my boxes of war "loot" get there O.K. If they don't I won't have many souvenirs. All I have with me is my pistol and German watch and a few insignias etc. But I've got plenty in those boxes. And I've got a sweet little pistol with me. The watch I have doesn't look perfect but it keeps good time. And it doesn't look bad. I took it off a German SS trooper. He was a wise guy. I couldn't understand why Bob wrote home and asked for you to send him a watch. We got a lot of prisoners with watches.*

*We'll still be here a few more days. We've got a complete new uniform including a combat blouse—SHARP. We're not doing anything much except just goofing off.*

*We got 4 bottles of coke the other day. First since we got here. We also got a bunch of candy and gum.*

*I had a date with a Czechoslovakian girl. It was just after the war ended and we were all so happy that we really had fun. I had a little trouble dancing with her. I can't even dance the American way so you can imagine how much trouble I had trying to dance European style. (We had fun though just trying to talk to each other.)*

*I didn't do anything except dance and talk with her. I didn't even kiss her although there's no doubt I could have. They regard the American doughboy as their hero and anyway we're a lot more handsome than their own men.—No remarks, Eldena*

*Well, guten tahh fer der abend. In other words—so long for tonight.*

*Stan*

*P.S. Mom we may have to bring our duffel bags and all home with us. I've got plenty of dirty socks and underwear in it too. Of course I won't hint for you to wash them for me.*

The voyage aboard the Marine Panther was almost like a pleasure cruise. We spent our time lolling about the decks. It was warm and we did a lot of sunbathing, improving on the tans we had begun in Czechoslovakia, so we could impress our girlfriends. At last, there was no fear of mines or artillery or submarines. We were just going home.

We landed in Boston on June 25, 1945, completely unprepared for the reception we received. There were parades, bands, photographers, and reporters. People in the streets hugged us, kissed us, and slapped us on the backs. Huge black headlines blared, 97th DIVISION COMES HOME. Since we were one of the first full combat divisions, if not the first, to return, we received a welcome that should have gone to some of the divisions who landed at D-Day or to the 101st Airborne, who blunted the German offensive during the Battle of the Bulge. Nevertheless, we certainly enjoyed every minute of it.

We left for home as soon as possible. What an indescribable feeling I had a couple of days later when my train pulled into Pennsylvania Station on a balmy afternoon. I stopped for a moment just to stare and enjoy the sign: FORT WAYNE. There had been many times during the previous few months when I doubted that I would ever see this city again. But here I was for thirty days. I intended to enjoy them, regardless of what I would face later.

Stan with Rocky, just after his return from Germany, July 1945.

My parents and sister greeted me like a conquering hero. I was so happy to see them that I had tears in my eyes. After repeated rounds of hugs, with everyone talking at the same time, we made it out to my cherished yellow convertible. As everyone piled in, I threw my duffel bag into the trunk and took the driver's seat. This was the life! Cruising down the street with the top down in the sunshine.

When I turned into the driveway on the Maysville Road, Rocky came running and another emotional greeting ensued. He was as excited to see me as I was to see him. It had been over half a year since we had rolled in the snow together—a long time in a dog's life, and in mine, too.

It seemed the finest luxury to sit in our old-fashioned porch swing on a gorgeous afternoon, sipping lemonade and eating Mom's cookies. So peaceful. No artillery shells, no machine gun fire, no explosions of any kind. The stillness of the day was pure joy.

The next day I was out and about. We were required to wear our uniforms at all times. Although I thought of sneaking into civilian

Stan, Eldena, and Bud with Rocky, July 1945.

clothes on occasion, I never did. As a result, with my Combat Infantryman badge and ribbons with two battle stars, every place I went I was treated like a hero. I knew that I had just tried to survive over there—not to be a hero. I also knew I was extremely fortunate to have experienced the things I did without being killed. I enjoyed the attention.

In fact, that uniform saved me considerable embarrassment just a few days after I got home. Around 1:00 A.M. I was driving down State Street, returning from a date, when I saw a red light at Crescent Avenue. As teenagers tend to do, I looked, saw no cars, and went on through. At Anthony Boulevard, another red light, no cars, so I went through it too, turning south. Flashing red lights and a siren soon reminded me I was not alone. When I got out of my car, one of the officers said, "You just ran two red lights, soldier."

"I know," I said. "I just came from Germany where we didn't stop for red lights, and since no cars were coming, I just decided to keep going."

Looking at my decorations, he asked what outfit I was in. "The 97th Division," I said. "We just left Germany, and I'm on my way to Japan."

Both officers wanted to know where I had served, where I was when the war ended, and when I was leaving for Japan. We had a very amiable conversation as they asked questions about my combat experiences.

Finally, one looked at the other and said, "I can't arrest this guy."

"Neither can I," he replied, and turned to me. "But remember one thing, soldier. This is not Germany, and we do stop for red lights here."

I thanked them profusely and promised it would not happen again.

As I started my car, one officer called out, "Good luck to you in Japan, soldier."

I certainly don't recommend such blatant disregard for traffic laws, but this story illustrates how insignificant a red light can be for someone who has just experienced the brutal realities of war, where one's main preoccupation is to live for another day. It also shows how much typical Americans appreciated what the young people in the military had done and were doing.

This was not the only instance of thankful friendliness, either. I was totally unprepared for the reception I received from friends, neighbors, teachers, ex-coworkers, and even strangers in the next month.

People were delirious with joy that the European war was over, and I happened to be one of the first combat veterans to return. When I parked my Ford convertible (top down, of course) in front of North Side High, where I had graduated two years earlier, I was immediately surrounded by kids, some who knew me, but many who didn't. They bombarded me with questions about what Germany was like, what adventures I had had in combat, and what I expected in Japan. One kid whom I barely knew even brought his cute younger sister up to the car to introduce her to me. Inside the building, teachers were eager to talk to me, often asking the same questions I had just answered outside.

I knew that all of this adulation was not meant for me personally. It was an expression of relief and joy that the horrible, costly war in Europe was finally over. Americans were so tired of seeing huge casualty lists every day in the newspapers. Everyone knew someone—husband, child, relative, boyfriend, neighbor—who had been killed or wounded. Many still had sons, husbands, or boyfriends languishing in prison camps someplace. At last, the European nightmare was history.

Luckily, two of my best friends were on furlough, too. Bob Putt

Stan and his friend Bob, after their return from Germany, July 1945.

and I had been friends since the sixth grade, and had become especially close in the eighth grade when we played on the St. Joseph Central basketball team together. Bud Foote was also in the 97th Division, but a different regiment. All three of us had gone to North Side together, but Bud and I only became close friends in the army.

Of course we all had war stories to tell, but Bob's was the most harrowing. He was a crewmember of a Flying Fortress bomber on a mission to Berlin in January 1945. About half an hour away from their targets, German Focke-Wulf fighter planes attacked them. The Americans tried to fight them off and even downed one, but the Germans took their toll. Finally, with two dead and the plane badly damaged and losing altitude, the pilot ordered the rest of his crew to jump. Since the bomb bay was in flames, Bob followed the pilot and co-pilot through the nose hatch. They were still up over 20,000 feet where the air is thin, so he dropped a couple of miles before pulling the ripcord. When he did, nothing happened. He tried not to panic and pulled again, harder this time. Nothing happened.

"I knew I was falling faster and faster," he said. "As I pulled for the third time, I felt a little drag at first and then the heavy jerk on the harness as it opened. I was probably only a thousand feet above the ground when it did, but that was good enough for me."

The danger wasn't past, though. Floating through the air, Bob could hear bullets ripping past him as Germans on the ground were shooting at him. Although it was a violation of the Geneva Convention to shoot parachutists in the air, it was common practice among both the Germans and the Japanese.

Fortunately, he made a soft landing in snow and found himself lying in a cold, deserted pine forest. For two days Bob stayed in the same spot, hoping to escape detection, but he finally realized that he had to move or die from exposure, starvation, and dehydration. Ironically, capture was the only thing that could save him, even though the very thought of it was scary. His bulky flying clothes made walking difficult but they were what kept him from freezing, so he had to leave them on. Not knowing where he was or where he wanted to go, he traveled at night and hid during the day. Eventually, he started brazenly walking through small villages, hoping to find some food, but nothing happened.

Finally, civilians in a small town captured him, but his troubles were not over. They were unfriendly and he feared they might lynch him. They put him in an open cell in an old barn, where they mocked and threatened him. It was a great relief when German soldiers came and took him to Berlin. Once there, however, he was assigned only a single guard to protect him from the crowds in the subway. People were threatening, waving their fists, spitting, and shouting at him. Things quieted down once they boarded the train, but that night the Allies attacked the train and made several direct hits. Bob was nearly killed again.

When he arrived at the prison camp near Frankfort, surly SS officers began interrogating him immediately. He was hungry and exhausted, but of course they would allow him no rest. When he finally got food, it was grass soup, which turned out to be a staple of the prison diet. Since he would not tell them what they wanted to hear, he was made to sleep on the concrete floor of the unheated barracks. During one of the coldest winters on record, he was forced to stand outside in the snow for hours at a time and then the rounds of questioning began again.

When the U.S. 3rd Army arrived the SS put up stiff resistance, and there was fear among the prisoners that they would be killed in revenge. American infantrymen, however, overran the Nazis before they could commit any more atrocities, and liberated him on April 29, the same day Hitler married Eva Braun and made out his will, and the day my outfit was moving toward the airport at Cheb.

Like all the rest of the prisoners, Bob was emaciated and exhausted by starvation and maltreatment. It took weeks for him to get strong enough to make the trip home.

Neither Bud nor I could top that story.

Bob was lucky enough to be on a 90-day furlough, and was home when the Japanese war ended, so he was simply discharged. Bob wasn't worrying about Japan, though. As a former prisoner of war, he wasn't likely to be sent back overseas.

I saw a lot of Bob Putt after the war. He became one of the best painting contractors in town, and I started an insurance agency. I insured his business as well as his home and autos. He painted my homes and apartment buildings.

In fact, I called him in December 1949 to paint an apartment I owned, and he told me later that he had had no money for Christmas that year until I gave him that job. Sadly, a few years ago Bob came to my office and told me he had leukemia, but he could live for several years. He fought the disease with the same courage that he had fought the Germans fifty years earlier, but he lost this one. He died a couple of years later, ending a friendship that had started 58 years previously, in the sixth grade.

None of us knew that would happen, of course, and we made the best of our 30 days, going to house parties at the lake, dating a lot of pretty girls, and generally having a great time.

One beautiful July afternoon when the sky was that infinite blue with small white tufts floating lazily through it, Bob and I were lying face up on a beach at Lake James drinking in the warm sun with our bodies. Our dates were in the water. I closed my eyes, feeling for the first time in months a sense of total relaxation.

Bob broke the peaceful silence. "Stan, isn't it hard to believe what you and I were doing just three months ago?"

My first recollection of April was the day I had taken the Russian watch from the SS officer. Coincidentally, Bob's thoughts also involved a watch, but in a much more desperate situation. Driven by hunger, he had offered a guard his watch in exchange for food. The German smirked and walked away, but he returned in a few minutes holding out a small, half-rotten potato. Hands shaking, Bob took it and gave up his watch. He considered it the best business deal he ever made.

As I closed my eyes again, the thought came to me that, if today was so different from three months ago, it could be just as different three months into the future. Very clearly, I could see myself working my way down the landing net into an LCVP (Landing Craft-Vehicles and Personnel) for a beach invasion of Japan.

I remembered how we were taught in training to always keep our hands on the vertical strands of netting and NEVER on the horizontal, where the guy above you could step on them. Combat boots under 300-plus pounds of man and equipment can do a pretty good mash job.

The nets swing out six to eight feet as the ship rocks. When they come crashing back into the side of the ship we could be knocked off, which means plunging as many as 75 feet either into the LCVP or, worse yet, between it and the transport. Either scenario meant death or serious injury.

Once in the LCVP, we wait for it to fill before joining the ever-increasing circle of others ready for the dash to the beach. In the sky above, American fighter planes swoop and dive, fighting off the pesky Japanese Zeros strafing us. Finally, the big guns on the cruisers and battleships open up a murderous bombardment, and our little flat-bottomed boats streak for a landing as far up on the beach as they can get. The front ramp drops down and I jump from the side,* as we had learned, into shoulder-deep water, just as at Merten, but the ocean current is stronger. I fight to keep from being pushed out to sea.

Once I get my footing and more of me is out of water than in, I realize that besides machine gun and mortar fire, the beach is mined. Our goal is to move forward as fast and as far as possible. In training, the sergeant always told us to take our choice—stay on the

---

*Exiting from the side rather than directly off the front was necessary because the sailors had to keep accelerating their engines to prevent the craft from being pushed back by the tide. Therefore, a front exit could easily result in a foot or leg crushed or amputated by the ramp.

beach and die for sure or move forward with at least some small chance of surviving. . . .

"STAN! BOB! COME ON IN. THE WATER'S GREAT!" The voices of Doris and Bob's date interrupted my reverie. The projected invasion left my mind for the moment, displaced by peaceful blue water and children frolicking in the sand. We jumped up and followed the girls.

When we had had our fill of swimming and sunbathing, we piled into the trusty convertible for our trip back to Fort Wayne. In the little town of Auburn we stopped at a drive-in restaurant, a popular fixture of the 1940s. Carhops, as they were called, came up and took the orders, and we were served our food on trays hooked to the windows of the car. We ordered the usual hamburgers and milkshakes for a total of about thirty-five cents apiece.

And so passed my wonderful 30 days. All too soon I found myself saying good-bye once again. This time, it was much more difficult, though. I knew firsthand what war was, and I was not looking forward to an amphibious invasion of Japan. I knew a very large percentage of the guys in the first four or five waves would die or be wounded on the beach. Since our unit had been trained in amphibious landings, I knew we were going to be one of those waves. I could not stifle the awareness that this was very possibly the last I would see any of my friends or family.

I kept up a brave front, though, and tried to reassure my parents that the Japanese were so weakened that we would make short work of them. In reality, I knew better. Because of my previous combat experience, I really felt that I had a rendezvous with destiny. But I left Fort Wayne with as good a frame of mind as possible.

# PART IV

## THE JAPANESE OCCUPATION

# THE 20 WAR ENDS
## AT FORT BRAGG

O N ANOTHER BEAUTIFUL JULY DAY, MUCH LIKE THE ONES WE HAD spent at the beach, I boarded a train for Fort Bragg, North Carolina. I was rather somber after my family and the station were out of sight. On the one hand, this was a new adventure; but this time around I was a seasoned veteran (at 19!) and knew how many would be killed and maimed in the invasion of Japan.

I was not alone in these feelings, either. A lot of the guys strag-gled back to camp late, and, honoring an American tradition that goes back to the Revolutionary War, hundreds went AWOL (absent without leave). Many people may consider them cowardly, but I could not and cannot condemn them. Unless one has been through the horrors of infantry combat, one has no grounds on which to make judgment. Living outside in all kinds of weather, being hunted like an animal by deadly enemies, seeing humans slaughtered and severely injured day after day, discovering unspeakable atrocities, and observing the misery of civilians during war are experiences unlike any other faced by humans. They can't be explained, can't be felt, and can't be fully comprehended by anyone who hasn't actually had them. Some men just felt that they couldn't face it again. They had simply made the decision that they were not going back over-seas. They were willing to pay the price, whatever it was, for staying in the United States.

We were told to be prepared to ship out at any time. Since each company was increased from 190 men to 250, we had quite a few new guys coming in. But, we weren't really doing much training. We just looked forward to weekend passes. We certainly had not lost the capacity to have a good time. Bud and I spent the weekends in Raleigh, Fayetteville, and various other places around Fort Bragg. The local people treated us wonderfully. One time we rented a room from a lady who just turned her house over to us. When we went out for the evening, she gave us a key and said we should check the refrigerator when we got in and help ourselves to anything we wanted.

When we first heard a new bomb was being tested, we didn't realize its full significance, but it certainly sounded promising. We were for anything that would shorten this war and save us from having to go over for an invasion. We had read about the attack on Okinawa the previous April, and knew that the mainland would be even more dangerous.

In late July, while we were still on leave, the Allies demanded an unconditional surrender from Japan. On selected Japanese cities, the Air Force then began dropping millions of leaflets, including the ultimatum and announcements that they would be bombed. After each leafleting, several, but not all, of the targeted cities were bombed heavily. On August 5, Hiroshima and Nagasaki were among the warned. On August 6, the first atomic bomb was dropped; three days later, the second and last.

On August 6, when I returned to barracks from guard duty, I ran into Dave Gerstlauer. "Did you hear the news, Stan?" he asked excitedly.

"What?"

"We dropped a new bomb on Hiroshima, Japan, and wiped out the entire city. One small bomb!"

"Yeah, right," I said. "How could that be?"

"I don't know, but it had something to do with splitting an atom," he explained.

Much as in Germany, hard-line military fanatics tried to prolong the war, but on August 10 the Japanese government agreed in principle to surrender, and it did so officially on August 14, 1945, after some negotiations about preserving the emperor.

Huge celebrations broke out across the country. The people in the United States and the rest of the Allied countries went wild with excitement and joy. A little over three months after the German surrender, this most horrible of nightmares, World War II, was over.

We were ecstatic! Our immediate hope and assumption was that we would stay in the states and be discharged. We couldn't believe they would send us all the way to Japan when there were already millions of Allied troops in Asia.

Of course, we were wrong. We were soon told not to get too excited because we were going over anyhow. The mood of the guys got ugly, as there were no indications the orders would be canceled. We were so sick of the Army, and this seemed like just another example of stupid decision-making, with us as the hapless victims.

One night, Vonksky, Schlesselman, and I decided to take our frustrations out on our almost universally disliked platoon sergeant. We threw ropes over the rafters in the barracks and lifted his bed up, leaving it there. When he found his bunk, he exploded. After an angry inquisition, we felt that we had to confess so the entire platoon wouldn't be held responsible and punished. The three of us spent a long day on KP. It was still worth it.

As the disappointment deepened, I also began to accept the fact that I was going back overseas. I was at least relieved to be going to occupy Japan rather than invade.

The letters from this period are interesting, both because of what they say and because of what they leave out. My ability to predict the future had not improved.

> Postmark: Friday, August 3, 1945
> Fort Bragg, North Carolina
> *Dear folks (and Eldena),*
> *Here I am back in the same old rut. My morale is a little higher than it was at Atterbury though. This is a pretty good camp. Plenty of stuff to do. Basketball courts, a golf course, a lake with rafts, slides and everything right in camp. They also have a*

*dance here every night. Glad I didn't do anything rash while I was home such as get engaged like Glenn did.*

*Everyone has a million things to talk about his furlough—lots of guys get married or engaged.*

*Boy it sure is hot down here. You sweat all the time. We're about 70 miles from Raleigh, NC. Pretty good transportation too.*

*It hardly seems possible that the 30 day furlough I was looking forward to so much is already over. But although it's over, no one can take the memories away from me. All the guys were laughing about how all the civilians think the war will end in a few weeks. I guess infantrymen were just born pessimistic. . .*

*Well, guess I'll write Stony a couple lines (or pages).*

*Love, Stan*

∽      ∽

Postmark: August 4, 1945
Fort Bragg, North Carolina
*Dear Mother & Dad,*

*Saturday morning and a little cooler than it was yesterday. I hope it stays cooler.*

*Well I guess Bud had to leave yesterday and Glenn today. I hope they like it better than the guys here. I never saw such disgusted, homesick guys in my life as they are now. Everyone seems to have lost all interest in the war and just looks forward to one thing—a discharge. So don't worry about me if I sound disgusted and homesick. Everyone is that way.*

*I haven't done anything since I got back. I just get up in the morning and take off for the Service Club. They haven't caught us yet. Yesterday there were 11 of us from L Company goofing off. They couldn't do anything if they did catch me except bust me and I'm certainly not worried about that.*

*I'd just as soon be a Pvt as a General in this screwy army. All I want to be is a good old civilian where a guy can get somewhere if he has the ability.*

*They're starting to give out 3-day passes. I may try to wait and see if Bud & I could get one at the same time & go to Washington DC. I doubt it though. Bud doesn't get along with his 1st Sgt. very well. He said he gets put on KP about every other Sunday. That's one thing I haven't had for a long time and don't particularly want.*

*Well guess I'll close & go read Newsweek and find out when the war is going to end.*

*Love, Stan*

ᔐ      ᔐ

Postmark: Sunday, August 5, 1945
Fort Bragg, North Carolina
*Dear Mother, Dad & Eldena*

*Well, it's Sunday morning. Dad, are you playing golf? A couple of us guys were going to go but it's real cloudy and ready to rain. It rained last night and the course would be all wet even if it doesn't rain today so we decided against it.*

*Guess I'll just stay in camp and screw around today. Probably go to a show this afternoon. Last night we went and saw (don't faint) "Pride of the Marines." Boy the group almost tore the show down when they started showing that.*

*We're getting a bunch of new men in the outfit. We're supposed to go back overseas with 250 men per company instead of the usual 190. They're also putting a 37-mm and a 75-mm gun in each rifle company. I think the Japs have a surprise in store for them. Don't talk about that though as it's not supposed to be broadcast.*

*Eldena, I've got a carton of Dentyne gum and I'll send it as soon as I get a box. You can get all you want around here.* [Items like gum went to the armed forces first and so were often in short supply in the civilian world.]

*Mom did you know that you forget to put in my socks and handkerchiefs? Anyway I can't find them anywhere.*

*I suppose Bud will get here tomorrow night sometime. I bet he's a sad sack this morning.*

*Well I guess I'll go in the cafeteria & get myself a sundae.*

*Love, Huff*

The next letter was written on the day Hiroshima was bombed. Clearly, I didn't know about it. The letter was probably interrupted by the arrival of a superior. Note the understated response to the bombing in the following letter.

Postmark: August 7, 1945
Fort Bragg, North Carolina
*Dear Mother & Dad,*

*You can thank Bud for this classy stationary. He's sitting here across from me writing too. He came down to my barracks tonight but I wasn't there so he left a note telling me he'd be at the Service Club so I went up there when I got back and there he was. We talked about an hour then came back to my day room to write. It was good to see him again.*

*We're going to try to go to Raleigh this weekend. Bud got put on KP tomorrow for goofing off this afternoon. I might be on this weekend because I didn't salute the Colonel this morning. He took my name and said he was going to get me busted but I don't think Captain Lee will bust me. Even if he would he'd make me a Pfc. again right away. Anyway, I don't give a darn.*

*That new bomb really sounds like the stuff don't it? I may be a civilian in six months.*

*Well bye for now.*
*Love, Stan*

Coincidentally, this letter was written on the date of the Nagasaki bomb, but again, I seem to be unaware of it. My concerns were much more immediate.

Postmark: August 9, 1945
Fort Bragg, North Carolina
*Dear folks,*

*Just a few lines tonight to let you know I'm O.K. Bud & I have been together for the past 3 nights.*

*Now for the bad news. All 97th Division Training has been canceled and we're supposed to ship out in about 10 days. Where we're going no one knows but the latest rumor is the West Coast. You know what that means.*

*The Army is pretty good. They put in the papers that the ETO veterans will get 8 weeks training but you can see what happens.*

*Bud and I are going to try to go to Raleigh this weekend. I hope we both get passes.*

*Love, Stan*

෪    ෪

Postmark: August 10, 1945

*Dear folks,*

*Bud and I just got back from the show. We're in L Company's Day Room now and Bud is reading the paper.*

*Well it looks like we won't be here for long. We made out our change of address cards today.*

*It begins to look like the war may be over soon. I certainly hope so. I can't see myself going back into action as an infantry scout. But it looks like we may get stuck for occupying awhile.*

*Bud & I are going to Raleigh tomorrow. Wonder if we'll have as much luck with the women as we had in Ft. Wayne. We're planning on getting us a room as soon as we get there, then go out Saturday night. Then we'll get up Sunday morning and play golf then go horseback riding or something Sunday afternoon.*

*Well guess I'll close for now.*

*Good night, Stan*

෪    ෪

Postmark: August 14, 1945

V-J Day

*Dear Mom, Dad & Eldena,*

*Well peace has come once again to the world. Now all I'm waiting for is when Huff gets his discharge. But I'm afraid I've got a while to spend in the Army yet. It looks like we'll ship out the latter part of the week. But everyone is still hoping that our orders will be canceled. Anyway, I'm not going to fight. It feels good to know that I'll be just as safe over there as the rear echelon (Ha).*

*The division band is playing The Infantry Song, the fire trucks are running around with their sirens on and the guys are all going crazy. Bud and I are celebrating with a bottle of Coca-Cola. The reason—the beer line was about a block long. Boy, you can't imagine how happy the fellows are even though it looks like we're going over again.*

*Well, I'll close for now. I didn't get a letter from anyone today incidentally.*

*Love, Huff*

Postmark: August 15, 1945

Fort Bragg, North Carolina

*Dear Mother, Dad & Eldena,*

*Well the war's over but I haven't noticed any drastic change yet. Today I didn't get up for reveille so they put me on KP. Of course that wasn't the only reason. Last night we put the platoon Sgt. bed up in the rafters. But I didn't mind KP. I didn't do much work anyway . . .*

*Well, guess I'll close for now.*

*Love, Stan*

Postmark: August 16, 1945

*Dear Eldena,*

*Well! What a surprise!! You're sure you're not sick or something. When I saw that letter from Eldena Huff I couldn't believe my GI eyes. But I was glad to see it.*

*Don't forget that I'm still mad at you for not going out with me while I was home. Now I'm gone and you can't go to the show with me. I know that makes you very sad.*

*Eldena, what do you know about Doralie Place? Bud is interested—not me. You should see the little North Carolinian I had out the other night. She was sharp. She said she never trusts a Yankee but when I left her she almost begged me to write. And she wants me to come up again this week—which I will probably do. She was pretty hard to get acquainted with but she finally broke down (cough cough). The southern girls are not nearly so wild as they are in Ft. Wayne. And they insist on being home pretty early.*

*Well be good and don't forget to write again sometime within the next year. Good night.*

*Your brother, Stan*

*Write Bob.*

Postmark: August 16, 1945
Fort Bragg, North Carolina
*Dear folks,*

*Here I am again. As regular as the clock. It's raining so Bud &*
*I didn't go to the show so we're writing letters again.*

*We're going to try to go to Raleigh again this weekend. Hubba*
*Hubba. That's a pretty cute little gal I've got up there. We'll prob-*
*ably play another game of golf, too. . . .*

*Poor sad sack 97th. The TS Division.*

*Oh well, I'll only be 20 so I've still got time to get started in*
*life. When I think of the poor guys who'll never come back or else*
*come back maimed, I feel that I've got off easy. Anyway I'll spend*
*my time studying and keeping myself healthy. I should be able to*
*save $500 in 9 mos.*

*Well I guess I'll close for tonight.*

*Love, Stan*

᪘      ᪘

Postmark: August 17, 1945
Fort Bragg, North Carolina
*Dear folks,*

*Just got out of the show and also just finished consuming a*
*chocolate sundae and a couple glasses of milk. Now, as an after-*
*math, we're writing letters. (Interesting, huh!!!)*

*We're in the Day Room writing and there's about 20 of us here*
*all griping about the 97th, the Army, the generals, and anything*
*else militaristic. The guys' morale is so low that if they don't hurry*
*and send us over, the whole bunch will be AWOL. The 86th*
*Division has 4000 AWOL but I think our record is better. Two*
*of our Lieutenants never came back from their 30-day furlough so*
*we've only got 3 officers in the Company. And there are lots of Sgt.*
*Pfcs & Pvts that didn't come back.*

*As for me I'll stick it out for another year or so but I'll be*
*damned if I'll stay in the Army the rest of my life. Now don't get*
*me wrong—I'm not being overworked. In fact, I doubt if the*
*Army will ever get another day's work out of me. I just do enough*
*to keep out of trouble and that isn't much. But the idea is that I'm*
*just tired of this Army and lonesome for home. I'm getting good*

*food, clothes and all other necessities of life so don't worry about me if I gripe. But our morale is lower than ever before and it probably will be until we get out. For a lot of people the war is over, but for some it's far from it.*

*Well guess I'll quit for tonight.*

*Love, Stan*

*P.S. The guys sent a long letter to Drew Pearson explaining our plight. Bud's Company wrote Walter Winchell.* [Pearson and Winchell were well-known newspaper columnists and Winchell had a radio program. Clearly, this was a time when average people still felt that journalists had some clout and would speak out for a good cause. How times have changed.]

Since the 17th was a Friday, this letter would have been written on the 18th.

Saturday Night

Fayetteville, North Carolina

*Dear Mother Dad & Eldena,*

*Just a few lines as I haven't much time before we go back to camp. I just wanted to write this as we're leaving tomorrow morning for Seattle, Washington. So don't expect any mail from me for awhile. I hope we don't go through Ft. Wayne because I think I'd hop off the train.*

*Bud and I have been to a dance. Eldena I actually think I'll be able to jitterbug someday.*

*We both had dates in Raleigh but couldn't get there as my pass is only good for tonight. But it didn't matter because it didn't take us long to find some more. All we did was dance with them though so don't be worrying about me picking up "bad girls".*

*Well, I'll close and I hope to see you in a year or so. And then I won't have to count the days of my furlough as I'll be a civilian.*

*Bye.*

*Love, Stan*

# WEST TO 21 FAR EAST

AFTER A LITTLE LESS THAN THREE WEEKS AT FORT BRAGG, WE BOARDED a train for Seattle. It was crowded and hot at first, but the further north we went, the better the weather. The scenery was breathtaking. Unlike ravaged Europe, this was open countryside with deer, elk, wolves, antelope, and coyotes. The Rockies were stunning, with their sheer rock walls, rapid streams, and magnificent vistas.

Even America the Beautiful couldn't keep our minds off our destination, though. We hoped all the way out that our orders would be changed. Newspapers across the country encouraged us by talking about the unfairness of sending us, but apparently the Army brass weren't reading those papers. By the time we got to Puget Sound, it was cool and rainy. We stayed in a camp outside town for a couple of days, and then, in a slow, steady drizzle, we boarded the USS General Pope, which sailed on August 27th.

There was no great armada this time, no U-boats, just a huge troop ship steaming across the sunny Pacific. On September 2, as we passed Hawaii, where it had all started, the news came over the radio that the official surrender had been signed in Tokyo Bay on the battleship *Missouri*. The news brought us little comfort. Heading southwest, we spent our days reading, getting tans, playing cards and other games, and looking out on the seemingly endless ocean for the occasional fish sighting.

My biggest adventure of the voyage came in the form of near microscopic vermin. As we neared the equator, I started scratching some little red pimples on my skin. The next day, however, they had spread, so I reported on sick call.

The diagnosis was scabies—a tiny mite, which burrows into the skin to eat and lay eggs. Since they are highly contagious, I was admitted to the ship's hospital and all my clothes were put in an oven for decontamination. Unfortunately, no one removed my fancy California sunglasses from one of the pockets, and they were melted into a big lump, useless albeit scabies free.

I actually enjoyed my stay in the hospital, as I slept on a mattress on a bed rather than in a hammock, and there was a considerable upgrade in the food. I was a little sad when, after only a few days, my scabies disappeared and I had to return to my squad.

Our first stop was Ulithi Atoll, where we were to refuel and rendezvous with the fleet originally gathered for the invasion. One of the Western Caroline Islands, Ulithi consisted of a large atoll, or barrier reef, with a number of lagoons and detached reefs, near the equator at 140° E 10° N. It was a tropical paradise.

As we approached, the ship disturbed hundreds of flying fish that darted out of the glass-smooth ocean and skimmed over the surface to escape the oncoming bow. We saw brilliant white beaches surrounded by deep green palm trees reaching into the clear blue. The air was salty, fresh, and warm. As we glided between the numerous little islands at the mouth of the lagoon, we could see deep into the clear water to the bottom of the ocean—a truly marvelous sight.

The lagoon was filled with the mighty invasion fleet. The *General Pope* pulled alongside a tanker, and we were able to talk to some of the sailors. Veterans of long service in the Pacific, they had deep tans. They had been sitting practically on the equator, refueling other ships. Despite the beautiful setting, this was a boring life, and they were anxious to talk to us, especially to get news of home.

We must have been one of the last ships to join the occupation fleet because after only a few days we headed north to Cebu, one of the thousands of islands in the Philippines. We were able to go ashore and see the town of Cebu, a totally foreign culture. The buildings looked both Spanish and Asian. The signs were in several different languages. The smell of Filipino food was much less than appetizing, but there were all kinds of strange things for sale in the grocery stores, which opened onto the streets. The people were very small—Americans towered over them—but they were very friendly and outgoing, often talking to us either in their native languages or in broken English.

One young man approached me with what he called a "natural" pearl. He named a price in what I think was Filipino money, which I didn't have a clue about. I also had no idea what the value of the "pearl" was, or even if it was the real thing. It did look beautiful, though, perfectly round with a brilliant, translucent whiteness. So, I offered him my Russian watch in trade. He eagerly accepted.

I managed not to lose the pearl, and a few years later had it appraised. It was indeed flawless and natural, so I had it surrounded with a cluster of diamonds in a necklace for my wife, Alda. It became her favorite piece of jewelry. Many years later, however, she lost it while skiing, and never got over her disappointment.

After only a couple of days, we again sailed north, but this time to Japan. Just before arriving we had an orientation session, during which we were warned not only about VD but also other diseases that we would be more susceptible to because our immune systems had not been exposed to them. They mentioned foreign sounding diseases such as elephantiasis, a swelling of body parts caused by parasitic worms in the lymphatic system. I decided that I wasn't going to challenge my immune system to fight off some exotic Far Eastern disease. Consequently, I didn't eat meals in Japanese houses, didn't drink homemade Saki, or date the girls. Some of the guys who weren't quite so careful did pay the price.

We had been on board ship for 28 days when someone yelled, "LOOK! THERE'S LAND!" It was September 24.

Over a month after leaving Fort Bragg, we had at last arrived in Yokohama. This was very close to the area where we had been scheduled to make an amphibious invasion. Instead, we sailed into the harbor untouched. No fighter planes, no artillery, no machine gun fire. No one in history had successfully invaded Japan until we did it, without a shot being fired. And the reason for our success was the bombs dropped almost two months earlier.

American troops had originally been scheduled to launch an amphibious assault on the island of Kyushu on November 1, 1945.

MacArthur's Chief of Intelligence was conservatively predicting one million casualties. Information made known after the war indicates the actual number could have been far greater.

In the last months of the war, Japanese Kamikaze suicide pilots, who attempted to crash their planes directly into ships, had often been successful. During the battle of Okinawa alone, fewer than one in five got through anti-aircraft and fighter attacks, but the 475 who were successful sank 42 ships and damaged 216 more.

American intelligence had estimated the Japanese had 2,500 aircraft left. However, they actually had over 12,000 planes and were building over 1,000 per month. They were also building suicide-pilot rocket propelled bombs, much like the German V-1, to be used against troop transports. The Japanese concluded they could kill far more Americans by sinking one troop transport rather than 30 destroyers. Their plan was to sink 700 to 800 troopships along with their soldiers.

The Japanese planned to coordinate Kamikaze strikes with attacks by 40 submarines from the Japanese Navy. In addition, they had 300 two-man suicide subs, each carrying a 1,320-pound bomb in its nose. They also were prepared to use human torpedoes over 60 feet long, carrying a warhead of 3,500 pounds and capable of sinking our largest ships.

In the initial invasion, even if all 550,000 American troops had gotten ashore, they would have faced 790,000 highly trained, fanatical Japanese defenders. All along the invasion beaches, our troops would have faced coastal batteries, anti-landing obstacles, bunkers, pillboxes, and underground fortresses. On the beaches there also would have been hundreds of machine gun positions, mines, and booby traps.

In addition to all of this, the Japanese were experimenting with poison gas and bacteriological warfare. The national slogan was "One hundred million will die for the Emperor and Nation."

The atom bombs made these further horrors unnecessary. By concentrating the casualties in two cities, they spared millions of other Japanese, as well as their American opponents. The number of casualties in the conventional invasion can only be pure speculation, but we do know that every foot of Japanese soil would have been paid for many times over, by both Japanese and American lives.

In fact, the atom bombs seemed a peculiar twist of fate for the Japanese. In 1281 A.D., 4,400 ships sailed from China and Korea to conquer Japan. Hundreds of thousands of Japanese prayed to their Shinto gods for protection from the invaders. Miraculously, a savage typhoon sprang up and devastated the Mongol fleet. The invasion had failed, and all over Japan, huge celebrations were held. The Japanese believed this "divine wind" had protected them, and would do so again.

The American invasion was to take place November 1, 1945, but in early October, out of season, a gigantic typhoon had sprung to life. Winds over 150 miles per hour hit Okinawa, completely devastating the island. Tent cities housing 150,000 American troops ceased to exist. The toll on ships was huge. Over 250 were sunk or damaged beyond repair. It was said to be the most furious storm ever encountered by the U.S. Navy.

Few people, then or now, have realized that an American invasion fleet of thousands of ships and planes and hundreds of thousands of men might have been in that exact spot had the war not ended in August. The losses would have been that much worse, and once again, the Japanese might have gathered in large numbers to pay homage to a "divine wind" that centuries before they had named Kamikaze. As it turned out, the divine wind was instead two nuclear bombs directed against them. Different divinity, different kind of wind.

Today, some criticize the dropping of atom bombs in Hiroshima and Nagasaki. Yes, 140,000 casualties are horrible, but compare that to the millions that might have died had an invasion taken place. Compare the peaceful invasion they made possible with the phenomenal death and destruction without them.

As we docked, far below us we could see little Japanese men scurrying around. We had not wanted to come, but we were there, anxious to get off that ship and see this country that had caused so much misery and death over the previous fifteen years.

My letters from this period pretty well reflect the variety of conflicting emotions all of us had.

Postmark: August 25, 1945

*Dear Mother, Dad & Eldena,*

*Well, here we go again. But we aren't going over to fight, so I guess it won't be too bad. Anyway, a lot of guys in this outfit are getting a lot worse deal than I am. Some have been in the Army 4 years and for some, this is the 3rd time they've gone over. But that's the stupid Army for you.*

*Anyway, we got a little publicity on the way out here. They had articles in every newspaper in the country. I'll send some of them to you. You can put them in your scrapbook.*

*I could tell you a lot more about it, but these letters are censored so you know how it is. Needless to say, the morale in the outfit isn't too good. But going over doesn't mean we'll be over there for an extended period. Some of the fellows have 74 points and you know they can't keep them over there very long. I guess when our time comes, we'll get out.*

*Well, be prepared for some more souvenirs. Those Japs will think another atomic bomb hit them when the souvenir hunting 97th gets there.*

*Well anyway, the war's over and my time to get out has to come sometime so I guess I shouldn't feel too bad.*

*Bye. Love, Stan*

This next letter would have been written on the 26th. The war was officially over, but for some reason the censorship persisted. It was apparently not very stringent, since the discussion of low morale was not excised from the previous letter. Nevertheless, no one could figure out who would possibly benefit from it.

Postmark: Sunday, 6:15 P.M.

*Dear Mother, Dad & Eldena,*

*Well, I'm going to write you a letter from town so it won't be censored. We aren't supposed to do this but that censoring is a lot of bull anyway.*

*As you probably know, we're in Seattle. We're staying about a mile from town so you can see what a wonderful deal it is. I'd sure like to stay here awhile. We just stepped out of the gate and a sailor picked us up and brought us right up town. The girls here almost come out and ask you to pick them up but so far we haven't honored any of them—poor things!!!*

*Boy they're having a time getting us on the boat. We've really got a lot of AWOLs. But I guess it won't be long. Probably within a week. So when my letters stop, don't worry and don't expect any for a good while. We're supposed to be on the ship for 28 days. Our destination is probably the Philippines or Okinawa. Then after a few weeks there we'll probably go either to Japan or Korea.*

*I'm sending another clipping. We're getting a rough deal but guess I shouldn't kick too much. I haven't even been in the Army two years yet. Boy, the people of Seattle are mad cause we're going too. A lot of them are writing their Congressman and most of them don't even know anyone in the 97th. But I still think I'll be out of the Army in a year or so.*

*Anyway, I'm getting to see the world. The only 2 outfits in the U.S. Army to see action in both the ETO and S. Pacific will be the 86th & 97th. I'll have so many ribbons they'll think I'm Gen. Patton.*

*We had a good trip across the country. Went through N. Carolina, Alabama, Georgia, Tennessee, Mississippi, Illinois, Iowa, Minnesota, Montana, & Washington. We had our train just full of signs protesting against going to the Pacific. Naturally, every big town we came to, a bunch of people would gather and ask us questions. Then the next day that town's paper would be full of articles about the 97th. Our name was in every paper in the U.S.*

*But it won't do any good. We're going and that's that.*

*But whatever and whenever I can, I'll write so don't worry. There won't be any fighting over there this time. I hope. . . .*

*Bye with love, Stan*

෨      ෨

Postmark: September 6 (?), 1945
San Francisco, California
*Dear Mother, Dad & Eldena,*
*It seems almost hopeless to think this letter will ever find its way back to that wonderful place on R#9 called home, but here's*

*hoping. It seems we've been on this ship forever. We're supposed to stop somewhere (probably Guam) within a day or two to refuel, so maybe they'll drop our letters off too. I hope so because it'll be another 8 or 10 days before we get to the Philippines.*

*Boy, it's really hot down here. Everyone on board—even me—is beginning to get as dark as a native (I haven't seen any natives yet, but I always heard they were dark).*

*Guess what! Today is the 6th of September and yesterday was the 4th. Sounds screwy, doesn't it? We crossed the International Dateline yesterday so we automatically skip a day (which suits me fine—the faster they go down here, the better I like it).*

*You know, I bet I've got more sea time than 75% of the sailors. 13 days, 12 days, 9 days and God only knows this time.*

*They're playing "Stuff Like That There" on the P.A. system and that makes me lonesome as heck. That last Saturday night Stony and I played it over and over.*

*There are some Marines on board and we've really been giving them and the sailors a bad time.*

*Boy, the heat down here is terrific. OK, I guess I said that once, didn't I. I guess that's the thing utmost in my mind now.*

*I wish we'd hurry and get to Japan or Korea or wherever we're going. It's not so hot up there as it is around the Philippines.*

*Mom, get a map and just look at the distance we've traveled from Seattle to where we are now (near Wake Island).*

*Well, I'll close for now. Good night.*

*Love, Stan*

*P.S. I read this over and decided I better explain something. On page 2, I said I wish we'd hurry and get to Japan or Korea. Well, we aren't going there now, but probably will after we're in the Philippines a few weeks. We're hoping there is a change of orders waiting for us at Guam sending us to Japan instead of our present destination (Philippines).*

ⵗ     ⵗ

Postmark: September 14, 1945

*Dear Mom and Dad,*

*Guess I better get on the ball and get this written. We dock this afternoon in Cebu Harbor so I want this letter to get started back as soon as possible.*

*It's about 8 am and we just finished breakfast. Now everyone is lined up against the rails looking at the scenery. We're going past Leyte Island now and it can be seen very clearly. It's rather mountainous and makes me very happy to think I was fighting in beautiful Germany and Czechoslovakia rather than this ugly island. They claim Cebu is very beautiful though. I'll soon know and tell you.*

*I guess we'll only be in the Philippines a short time (week or two) and then another boat ride. I guess it'll take about 8 days to get to Japan or Korea, whichever one we go to.*

*Well, I'll close and go see if I can see any beautiful native girls bathing on the beaches (big joke).*

*Love, Stan*

ﻌ　　ﻌ

Postmark: September 23, 1945

(aboard the *U.S.S. General Pope* near Japan)

*Dear Mother, Dad & Eldena,*

*Well we're finally nearing the end of our little voyage. We've been aboard ship for 27 days. We did get a chance to get off for a couple days down in the Philippines but we came back to the ship at night. We stopped at Ulithi Island in the Carolinas and Cebu and Leyte in the Philippines.*

*We had a lot of fun at Cebu. It was a swell place and we went for a tour of the entire island.*

*I got a couple little souvenirs from the natives and some Filipino gave me some Philippine money. We had a lot of fun in the harbor throwing pennies and nickels in the water and watching the natives dive for them. They can really swim.*

*We are supposed to land at Yokohama, Japan tomorrow. I'll be glad to get off this ship. It's a good ship and we don't have to work, but it's getting rather monotonous. During the day, we just lay around on the deck in the sun and usually go to the show in the evening then come back on deck and just lay in the tropical breeze and look at the moon and talk. The moon sure is pretty out here.*

*We've got two Army bands and a Navy band aboard, plus about a thousand records, so we've had a lot of swell music.*

*I'm sure glad this war is over and we're on our way to Japan to occupy rather than invade. I'm afraid it would have been a bloody job.*

*Those Filipinos had some harrowing tales to tell of Japanese atrocities.*

*We made friends with one Filipino who was really a good Joe. He took us to his house and introduced us to his wife and daughter. Boy, his daughter was cute. I could have had a lot of fun if we would have stayed there. He said the Filipinos had to bow 90 degrees every time they met a Jap soldier. There were 20,000 Japs on the island of Cebu, so you can guess what kind of a life they had.*

*The Filipino kids don't wear much, if any, clothes until they get about ten years old.*

*We've traveled 14,000 miles since leaving North Carolina. I guess I'll be more than glad to settle down when I get back.*

*You should see the tan I've got. After 28 days of lying in the sun, I'm getting pretty brown.*

*Well, I'll close now and I'll write as soon as we get settled down in Japan. I've always wondered what Japan is like and now I'll soon know.*

*Love, Stan*

# After the Sunset—
# First Impressions

THE TWO DAYS WE SPENT ON BOARD THE SHIP IN YOKOHAMA WERE frustrating to say the least. We were stir crazy, had cabin fever—call it what you will. We had absolutely nothing to do except what we'd been doing for the previous month. We were in Japan—but we weren't. When the trucks finally lined up on the dock, we practically ran down the gangplank. They drove us just a mile or two to a railroad station where we boarded an ancient Japanese passenger train. It was beat up and run down, but it got us to the airfield near Kumagaya, about 50 miles northwest of Tokyo.

The destruction we saw in the once great capital city was a replay of the German cities, especially Dresden. Incendiary bombs had caused huge, uncontrollable fires that destroyed most of the buildings constructed of wood. Only the Imperial Palace seemed undamaged. With its imposing, ornate architecture, it stood like Emperor Hirohito himself, with the surrounding wreckage bowing to it. As far as the eye could see, chimneys and smokestacks rose like monuments in fields of rubble.

The people we saw from the train windows were in equally bad shape: threadbare, haggard and dirty, with blank faces. At one street corner, people were simply stepping over a body in the gutter. I could only assume they had too many problems of their own to worry about something that didn't directly pertain to them. Like the

Germans, they were paying the price for bad leaders and an immoral government.

Only three months earlier we had been in Czechoslovakia, and now we were billeted in an airfield barracks that had been occupied by Japanese troops only a few days previously. In fact, the timing proved to be perfect for a last bit of Nipponese revenge for their defeat. Shortly after going to bed, we began to feel small things crawling and dining on us. After considerable slapping and flopping around, we gave up, got up, and turned on the lights. The place was alive with starving fleas! There wasn't much we could do right then, so we went back to bed and spent a miserable night as parasite feasts. The next morning everything in the barracks, our clothes and all of our belongings, had to be fumigated.

The airfield itself was a grim reminder of what it might have been like had we invaded. There were hundreds of the famous Japanese Zero fighter planes lined up wingtip to wingtip—fully gassed, heavily armed, and ready to fly. They would have met our invasion forces.

In the early days of the occupation, American soldiers lived in a surreal world with few inhibitions. Although the Japanese military had fought ferociously for every little island on the way to Japan, after their leaders surrendered, the Japanese population accepted defeat and tried very hard to please us. This was a sharp contrast with the Germans, some of whom continued to organize and fight in isolated groups for months after the war ended. Japan had been at war for over fifteen years with China, Korea, France, the United States, England, and several other countries. The people were war-weary and seemed eager to get on with their lives peacefully.

It didn't take us long to learn we were the new law in Japan. At first, average people were very much afraid of us. In order to keep them fighting until the end, they had been told Americans would be brutal and sadistic. They really expected that we would treat them as they had treated the hapless Chinese, Filipinos, Koreans, and other Asians. When we walked down the street, they would stop and kneel until we passed. If they were on bicycles, they would stop, get off, and kneel. Even though we made the rules, they accepted them without question, and soon found out that we were not going to treat them cruelly. They were greatly relieved by our fairness, and I believe they were so pleasantly surprised that they actually over-compensated in their kindness toward us later on.

The culture was so exotic to us that we were fascinated by it. Like the Filipinos, the Japanese were extremely short by our standards, and the women were about the same size as the men. Most of the men wore knee britches, like our old-time knickers, with straps of cloth wrapped around their calves. For tops they mainly wore short jackets. Also little bill caps that looked somewhat like those of our Civil War were very common. To make the caps fit tight, there were three or four eyelets in the back that they laced up, as we would our shoes.

The women wore the traditional kimonos, although some of the younger ones wore slack suits. In the poorer districts, the women wore long pants, and we saw women working in the fields stripped to their waists. It seemed the clothes of both sexes were almost all khaki color.

Most Japanese had never seen six-foot blonde, blue-eyed men before, and the girls were extremely impressed with the American soldiers. After they got over their initial fears, many became extremely aggressive and would sometimes grab Americans by the arm and try to coax them to go on a date. Since it was possible to go into town and meet ten very available girls within an hour, many of the guys had Japanese girlfriends soon after we arrived. I was not one of them, however, as I had made the decision before we arrived that I was not going to have any kind of relationship with the Japanese girls.

People were jammed in every place. In the areas where no bombs had fallen, homes were placed almost on top of each other with narrow dirt alleys between the rows. The pyramid-shaped roofs were of tile or thatch. It seemed every square inch of land was being utilized to the greatest extent possible. Everywhere there were immaculately manicured gardens laid out in neat rows.

There was little furniture, except for stools and mats. Sitting on a matted dais in the middle of the room, gathered around one little pot, families ate with chopsticks. (Of course we tried to learn to eat with chopsticks, too, but, after varying degrees of failure, we reverted to more familiar utensils.) At night, they slept on mats on the floor. Also they did not wear their shoes in the house, and they never could get used to Americans walking in with shoes on.

In many places the sanitation facilities were unbelievably crude. Only a few houses had outhouses. The rest used an open gutter along the street. In some areas, people appeared simply to use their own backyards. The stench was often unbearable, sometimes so strong it brought tears to our eyes.

We lived a completely different kind of life as occupation troops than as combat soldiers. We pulled guard duty, but had lots of free time. We formed basketball teams and played teams from other parts of the service. We also played Japanese teams. I was able to go to the Tokyo Country Club several times for several days. We played golf and tennis and ate wonderful meals there. We traveled extensively throughout Japan, primarily by train. We had Japanese civilians to do our work. We visited schools, where we were treated as celebrities and given tours of the classes.

One day, several of us decided to go to Tokyo for the day, so we walked about a quarter of a mile to the railroad tracks. When the next train came by, the engineer saw American soldiers with guns and immediately stopped. The car was jammed, but when we got on, people moved out of the way and left seats for us. This turned out to be normal treatment to us.

The trains were always crammed full, and when one pulled into the station the waiting crowd made a mad dash for seats. They kept pushing in until not one more person could squeeze in the door. Those remaining would then hang on the outside of the train. Once I saw a man trying to force a woman through a window, but her backpack was so large that it wouldn't have fit, even without her. Nevertheless, he continued grunting and pushing. When Americans were present, however, everyone would wait until they got on and were seated. Then the wild crush began.

When we arrived in Tokyo we rented rickshaws, little two-wheel carriages pulled by men. For pennies, the rickshaw driver would take us wherever we wanted to go, wait for us, then take us to our next destination. In the evening, he would finally take us to the train station for our return trip to wherever we were living at the time.

192

Walking down the street, we once saw a large crowd making a lot of noise, yelling and screaming. Curious, we ran up and pushed our way to the center. Several men were unmercifully beating a guy who was bleeding profusely and obviously hurt. We pulled the assailants off and threw them back into the crowd. Then I asked if anyone could speak English. One young man volunteered that he could. I said, "Tell me what is going on here. Why is this crowd encouraging these men to beat this person?"

The young man replied, "This man was caught stealing food. Because of the

Stan in front of the Imperial Palace, Tokyo, September 1945.

shortages, we cannot allow anyone to steal food from another."

We could see two sides to this incident, but didn't feel we could walk away and let the crowd kill this man. We told the young translator to explain that we would allow them to call the police but we would allow no further beatings. They accepted our instructions without question and no one attempted a continuation of mob rule. The man was turned over to the police and we left.

At Fort Bragg, I had decided to enroll at either Purdue or Michigan to study engineering after the war. (The so-called GI Bill had been passed in May 1944, and we were well aware of the opportunity it offered us.) I realized I didn't have enough math and science in high school, so I enrolled in an Armed Forces school, which furnished textbooks for self-study. I continued those studies the entire time I was in Japan.

We stayed at the airfield for ten days, but, needless to say, we were more than happy to leave. Our next station was a lot more fun.

Postmark: September 27, 1945
Japan
*Dear Folks,*
*I haven't much time, but I'll try to get a few lines out.*
*We landed at Yokohama 3 days ago. After staying there a couple days, we got on a train and came here. We're about 40 miles east of Tokyo.* [A little bad geography here. It was actually about 50 miles northwest.]
*The climate here at this time of year is perfect. I haven't decided whether it's summer or some season we don't have. Some gardens are just planted, some are 3 or 4 months old and some are just about finished. About all they grow is rice.*
*The Japs are funny. They kneel to you, salute you and practically worship you. And they're real polite but have a sneaky look and smirky sneer and I wouldn't trust them as far as I can see.* [My thoughts about the Japanese came from three years of adverse publicity in the news by the press and comments from fellow soldiers.]
*Well I'll have to close for now. I'll tell you all about Japan as soon as we get settled.*
*Love, Stan*

      ℘    ℘

Postmark: September 30, 1945
Somewhere in Japan
*Dear Mother, Dad & Eldena,*
*Well, today is Sunday—not that it makes much difference. We don't have to work today, but then we don't have to work any other day either, so one day is no different than any other.*
*We've got 60 Japs per battalion to do our work. We just eat and sleep and take sunbaths and play football and basketball.*
*We're at an airport now, but this is just a temporary setup. We're going to move to towns next week. There will be about one*

*company to a town and we'll be living in Jap houses and hotels with Jap servants to clean our rooms.*

*Sounds pretty good, doesn't it?? Well, if you think so, you're wrong. In the first place, so much time on our hands just gives us more time to lay around and think, and the more we think, the more homesick we get. I've been away from home quite awhile now, but I miss it and all of you just as much as that first lonely Thanksgiving at Fort Benjamin Harrison.*

*Well, I've got over 30 points* [Soldiers were sent home for discharge according to the number of points they had accumulated. The points were determined by a formula based on the number of months of service, time spent overseas, and the number of battle stars, etc.] *and it should be down to that by March* [Finally, my predictive powers were improving!] *or April. That would be a swell time to get home. I think I can get my job back at The Harvester and I'll stay at home and work until September, then go to college. At the present I'm planning on going to Purdue or University of Michigan.*

*The reason I think I can get my job back is that The Harvester keeps writing me and telling me it's open. I realize there are lots of veterans coming home and a lot of unemployed, but I think The Harvester is pretty square. Anyway, I only intend to stay there until fall. I'll have fun next summer. Just think, I'll be at home without worrying about coming back to the Army and I'll have money for spending and I'll try to save some too. Is the Ford still running? It's getting pretty old now, isn't it? I want a car for college but I want about a '39 or '40.*

*Mom, I know you won't be particularly happy about that, but if you'll stop to think, you'll see that it'll be almost a necessity. From Purdue, I could drive home about once a month and I'd be almost lost in a strange city without a car. The government will pay for my tuition, books, fees, etc. and give me $50 a month besides and I can pick up a part-time job for a little more, so I shouldn't have any financial worries.* [I was pretty typical. Far more vets than Congress had estimated took advantage of the GI Bill to get a college education.] *Anyway, I figure I'll have almost $1,400* *when I get out including the money I have in War bonds, the car and my mustering out pay and what I'll save over here.*

*Well, whatever happens, I'll sure be glad to get home and live a civilian's life again and start doing something useful. Some guys might like this Army but if they do, it's because they have no ambition and are too lazy to work.*

*Love, Stan*

*Sorry, but I'll have to send this free, as I have no Air Mail stamps. I hope we get some soon.*

*Eldena, how about a letter? You know I like to hear from my cute sister. If you've written, just ignore this request.*

*Tell me what you have heard from Bob when you write, Mom. Hope he gets home for Christmas. He's had a tough row to hoe in this Army and he certainly deserves a break in civilian life.*

ᔏ    ᔏ

Postmark: October 2, 1945
Japan
*Dear Mother, Dad & Eldena,*

*Finally got a letter. I got the one you (Mom) wrote on Sept. 14. I should have quite a bit more somewhere. But all that was written before September 12 went to the Philippines so it'll be a while before it catches up with us.*

*We're still laying around this airport just sleeping and eating. I played volleyball all Sunday afternoon and now I'm so stiff I can hardly walk.*

*We're supposed to leave here Friday, Sept. 6* [Should have been Oct.] *We're going about 20 miles from Tokyo. It's supposed to be a pretty good deal. We'll have about 4 men to a room and electric lights and all modern conveniences. I guess I can stand it until my turn for discharge comes up. . . .*

*Did you ever hear of Japanese Geisha girls? WOW!! There are a couple Geisha houses in Tokyo and Yokohama. Some of the guys have been going there, but not this kid. I've already promised myself to leave all Jap women strictly alone. I didn't monkey with the American, French, Belgians, Germans, Czechoslovakians, or Filipinos so I guess there's no use starting.*

196

*Well, I guess I'll close and work on my schoolwork awhile.*
*Love, Stan*
*You should see these Japs work. Whenever we tell them to do*
*something, they really snap to.*
*P.S. I haven't written Stoney yet. Guess I will pretty soon.*

# 23

# MATSUYAMA—
# THE FRUITS OF VICTORY

THIRTY-TWO OF US WERE TRUCKED EIGHT MILES DOWN TO MATSUYAMA, a city about 40 miles from Tokyo. We were quartered four men to a room in a former hospital, and when we arrived, a group of ex-Japanese soldiers saluted us, unloaded our trucks, and carried our belongings into our rooms. They continued saluting us for the balance of our stay. We also had cleaning women who bowed to us each time we passed or when they came into our rooms. The food was good and we actually did not have to work very hard. We soon began feeling like conquerors.

Our first job was to disarm about 300,000 Japanese soldiers. As they turned in their equipment, we stockpiled mountains of army clothing, swords, gasoline, rifles, etc. Since the 97th was occupying over 9,000 square miles, we soon had huge amounts of war material under our control.

Gasoline turned out to be the most valuable commodity we had. No one really had any use for guns or swords, but there was a critical shortage of gasoline in Japan, which produced no oil of its own. While we were sitting on thousands of barrels that had been turned in by the Japanese Army, gas was badly needed to provide fuel for trucks and cars, as well as for heating homes and cooking. Enterprising Japanese men started sneaking into our supply depots at night to steal gasoline and other supplies that could be sold on the black market. This was a risky maneuver, but very lucrative. We were given orders to double our guard and stop the theft.

One night, while I was on guard with another soldier, we heard barrels clanking and men speaking Japanese. We followed our ears until we saw the outlines of a large number of men rolling barrels. They were probably ex-soldiers so we considered them armed and dangerous. We were both armed with BARs (Browning automatic rifles, highly accurate semi-machine guns), so we felt that we had three alternative courses of action.

We could: (1) challenge them with the command "Halt" and hope they would surrender; (2) start shooting at them (we quickly vetoed this alternative because it seemed to be far too aggressive a response, even though we had been given orders to stop the theft of supplies); or (3) fire over their heads. We took the third choice, and split up so our fire came from different directions to give the appearance of a larger number of men. (We were not anxious for them to know there were only two of us.) The moment we fired our first volley, they ran headlong into the night. They must have gotten the message that this was a dangerous practice, because gasoline theft stopped. The next day we searched the village and located about 200 more stolen barrels. We recruited some Japanese men and made them return the gasoline to our storage facilities.

Since the former soldiers were doing all the real work, we had plenty of time to travel and enjoy ourselves. Trains were free for us, so we often took them to Tokyo and anywhere else we felt like going. One day Joe Vonksky and I decided to pay a visit to the local school. When we walked in, everyone went into a state of panic. Their frightened faces flashed the question, What are these two American soldiers going to do to us? We finally found a teacher who could speak a little English. We told him we only wanted to observe and that we would not harm anyone. Flattered that we were curious about their school, the principal and the English-speaking teacher took us on a tour.

The rooms were quite small. At the front of each classroom were a small, raised platform and a blackboard. At the back was a row of cabinets where they kept their books and supplies. The desks were small, low benches with room for two little chairs behind them. There were 25 to 30 pupils per room, all wearing short pants and blouses. Everyone left their shoes outside the building, as they did in their homes.

After the tour, the principal insisted on having pictures taken with Joe and me. We parted with very friendly feelings all around. Incidentally, in Japan at that time, unlike the United States, teachers seemed to be highly respected and highly ranked socially. This respect carried over into the classroom as well as all other areas of the school. Children were very well behaved.

Dave Gerstlauer discovered what was to become one of our greatest pleasures in Japan. He heard there would be three-day passes to Tokyo Country Club and told me. We signed up, and a few days later we were part of one of the first groups to go. Today, Tokyo Country Club is one of the most luxurious and expensive clubs in the world, with a membership fee of over $1,000,000. In those days, of course, it was free to American troops, so Dave and I played golf with the help of Japanese caddies, played tennis, and thoroughly enjoyed wonderful food. I still have a scorecard. I'm a little embarrassed to admit that those caddies must have thought we were the worst golfers they had ever seen.

Despite the good times, we were all eager to get home. As a result, many of the letters from this period reflect frustration and impatience.

Postmark: October 5, 1945
The Co. "L" Hotel in "The Land of the Setting Sun"
*Dear Mother & Dad,*
*Well, for the first time since our unprecedented arrival in this miserable country, we have tasted the fruits of victory. We are finally living like conquerors instead of peons. We moved to this place yesterday and it's pretty sharp. We're living in a former Jap hospital and we're fixing it up pretty good. There are four guys in my room and it's just right. We have all been together so long that we just leave our stuff laying around and don't have to worry about anyone stealing anything.*

*We've got a nice writing desk and places to hang our clothes*

Stan and Joe Vonksky with Japanese school authorities, Tokyo, 1945.

*and electric lights. We also commandeered a Jap radio so we lis-
tened to the World Series yesterday.* [The Detroit Tigers beat the
Chicago Cubs 4 games to 3 and the Cubs have never been to
the series since.] *The Armed Forces Radio Service brings us all the
popular American programs and latest news.*

*The only work we have to do is guard a couple ammunition
dumps and a clothing warehouse. We've got Japs—former soldiers
who were going to conquer the world—to do our dirty work for
us. When we got here yesterday, they unloaded our trucks and even
carried our bags in. They salute us every time they pass and the
Jap women bow to us. I'm beginning to feel like a king . . .*

*We went over to that clothing warehouse and I got a pair of
brand new Jap house slippers. Some deal. Right after chow in the
evenings, I'll put on my house slippers and do my schoolwork and
read the* Stars and Stripes [U.S. Army newspaper].

*They're trying to make it as nice as possible but of course it can
never come close to being at home. I'm just counting the days until
my number comes up to be discharged. . . .*

*We heard over the radio where some Congressmen were demanding the immediate return on the gallant 97th Division. It won't do any good, but at least some guys have some sense of fairness. Everyone knows we got a dirty deal.*

*Love, Stan*

ରେ   ରେ

Postmark: October 5, 1945
Thursday Evening
Matsuyama, Japan
*Dear folks,*

*I wrote one letter this morning but I received a letter since then, so I'll answer it now.*

*No, Mom, I didn't have to do K.P. on board ship. All I did was eat, sleep, and take sunbaths for 28 days. Bud always gets hooked, it seems.*

*Bing Crosby is singing "The More I See You" on the radio now. That's really a swell song.*

*Mom, I was glad to hear about the camera. I was going to ask you to send one, but was afraid you couldn't get any. Send it as soon as you can. I can really get some swell pictures of Japan and Japanese life.*

*The Jap people are a bunch of queers. They treat their women like they were an animal and good for only one thing. The only girls who are considered as equal to the men are the Geisha girls and the main ambition of the girls is to be a Geisha girl. They are all real pretty and live in pretty houses. They entertain the rich men of Japan. . . .*

*As for our work, we pull guard about every 3rd day. We get about 4 days off a week and during that time, we fix our basketball and volleyball courts up. We're also making a baseball diamond and a horseshoe rink. We also do our share of sleeping. I think I'll get fat around here. We're getting good chow.*

*I'll have lots of souvenirs before I get home. Mom, I'll get you a Japanese silk kimono. They make them near here—real silk, too. They sell for about $15.00 but I can get one for a carton of cigarettes. Cigarettes don't cost us hardly anything. We get all our candy and gum free. I'll have quite a bit of money to send home* *soon. We haven't been paid for two months. We don't care, though, as we don't need the money. We had all the money we had changed to Japanese yen. One yen is worth 6 cents.*

*It's been raining all day today. Glad we got here when we did. Well, I better stop for tonight.*

*Love, "The Globetrotter," Stan*

ᔕ   ᔕ

Postmark: October 6, 1945

Matsuyama, Japan

*Dear Mother, Dad & Eldena,*

*Here it is Saturday afternoon and instead of planning on a date tonight, I'll probably spend a very exciting Sat. night playing pinochle or bridge (or blackjack). Probably not the latter, though, as I very seldom gamble (angelic little guy, hain't I???).*

*There was a swell piece in the* Stars and Stripes *tonight about the 97th. It told about us coming from Czechoslovakia and said we hold the record of the most traveled division in the US Army (over 35,000 miles).*

*I've got a Jap book. I'll send it home some time when I can get enough stuff to make it worthwhile. I've also got a Jap saber, Jap Army hat, gloves and a beautiful silk mosquito net.*

*Well, that's all the news there is for today.*

*Love, Stan*

ᔕ   ᔕ

Postmark: October 8, 1945

Matsuyama, Japan

*Dear folks,*

*Just a few lines tonight. I got a couple letters from you today. Also one from Bob.*

*We're still laying around just living and that's about all I can say about it. We worked on a basketball court today. It'll be O.K. when we get it finished.*

*We walked up to a house yesterday and a girl about 20 came out and kneeled to the ground in front of us. I didn't know what to do. These people think we're gods. They never wear shoes in the house and almost faint when we go bouncing into the house with our combat boots on.*

*I got a good Jap bayonet today and I've got my saber. Bob asked me to get him some Jap books. I'll get him some, but if he can read them he's a darn good man.*

*This occupation deal will get awfully monotonous in darn short time.*

*Mom, don't worry about me getting sick. I'm just naturally healthy. And if you're worrying about VD, forget it. I don't indulge.*

*Well, so long for tonight.*

*Love, Stan*

ℰ    ℰ

Postmark: October 12, 1945

Matsuyama, Japan

*Dear Mom and Dad,*

*Friday night and I'm about ready to go to bed. I'm pretty tired tonight, although I didn't do much today. We worked on our gym awhile this morning. We've got 20 Japs to work for us here. They do most all of our work except guard. I don't suppose we better let them guard our buildings—ha. . . .*

*We heard over the radio where the 97th was going home in June. That's a long time to wait. But if I stay over here that long, I'll go home rich. I sold my $4.00 Thom McAnn shoes today for about $25.00. They didn't even fit the Jap I sold them to, but they go crazy for American shoes, whether they fit or not. They're also crazy about American cigarettes. They'll give $2.00 a pack for them.*

*I got a Jap rifle today. I was lucky to get it. We only had 9 for the platoon so we drew for them. My name was the last one called. It's a pretty good rifle.*

*Well, guess I'll hit the sack.*

*Love, Stan*

ℰ    ℰ

Postmark: October 15, 1945
Matsuyama, Japan
*Dear Folks,*

*Well, I'll start this letter now as I have to stay in here a while yet anyway. A Jap is sweeping our room out and I have to watch to see that he does it OK. The other 3 guys from this room are on guard. These Japs do a good job. He's picking up every piece of furniture to sweep under it. We have to get up about 7:30 in the morning so the Japs can clean up the place. We eat breakfast at 8:00 a.m.*

*We finally finished our gym. I played basketball yesterday afternoon until I was about dead. After awhile we'll get back in shape.*

*Dinah Shore is singing "I'll Get By." Bob should be here. He always liked her.*

*I got a Japanese flag yesterday. It is about 3-feet square and made of silk.*

*This is a pretty good deal here at Matsuyama. It's a town of 14,000 and there are only 32 of us Americans here to run the place. We haven't any officers around and can do about as we please. The only thing we have to do is pull our guard duty and that isn't much. A Jeep comes here from the Company HQ, which is in the next town, every day to bring our food rations, mail, and see that everything is going OK. We've got a medic with us in case anyone gets sick.*

*Well, guess I'll close and wash.*
*Love, Stan*

ᕗ    ᕗ

Postmark: October 16, 1945
Matsuyama, Japan
*Dear Folks,*

*Got 4 letters last night and five today. Finally starting to come through. I got a letter from Hill. He was on Okinawa but said he was going to Yokohama October 8 so guess he's here somewhere. He told me to tell him where we are and he said he'd try to find me.*

*Well, they took some guys out of here so now we've only got 24*

205

men here. We've got 20 Japs working here so we've practically got a servant for each man.

. . . I heard where anyone with 44 points in the ETO would be home by January. Bob should make it by Christmas . . .

Well, Eldena, did you get that record player from Mrs. Coil? If so, you haven't anything on me. We got one too, but you should hear the music. It's Japanese jazz and what slop.

Yes, Howard's right about the Japs being nice to us. I went into a Jap bank in town today to get 60 ten yen bills changed into 3 two hundred yen bills so I wouldn't have so much to carry and the bank teller didn't even count it. She just bowed to me and asked how much I had to be changed. I told her and she gave me what I wanted. I could have cheated her, but that isn't my way.

The mayor of Matsuyama invited us to a party given by the city for us, but we refused. After all, we didn't come over here for tea parties. I still can't forget what these miserable Japs did to lots of Americans, including Homer Baumgartner. [See War and Its Myths.] Besides, I know darn well they're just being nice because they want to get off as easy as possible and that's the best way to do it. We've already decided that if just one American is hurt here in Matsuyama, these Japs will really pay. They know it, so there's very little chance of any trouble.

Well, bye for tonight.

Love, Stan

I've got high hopes of being home by April now.

ぴ     ぴ

Postmark: October 17, 1945, 4:00 P.M.

Matsuyama, Japan

Dear Folks,

Just got through taking a hot bath and washing my hair so I feel all set for writing a letter. I was going to write first, then take a bath but the Japs had the water hot so I didn't want it to get cold.

Boy, we're getting popular around here. A reporter and photographer from the Nippon Times came here today and took our *pictures. They're going to put it in the paper.* The Nippon Times *is Tokyo's leading newspaper.*

*Also, the mayor of Matsuyama and the chief of police came and brought us each gifts from the people of the city. Among them were some cute little fans fixed in a holder to tack on the wall. On the holder were Japanese murals and drawings. The kids at the Matsuyama school made them.*

*But here's the big item. The Japs saw us playing basketball so now their high school team wants to challenge us to a game. We can't refuse. The Japs practically worship us as gods and think we're greatly superior to them. So we've got to beat them if it's the last thing we do. We should be able to win, as we'll have a lot more height than they. They're fast though, and tricky and they never get tired. We practiced a couple hours this afternoon . . . .*

*Well, bye for now.*

*Love, Stan*

∽　　∽

Postmark: October 18, 1945
Matsuyama, Japan
*Dear Folks,*

*There isn't much to write about today, but I'll write a few lines anyway. We're just laying around as per usual watching the Japs work. It's almost as hard on us as it is them, though. It keeps all 24 of us busy all day trying to think up stuff for them to do to keep them busy. We've already had them cut every weed within a mile of here and do a million other things which there were no need of. But, they told us to keep them busy. If you've got any suggestions as to what they could do, just tell me. . . .*

*One kid here got a "Dear John" letter from his girl yesterday and it really hit him hard. I guess he feels about the same way Ed Long did. This kid has been engaged for about a year and they had made all the plans for their wedding and everything . . .*

*Mom, what kind of a Japanese kimono do you want? They've got long ones and 3/4 length and come in almost every color. They're pure silk and really pretty. A lot of the guys have bought them already, but I figure it's better to wait as I'll always be able to get it and I won't have to carry it around. Also, I'd rather find out if you have any preference as to the color.*

*(One hour later)—Just finished chow. Had chicken, mashed potatoes, beets, peas and applesauce.*

*Bye for today.*

*Love, Stan*

ဢ        ဢ

Postmark: October 20, 1945, 6:30 P.M.

Matsuyama, Japan

*Dear Folks,*

*Here it is Saturday night and everyone is sitting around wondering what to do. One thing is sure, it won't be anything extraordinary. It's raining like heck outside so we definitely can't go to town. We'll end up by going to bed about 8:00 pm.*

*The old 97th got in the paper again. It seems there is an article in about every day. We've got quite an area to cover, haven't we? That's why we've only got 24 of us here in Matsuyama.*

*We were lucky to get this area right by Tokyo. It's the best place in Japan. And there's really a lot of silk around here. Some of the stores are packed with silk of all kinds. I'll bring some home with me.*

*Boy, we really had an experience today. Joe and I decided to get a haircut so we stopped in the main barbershop in town. When we walked in, the head barber ran over and grabbed our field jackets and hung them up (he bowed first, of course). Then he kicked the guy out that he was shaving and told me to sit down. I can't describe it to you in a letter, but it was really comical. He was so nervous that he was shaking. It took him about 45 minutes. When he got through cutting, he brushed my hair with a stiff brush like he was brushing a pair of shoes. It felt good, though. When I ask him how much it was, I really got a surprise (it cost .04).*

*Mom, you said I probably wouldn't be able to get a Jap flag. Well, I wish you could look in my duffel bag now. I've got 19 pure silk Japanese flags. We were pretty lucky as we found about 50 of them in an old warehouse. I'll keep about 5 and sell the rest to the sailors. They go crazy for souvenirs. But they only get 5 hours leave when they come ashore so they usually have to buy any souvenirs they get.*

*After being on board that ship for 30 days, we all were convinced that we wouldn't want to be in the Navy.*

*Well, guess I better close.*

*Love, Stan*

⌐∾        ⌐∾

Postmark: October 24, 1945, 3:30 P.M.

Matsuyama, Japan

*Dear Mother, Dad & Eldena,*

*Just got back to the barracks. We've been up town all afternoon. We were walking down the street when all of the buildings and trees and everything started shaking and we could hear a big rumbling noise. We couldn't figure out what was happening but found out it was an earthquake. It wasn't too bad, but I hope we don't get any worse ones.*

*I've got some pictures of Matsuyama. Some Jap girl gave them to me.*

*Gee, I'm stiff as heck today. I bet you couldn't guess what from—playing ping pong. That shows you what good shape we're in.*

*This life gets more boring every day. All I do is count the days and weeks.*

*Well, I can't think of anything else to say, so I'll close.*

*Love, Stan*

⌐∾        ⌐∾

Postmark: October 25, 1945

Matsuyama, Japan

*Dear Folks,*

*Well, I've got something pretty important to tell you tonight. Just wait till you hear this. I got a roll of pure silk today. It's a roll of 36" wide and over 100 yards long and it's reputed to be worth over $300. It's really pretty stuff. It didn't cost me anything, either. We took over a Jap silk factory and most all of us got some. I'm not going to send it, as I don't want to take any chances on it not getting there, so you'll have to wait until I get there to see it. From* the way things look over here now, I'll be home by March. If you have anything you want to make out of it, you can have as much as you want and I'll sell the rest. If you want all of it, you can have it.

I'm going to send a box about Saturday. There's nothing important in it but just a bunch of little things. I'm going to keep my rifle and saber and bring them with me too.

Incidentally, I've got something else to tell you. I didn't tell you before because I wasn't sure about it. I'm still not sure, but I'll tell you anyway. I got a pearl when I was in the Philippines, which may be worth some money. One jeweler in Cebu said it was worth over $100, but I'm not sure so I didn't mention it. I've still got it and I guess I'll keep it until I get home. If I can't get much out of it, I'm not out anything because it didn't cost me anything.

Don't you think this is pretty sharp stationery? It's Japanese.

Some American soldiers came to Matsuyama last night and really raised hell. They robbed some stores and smashed the Japs' furniture up. They (Japs) called us out to stop the other Americans, but we didn't get there in time. The Americans were from the 1st Cavalry Division. They're a rough outfit and think they're hot stuff because they were first in Tokyo and first in Manila. They really hate the Japs, too. I really don't care how much Jap stuff they smash or how much they steal from them just so they stay out of here because Matsuyama is our town and all other outfits are supposed to keep the heck out.

Well, I'll close for tonight.

Lots of love, Stan

∽         ∽


Postmark: October 27, 1945

Matsuyama, Japan

*Dear Folks,*

It's about 8:00 P.M. and getting cold as heck. Everyone is sitting around writing, reading, playing cards, or getting their box ready to send home and they've all got on about 5 layers of clothes. Don't get the idea that it's zero or anything like that, but it's just damp and chilly. We don't have stoves here yet, but we're supposed to get them Monday.

*Happy birthday, Dad! Course it'll be way past your birthday by the time you get this, but that's OK. . . .*

*Boy, have we been having troubles out here! I guess I've already told you we're (24 of us) living at a former Jap air base (Karoko Airfield) just about a mile from Matsuyama. Well, we've got a few Jap bombers and fighters here, a bunch of bombs and ammunition and 500,000 gallons of gasoline. The last item is our headache. The Japs sneak in and steal a barrel at a time and sell it for 2,000 yen. They know we've only got a handful of men here and they watch us while we're walking guard and as soon as we are out of sight about 2:00 am in the morning, they sneak in and steal the gas.*

*Well, they got gas every night last week and we couldn't catch them. We even doubled our guard, but they're the sneakiest little sons of guns. Well, anyway, Joe Vonksky and I started out this morning to try to track them down. We could see where they rolled the barrels away through the woods so we just followed the trail. After awhile we came to a small village so we went in and searched every house without luck. We were ready to give up when Joe saw something sticking out of a straw pile. We uncovered it and found 18 barrels of gas. But the place was deserted so we still didn't know who did it. So we are going to stay with the gas tonight (each guy stands guard for 4 hours) two guys at a time. We're on from 10 to two. I think we'll catch that stinkin' Jap (or Japs) tonight. It'll really be rough on him, too. Even if we don't catch him, we at least know where our gas is so we'll take a bunch of Japs down there tomorrow and make them haul it back.*

*Well, guess I've talked enough for tonight. I'll let you know if we get those guys tonight.*

*Love, Stan*

෨      ෨

Postmark: October 29, 1945
Karoko Airfield, Matsuyama, Japan
*Dear Folks,*

*Boy, this is really a beautiful day here in Japan. Guess it's because it's my birthday. I bet you didn't think 20 years ago that I'd spend my 20th birthday in Japan. Funny how things happen.*

211

*Well, we almost caught our gas thieves. They came back Saturday night about 9:30 P.M. Fleming and Grounds were on guard and they were hiding in the bushes. They heard them sneak up to the barrels of gas and start rolling 3 of them across the airfield. Fleming shined a light on one of them and said 'Halt' and all three Japs took off like a flash. Fleming fired twice but missed. Boy, did he ever get razzed when he got back to the barracks. That happened at 9:30. If they would have come a half-hour later, Erickson and I would have been on and I think we would have gotten them, as we both carry automatic rifles. Fleming and Grounds both had M1's. They'll be back, though. We're bound to get them sooner or later. . . .*

*We had quite a bit of fun yesterday. Joe Vonksky and I got on a train here in Matsuyama and rode for about 35 or 40 miles back into the mountains. We got off at Ogamachi and spent the afternoon looking the town over. I guess they hadn't seen many Americans there, as we had about a hundred people following us curiously down the street. Lots of people would run into the houses and bolt the doors but most of them weren't scared. In fact, there were quite a few Jap soldiers there and we thought they might try to give us a bad time. But they didn't. We both carried trench knives and we're about 8 inches taller than the average Jap so I don't think anyone will try to give us trouble.*

*Eldena, I got a letter from you yesterday written on August 23. That letter must have floated across the ocean in a bottle. But I was glad to get it anyway.*

*Well, after a month in Japan I'll try to tell you a little that I've noticed about Japan. First of all, it's the screwiest place I've ever been. The people all take off their shoes before they go into the house and it just about kills them to see an American come walking in with his big combat boots on. Very few of the houses have much furniture except for a small stand to eat off and a few little cabinets. They sit on the floor almost invariably and I wish you could watch one eat with those chopsticks. They really shovel it in. They never sleep on a bed but on mats on the floor. And very few of the women wear dresses.*

*Mom, you said the guys couldn't go to the Geisha houses anymore. Well, there's one in Matsuyama and it's going full blast.*

*There's an "off limits" sign in front but everyone goes in anyway. I haven't been in yet and I'm not going in. I wouldn't give the Japs 1 Yen for that stuff. In fact, I wouldn't if they paid me instead of wanting us to pay them.*

*Well, time for chow so I'll close.*

*Love, Stan*

ళ        ళ

Postmark: October 31, 1945
Matsuyama, Japan
*Dear Folks,*

*Well, the excitement for this morning is over so guess I'll take time out to write a letter. This morning we wheeled 5 Jap planes out into the middle of a field, poured 200 gal. of high octane gas on them and set them afire. What fun!*

(15 min. later)

*Well, here I am back again. Just as I finished the above para-graph, Dick Patrone came running in and told everyone to get out of the barracks. We didn't ask questions. When we got out, we found that a barrel of gas had caught on fire and they thought it was going to blow up, but it didn't. So now everything is quiet again.*

*Got 11 letters today. Pretty good haul, huh?. . .*

*Eldena, you can have the doll and that shell necklace from the Philippines. They're no good except for the souvenir value. Dad, the cannon cigarette holder is yours. None of the stuff in that box is much good but any of you can have whatever you want.*

*Mom, I'm going to send home 3 kimonos . . . one for you, one for Eldena and you can give the other one to Aunt Ruth. I won't send them for awhile as I want to just go in and buy them all at once as they're all picked over now. I know the Jap woman who has charge of all of them and she said she'd save mine back when she got some good ones in. The Japs all around here make them and take them to her and she sells them. They're awfully nice.*

*Wait til you see the saber I got yesterday. It's a two-hundred year old Samurai Sword. It sure wouldn't take much to slice some-one's head with that thing. I think we'll be able to send our sabers*

Stan guarding Japanese airplanes, 1945.

*in about a week. Bob asked me to try to get him one. I hope I'll be able to. I've got 2 sabers now but one is just a plain one. I've only got one Samurai.*

*That sign language we have to use with these Japs is a headache.*

*We went to another city about 40 miles from here and took some of the pictures there. We went to a school and the schoolmaster showed us all over the school and explained everything to us. Then we went back to his office and he had tea served to us. It was an all girls school and there were 800 of them there. We went to the Physics laboratory, the Home Ec. Room and everything. It was really interesting, especially since they treated us like we were President Truman. The schoolmaster begged us to come back and give a lecture to the whole school telling them about American schools, what the American boys and girls study, what they play and etc. Most of the pupils wouldn't be able to understand us but he said one of the teachers could speak English and would translate what we say. He (the schoolmaster) couldn't speak English but he could read and write it so we sat there and wrote back and forth.*

*Our 70 pointers left today. They are going to go to the Admiral Division and go back with them.*

*Love, Stan*

෨        ෨

Postmark: November 1, 1945
Matsuyama, Japan
*Dear Folks,*

*Just a few lines tonight. Haven't much to say. Everything is quiet as usual.*

*Do you remember me telling you about the gas being stolen from here? Well, altogether they got 35 barrels. But we fixed 'em. We went around and took every barrel of gasoline in the city and made the Japs haul it out here. Altogether we got over 300. So I think we got the best end of the deal.*

*I think I'm going to Tokyo to a recreation camp in a few days. It's supposed to be a good deal.*

*Well, this is enough for tonight.*

*Love, Stan*

෨        ෨

Postmark: November 3, 1945
Matsuyama, Japan
*Dear Folks,*

*Mom, I guess this is as good a time as any to get you straightened up on where I am. Neither of those two places you marked is right. That is a different Matsuyama. This place is only about 30 miles from Tokyo. I doubt if you'll find it on a map, as it's only a city of 14,000.*

*Did I ever tell you about Fuji (Mount Fujiyama)? It's that big mountain that kills so many people when it erupts. It's about 35 miles from here and on a clear day we can see it real plain. Today is one of those days and we were looking at it awhile ago. It's really a mammoth thing and all covered with snow. Really pretty.*

*Incidentally, I got another bolt of goods. It's rayon this time. Lt. Wimsatt found another warehouse and it was full of rayon so he got a bolt for everyone in the company. I've got about $500 worth of silk and rayon now. Let me know if you think I should mail it or keep it and carry it home. I'm going to have so much stuff to carry that I guess I'll have to bring a couple of Japs with me to carry it.*

*Well, I guess the Harvester didn't forget me yet. They sent me a swell Christmas box. It had a honey of an Eversharp, a Zippo lighter, a fruitcake, a box of candy, a jar of peanuts, a can of sandwich spread and some other little things.*

*Don't worry about our chow, Mom. We get plenty. And don't worry about the Japs starving over here. They don't have much but they don't need much. A bowl of rice is enough for them to be contented with for a day.*

*If they don't get us home pretty soon, we'll look like General Patton. My combat blouse has a Combat Infantryman Badge, five ribbons and 2 battle stars on it now. You know I told you we were supposed to get one for the Rhineland that we didn't get. Well, it came through yesterday so I've got 36 points now.*

*Well, I'll close for now. Here's some more of those little pictures.*
*Love, Stan*

∽     ∽

Postmark: November 5, 1945
Moosehead Country Club PRIVATE
*Dear Mother, Dad & Eldena,*
*Well, it looks like old Huff really hit it nice this time. I'm up at the Tokyo Country Club (now called Moosehead Country Club). This is really nice here. It's where all the Japanese big shots used to spend their time. The golf course here is reported to be the best in Japan. It's a hard course, too. We played 9 holes this afternoon and it made me feel almost like I was back at Municipal in Ft. Wayne, except we had Jap caddies.*

*The food here is swell and they just keep pouring it on until we couldn't eat another thing. Jap women do the cooking and they do a good job, too.*

*This is the only place I've been in Japan that looks really American. Nice, soft upholstered chairs, mattresses on your beds and all the comforts of home. (If we didn't have so much to do here, I'm afraid I'd get homesick.)*

*Wish Bud could have gotten to come here with me. But maybe he'll get here before he goes back. My buddy (Joe) is here anyway so I'm not alone.*

*I was pretty lucky to get to come. They only let 8 of us come from L Company. Lt. Wimsatt came all the way from Konosu to Matsuyama to get us this morning. I guess we'll be here about 3 or 4 days.*

*Dad, when I started playing golf on my furlough, I never thought I'd be playing the same course that Prince Konoyi of Japan played on. They've also got archery ranges, tennis, and a dozen other sports, besides movies at night.*

*This is supposed to be a rest camp, but I think it's just the opposite. We lay around so much that I think they brought us here for a little exercise. Well, guess I'll close for now.*

*Love, (Lucky) Stan*

*Guess I better change that. If I was really lucky, I'd be discharged instead of still in this Army.*

൭    ൭

Postmark: November 6, 1945, 7:00 P.M.
Moosehead Country Club
*Dear Folks,*

*Still here at this "Rest" camp. I was never so tired in my life. We played 9 holes of golf this morning and 9 holes this afternoon, then ping pong, tennis and then horseshoes between times. This is really a swell place. I got a beautiful tan today, too. We're going to play another 9 holes tomorrow morning then play tennis in the afternoon.*

*Some Jap cartoonist came here today and drew my picture. It's no good and doesn't look anything like me but I'll keep it as a souvenir. (I hope I don't look like the drawing.)*

*Dad, I wish you were here to go around the course tomorrow morning with us. You'd probably get the laugh of your life watching some of these guys. There's a creek that winds back and forth around the course and I've really been having a time keeping out of it.*

*Well, I might as well close. The movie's ready to start.*

*Love, Stan*

෨     ෨

Postmark: November 7, 1944

Moosehead Country Club

*Dear Folks,*

*Well, this is our last night here. We're going back tomorrow morning. But I think I can fix up a deal to get back up here in a few weeks.*

*I got a 57 today. These Jap caddies are really on the ball. He'd always hand me the club he thought I should use and I did better than I ever did.*

*I'll be glad to get some mail. That was the only thing wrong with this place.*

*. . . Well, I can't think of anything to write about, so I'll close. The next time you hear from me, I guess I'll be in Matsuyama.*

*Love, Stan*

# 24
# Konosu—
# No Substitute for Home

In mid-November, after the Japanese were disarmed at Matsuyama, we were moved about 10 miles east to the little town of Konosu, where we were quartered in a clock factory. The first time we were able to go into town and look around it appeared deserted. We walked the streets of this ghost town for a few minutes until, finally, several of us went up to a house and went inside. Twelve or fourteen prostrate people, bowing on the floor, greeted us. They were afraid to look up at us. Evidently they expected us to either shoot them or pillage their homes. We tried to assure them that we intended no harm, but it took a couple of days for them to relax and carry on with their normal activities.

Our lives were as pleasant as they had been at Matsuyama. Some of the men constructed a very nice movie theater inside the clock factory, so we had comfortable movie viewing. Soon films became available in abundance.

Some electrical geniuses rigged a camouflaged foot button in the sentry's guardhouse at the entrance. Whenever brass from battalion or regiment arrived, bells ringing throughout the area could warn all the men. By the time the brass arrived on the post, the men were busy cleaning their weapons and going about other matters of troop readiness.

We had experienced our first earthquake in Matsuyama. It was mild and we were outside at the time, so we really didn't see much movement. Besides, it was over in seconds. At Konosu, however, we were sitting around inside the clock factory when the entire building began shaking violently. The tremors were so strong it seemed likely that the walls were going to come down. In a panic, we all jumped up. It was difficult to walk because of the movement. We staggered toward the stairs, which we ran down as fast as we could without falling. Pandemonium reigned in the street as people streamed out of other buildings. Everything was shuddering. It seemed to go on and on. I expected the ground to open up at any moment and swallow us. Things were falling everywhere and a small crack opened up in one building. Then it stopped. We waited expectantly for several seconds, but nothing else happened. It probably had not lasted as long as it seemed. There was damage in the town; fortunately, our building held and the only losses were things like water glasses that fell off shelves.

I felt two other earthquakes while we were in Japan. However, after this one, I was used to the worst and simply accepted them as something that happened.

By December 1945, the Army started sending the men with the longest periods of service back home. This was the only reason I began my rapid ascent through the ranks. I became a squad leader, then platoon leader, and finally "Acting" 1st Sergeant of L Company. I served the last two months in that capacity, although my 1st Sergeant rating never came through because the 97th Division was deactivated in the spring of 1946. Finally, in March 1946, I was notified that I was going home. Needless to say, I was elated and not the least worried about rank.

Like the Matsuyama period, my time in Konosu was a mixture of fun, boredom, and yearning to be home in familiar surroundings. The letters reflect these conflicting feelings.

Postmark: November 10, 1945
Konosu, Japan
*Dear Folks,*

*Hope you can read this. As you can see, it's Jap paper and not much good, but it's all I have at the present.*

*I haven't written for the past few days as I've been pretty busy. We moved from Matsuyama to here. We're back with the rest of L Company now. This place is a little bigger than Matsuyama but not much. I liked it better back there, but this isn't bad either.*

*Mom, I guess I won't be able to send home 3 kimonos now. They're getting a lot scarcer now and since we left Matsuyama, I haven't had as much chance to get them. So I hope you didn't say anything to Aunt Ruth about it. The price on them has tripled since we first got here. But I've got one ordered. When it'll get here is beyond me, though.*

*I mailed my silk and crepe home today. Hope it gets there O.K. I had the silk wrapped in a Jap flag and a little red faded on it, but not much. It won't hurt it any, but I just told you so you'd know what it was.*

*I got a Japanese Flying Suit today and I'm having it tailored into a jacket. A lot of the guys already had theirs done and they're really nice. These Jap tailors will do it for $2.00.*

*Are the cigarettes any easier to get back there than they were? These Japs really go for American cigarettes. They'll gladly pay us 40 yen a pack. That's about $2.50.*

*Love, Stan*

✑     ✑

Postmark: November 15, 1945
Konosu, Japan
*Dear Folks,*

*I guess it's time I should write another letter or two. I'm getting so I hate to write letters. There's absolutely nothing to talk about. All we do is sleep, eat, and go to town and monkey around. Of course, we pull a little guard but not much.*

*Guess what I've got? Now don't get worried, but I've got ringworm. Joe got it, too. We got the Jeep driver to take us to Kagowa*

L Company basketball team in Konosu, Japan, 1945. Top row (l-r): Stan Szawara, Eugene Ervine, and Stan Huff. Front row (l-r): Dave Short, Norman Ruszanowski, John Marshak, and Leonard Bobcock.

*this morning to battalion and the doctor gave us some stuff for it. He said it would be O.K. in a couple days and if it wasn't, we should go back. We're going back anyway, even if it is well because I never take any chances with anything. That's what I hate about the Army and especially being overseas. Too many diseases. Coming over on the ship, an epidemic of scabies started and I had them. The Navy doctor got rid of it for me. It's just a skin disease.*

*Got a letter from Aunt Ruth yesterday. She wants a kimono. Said she'd pay me whatever it was. So I guess I'll try to get her one.*

*I'm going to send a Jap Flying Suit home. I can either keep it like it is or have it made into a jacket when I get home. I've got another here and I'm having a Jap tailor make a jacket for me and I'll wear it over here. They're electrically heated and fur lined.*

*There's a carnival in town. Something like our county fair. It's pretty interesting. All kinds of Jap dancers and stuff.*

*Well, bye for today.*

*Love, Stan*

~        ~

Postmark: November 20, 1945
Konosu, Japan
*Dear Folks,*

*I mailed your kimono yesterday. Also, I put in a couple sets of chopsticks. Can you imagine eating with those things?*

*Mom, I've changed my mind again. I'm going to go ahead and get Aunt Ruth's kimono. I'll send it to you and you can keep the one you like best, and send the other one to Aunt Ruth. If I wait till I get an answer from you, there may not be many left.*

*I weigh 165 now.*

*Did you hear that program about the 97th? It was 1/2 hour long and told all about our training, our trip to Europe, our combat experiences—how we captured Dusseldorf and our drive into Czechoslovakia, our trip back to the states, then over here.*

*Mom, you just didn't see the right pictures if you never saw a Jap laugh. They laugh at anything and everything.*

*Incidentally, I don't have to pull guard anymore. There are six of us who watch the Japs working in the kitchen to see that they get the pots and pans washed clean. Three of us are on each day as we only have duty every other day. Then all we have to do is tell the Japs what to do. And the 3 of us on every other day take turns staying over there so we only pull duty about every 4 or 5 days—rough.*

*But this life isn't for us. Some guys who have no ambition in life actually like this life. But for most of us, we hate it. All you have to look forward to is eating and sleeping and it drives one batty.*

*Love, Stan*

෴    ෴

Postmark: November 23, 1945
Konosu, Japan
*Dear Folks,*

*Well, Thanksgiving is over—now we can start sweating out Christmas. I got 2 packages from you Mom—yesterday. Thanks. I was glad to get that Colgate Toothpaste. I had been using some 2nd rate stuff that wasn't worth a darn.*

*Mom, you can send that first kimono to Aunt Ruth. I got one for you today. It's really a beauty. Sorry I couldn't get both of them like it but this one I got today was the first I ever saw like it. The first one I got cost $25 and the one I got today was $35 . . .*

*Dad, I just got a letter from you. You don't have to worry about the silk, crepe, etc. I got it all on the level.*

*As far as the black market goes, some guys are hauling in the dough but it's too risky for me to go in for it in any proportions. I want to get out of this Army some day.*

*Don't mind the stationary. It fell on the floor.*

*It's about time for the movie, so bye for tonight,*

*Stan*

જી          જી

Postmark: December 1, 1945, 11:00 P.M.

Konosu, Japan

*Dear Mother & Dad,*

*Saturday night and we just got back from the show. Incidentally, I guess this is a good time to tell you about this place we're staying at now. It is a former clock factory just a few blocks from the center of Konosu. We've fixed it all up so that it's a pretty nice place now. The Japs can't figure it out. Everything has been the same around here for years and they said when we came, it changed so much they can't believe it.*

*We've built one of the buildings into a theater and when you get in there, it seems just like a theater back home. Then we made one building into a recreation building with a bar and everything (of course there's not much beer, though—about 20 bottles per man per month) and that's too much for me.*

*On the front we've got a big electric sign—CLUB 'L'. And as for our barracks, we've got built in closets, shower and everything.*

*Don't get me wrong, though—I'm sure not in love with this place. In fact, it gets more boring by the day.*

*I got a letter in 7 days today. That's pretty good, isn't it?*

*Guess what's on the radio now—The Old Barn Dance* [a popular program that originated in Fort Wayne on WOWO]. *Just makes me think of Saturday night at home when we were younger.*

*We'd get our bath then go in and listen to the Barn Dance—remember?*

*They just announced that a play by play broadcast of the Army-Navy game would be on at 3:30 AM in the morning. What an ungodly hour to be listening to a football game—but I may get up. No—on second thought, we can all lay in bed and hear it. The radio is right here. We can have a guard wake us up. It should be a cinch. Navy hasn't a chance with that Army team this year. I predict a win by 26 points.*

*Well, the Hoosier Hot Shots* [a popular Fort Wayne country music group which was a big favorite on The Old Barn Dance] *are on now. Thanks for starting that bank account for me.*

*Bye for tonight.*
*Love, Stan*

ဖ     ဖ

Postmark: December 3, 1945, 4:00 P.M.
Konosu, Japan
*Dear Folks,*

*I've got about an hour before chow so guess maybe I'll have time to write a few pages (this kind of page).*

*I've been sitting over at the barbershop all afternoon shooting the bull (got a haircut on the sideline too). I also took a shower this afternoon so I'm all cleaned up. All I need now is a girl and a car and I'd be all set. There are a hundred girls around here but I wouldn't give a dime for the whole bunch. As for the car, I could probably get one of these Jap trucks we've got around here, but they aren't worth much.*

*Did I ever tell you they drive on the left side of the road around here? It seems funny as heck.*

*I hope we have a good show tonight. The one last night was Randolph Scott and someone else (???) in "Pittsburgh." It was good, even if it was old.*

*It was really a nice day here today. I read in S&S where there was a big storm in the Eastern States a couple days ago. I bet the little old Ford didn't like that a bit.*

*Well, I know you wouldn't want me to miss chow, so just to do you a favor, I'll close.*

*Love, Stan*

*P.S. I'm waiting on that picture of you, Al.*

ᓚ   ᓚ

Postmark: December 9, 1945

Konosu, Japan

*Dear Folks,*

*Well, here I am back at the company. We got back today.*

*Got your letter where you ask about the ringworms. Don't worry. I got over that already. And I didn't have it on my face. It was on my arm. That would have been a shame to mess up my handsome face, wouldn't it?? (That was for you, Eldena.)*

*We played basketball this afternoon. We've got a good gym. We took over the gym from Konosu High School.*

*Well, guess it's time to go to the show.*

*Bye, Stan*

ᓚ   ᓚ

Postmark: December 10, 1945

Konosu, Japan

*Dear Folks,*

*Boy, this is a lazy afternoon. The sun's shining and it's nice and warm. Some of the guys are sleeping, some are on guard and some are working the Japs. None are doing much work—especially me.*

*Well, I've got a new job now. I'm back on guard. But instead of Private of the Guard, I'm pulling Corporal of the Guard. It's a lot better because all I have to do is post the guards at their post then go back to the orderly room. I'm glad because it's starting to get cold at night and now I won't have to worry about that.*

*Sighonara, Stan [Note the phonetically accurate spelling!]*

ᓚ   ᓚ

Postmark: December 11, 1945
Konosu, Japan
*Dear Folks,*

*Boy, am I sitting pretty now. I'm on Guard now. As Corporal of the Guard, all I have to do is sit here in the orderly room while my men are on post.*

*I suppose you're wondering why I pull Corporal of the Guard when I'm only PFC. Well, they needed another non-com and since they didn't have any, they took me as I'm one of the ranking PFCs. If I'm lucky, I may get Sgt. stripes out of it. But the ratings haven't been going through Regimental HQ so well lately. Whether I get it or not doesn't matter much anyway. All I want is to get home and to hell with the Army.*

*Anyway, I've got a Sgt. job now which means I don't do much of anything and that's what I like.*

*Well, guess I'll close for tonight and read awhile.*
*Love, Stan*

ᔥ     ᔥ

Postmark: December 14, 1945
Konosu, Japan
*Dear Folks,*

*Well, I guess my days as an infantry scout are over. Yesterday I made ass't squad leader. See, each squad has a staff sergeant for squad leader and just a plain Sgt. for ass't squad leader.*

*Well, I didn't make sergeant yet, but I have hopes. It may take a month or more before it comes through. In fact, it may never come, but it probably will. Just keep addressing me as PFC and when (or if) I make it, you'll know it.*

*I really can't get very enthused about it. All I want is to get home and to hell with the Army and it's ratings and anything else militaristic.*

*Love, Stan*

ᔥ     ᔥ

Postmark: December 15, 1945

Konosu, Japan

*Dear folks,*

*Since I'm a CQ (Charge of Quarters) tonight, I've got time to write a few lines.*

*Well, I've been an assistant squad leader now for 3 days without getting into any trouble. But I'm afraid Marshak is pretty upset about it. He has been in the outfit longer than I and is 5 years older so I guess he thinks he should have gotten it. But he's starting to get over his disappointment now.*

*Well our company basketball team plays 3 games next week. We play I Company Monday night then we travel to Kumagaya to play M Company Wednesday. I hope I can get about 15 points.*

*Well, can't think of anything to say so adios, Stan*

⸋     ⸋

Postmark: December 20, 1945

Konosu, Japan

*Dear folks,*

*Well, I hate to do it but guess I better tell you about our game with M Company. To come to the point—we lost. But it really wasn't our fault. I know this sounds like the same old excuse but the referees were from M Company and we didn't get any breaks at all.*

*That was the dirtiest game I ever played in. We both wanted to win so bad because M and L have the 2 best teams in the Regiment. So we really played hard and rough. I went out of the game in the last quarter on fouls. So did Dave Short, the captain of our team.*

*We play them again on New Year's down here at our gym. We'll win next time.*

*Well everything's the same around here so there's not much else to talk about.*

*Love, Stan*

⸋     ⸋

Postmark: December 31, 1945
Konosu, Japan
*Dear folks,*

*Well, in about 45 minutes it will be 1946. New Year's Eve and I'm on CQ. That's life. Most of the guys are over at Club L tonight drinking the old year out. Marshak came all the way over here to the orderly room a few minutes ago and brought me a bottle of beer. He said he just couldn't let me get past New Year's Eve without a beer. He's the guy that was a little mad because I made assistant squad leader instead of him. But he's all over it now and happy as a lark. I guess my rating is supposed to go in next week. I don't know whether it will be Cpl or Sgt. but at any rate, I'll probably be a Sgt. before I come home. I'm still hoping to be home by March.*

*We've been having a little trouble with the Japs. They broke in a warehouse here last night and stole some rifles and a machine gun. But if they come back tonight, they'll get the surprise of their life. We've got it all wired up so they'll get 4500 volts of electricity.*

*Well so long until next year.*

*Love, Stan*

๑     ๑

Postmark: January 2, 1946
Konosu, Japan
*Dear folks,*

*I've got 15 minutes before the show so I'll write a few lines.*

*I guess the most important thing tonight is the damn Japs. A week ago at the 2nd platoon a few miles from here, a Jap tipped them off that 30 Japs were planning a raid on a warehouse. So they waited and sure enough the Japs came. The boys from the 2nd platoon captured 11 of them.*

*A couple days ago the same Jap that tipped them off before said 130 Japs were going to attack tonight or tomorrow. Well there's only 12 Americans there so they sent out 6 automatic rifles and a machine gun. And the rest of us are all restricted in case we are needed. They also snuck in here a few days ago and got away with a machine gun and some rifles. I guess they don't realize they're fooling with the 97th.*

*We've been teasing some of these replacements telling them they may get the Combat Infantryman Badge yet. They don't seem happy about it though. Most of them are scared to death. There are still enough of the old bunch left to give the Japs a bad time though.*

*Well time for the show so I'll close. Don't worry about this Jap trouble. It's nothing serious. I don't walk guard anyway since I pull Corporal of the guard. I just sit in the orderly room by the fire.*

*Love, Stan*

೧೩       ೧೩

Postmark: January 9, 1946
Konosu, Japan
*Dear folks,*

*I almost had to leave L Company. An order came down for me to report to Regimental HQ. The company commander talked them out of it. They wanted me to be a typist.*

*I don't really need that watch now. I got a good Jap watch today. It cost me 200 yen (or the equivalent of 6 packs of cigarettes). I'll sell the other watch when it gets here. It should bring me about 1000 yen or $70. The Japs don't get far when they ask prices like that. They know they better sell cheap or they may not get anything.*

*A bunch of us went to the Jap studio and got some pictures taken. They are 5" by 7". One with all of us and one of just me. I'm glad to have the group picture because it has all my buddies who have been with me since Leonard Wood. If they come out good, I'll send them right home.*

*Well bye for tonight, Stan*

೧೩       ೧೩

Postmark: January 13, 1946
Konosu, Japan
*Dear folks,*

*Since I'm on CQ tonight, I've got plenty of time to write. There isn't much to talk about but you'll know I'm still kickin'.*

*I'm still sweating out a transfer to Regimental HQ. They've*

*sent down two orders for me but Lt. Wimsatt got me out of both
of them because I'm an asst. squad leader but they're really short
on typists and they may get me yet. I'd hate to leave L Company
now that I've been with it so long. Then too, I'm on the verge of
getting a couple stripes here. The only reason I want the stripes is
for the money . . .*

*We had a lot of fun in Tokyo the other day. We went dancing
at the Oasis. Those Jap girls are getting to be pretty good dancers.
There were 7 of us and we had fun giving the 1st Cavalry a bad
time and taking their women from them.*

*Well so long for now,*
*Bye, Stan*

෩      ෩


Postmark: January 18, 1946
Konosu, Japan
*Dear folks,*
*I don't feel like writing tonight but here goes anyway. I'm still
disgusted at this crazy Army and guess I always will be till I get
out.*

*Guess where they were going to send me. Now I don't suppose
you'll believe this but it's the truth. This Army is really getting hard
up. They were going to send me to 1st Sgt.'s school for two weeks
to take over the 1st Sgt's job when he goes home. I almost fell over
when I heard it. But I told them I'd just as soon stay a squad
leader.*

*I've been an acting non-com for a month now and still no
stripes. There's a couple more in the same boat though. . . .*

*Well bye for now,*
*Homesick*

෩      ෩


Postmark: January 22, 1946
Tokyo Country Club
*Dear folks,*
*Back here again. I'll be up here for about 4 or 5 days. Then
when I go back I leave for Omiya on the 27th to go to 1st*

*Sergeants school. I told them twice that I didn't want to but the CO said I was the only man in the Company who qualified. When the present 1st Sgt. leaves on the tenth, I'm supposed to take over.*

*If I hadn't had to take this 1st Sgts job, I would have been acting platoon Sgt. of the 3rd platoon which is a good deal. There's too much to worry about in that orderly room. Oh well, I'll goof off as much as possible and I still think I'll go home in March.*

*The guys in the Company all tease me about that 1st Sgt. deal. It does seem funny for a 20-year-old guy acting 1st Sgt. I always pictured a 1st Sgt. as some mean old guy with hash marks all the way up his arm.*

*I got beat in golf today by one guy but beat the other two. I got beat in tennis too. Guess I'm not much good. But I'll win tomorrow.*

*Bye for tonight, Stan*

৲৲        ৲৲

Postmark: January 26, 1946
Konosu, Japan
*Dear folks,*
*Got back from the Country Club this morning. Day after tomorrow I have to go to Omiya to that 1st Sgt. school for a week. I went up this morning when I got back to try once more to get out of that but didn't have much luck. After February 15, there won't be a non-com in the Company and I'll be one of the high point men of the Company and they said I have the highest IQ in the Company so guess I'm hooked. They'll be sorry though because I'm going to be the biggest goldbrick in the division.*

*I'll tell you why I have such a poor attitude. The first reason is that an order came out that all men who will have 30 months of service by April 30 will be on their way home by February 15. Well I missed that by about 2 weeks. So now I don't know when I'll leave. I may have to wait until May 1st.*

*The other reason is that they act like they're giving you something when they give you a couple stripes. There are quite a few of us who have been squad leaders and asst. squad leaders for 6 weeks and over and we're still Pfc.'s . Now they want me to be acting 1st*

*Sgt. and I still might not get anything. They say now that there may not be any more ratings in this division because it's supposed to go home in about 3 months.*

*When I get home, I'm going to wait a couple weeks then drive up to Indiana U. and see if I can get enrolled and what credits I'll need etc. I figure I can find out more by going up and talking to them than by writing.*

*Well if they just keep taking the guys according to their service I'll be on my way by March 1st but if they stop after they get the 30 months men who are eligible—[it will be] May 1st. I'm just hoping and praying it'll be the former because if anyone was ever tired of this Army—I am.*

*Hi brother Bob,*

*I guess you're home by now. You certainly should be. How does it feel to be Mr. Huff? You don't have to answer that. I already know the answer.*

*Well, I'll write from Omiya next week when I skip classes at that 1st Sgt. school.*

*Love, Stan*

    ☙    ☙

Postmark: January 29, 1946
Umiya, Japan
*Dear folks,*

*Here I am at this no good 1st Sgts. School. I'm not learning anything though because I sleep through most of the classes. I don't care whether I hear what's going on or not. Anyway, a 1st Sgt's job is so simple a moron could do it.*

*I just don't have any spirit left for this Army or anything about it. I missed this 30-month deal by so close that I felt like stowing away when all the guys left that I've been with so long. Now I'm left here with a bunch of half wit rookies. I guess I've got more service than most anyone on Honshu except regular Army men.*

*All they have to do is bring it down one more month and I'll be on my way. But they don't act like they will for a while.*

*Well I'm running out of ink so bye for tonight.*

*Love, Stan*

∽   ∽

Postmark: February 1, 1946
Konosu, Japan
*Dear folks,*

*I really don't know what to write tonight. The last bunch left here tonight of that 27 month group. The next is me (26 1/2) but it's hard to say when it'll be. There are rumors that the division is going the 1st of March. I hope it's true. I'm definitely homesick.*

*Incidentally, don't be surprised if a stranger comes walking up some day. There are about a dozen guys from around Indiana, Illinois & Michigan who may drop in. One guy lives near Hartford City and is going to call you when he gets there. He left a couple of days ago.*

*How's the Ford running? Good I hope because it's going to get some mileage before long.*

*Bye for tonight & keep hoping I leave here soon.*
*Stan*

∽   ∽

Postmark: February 6, 1946
Konosu, Japan
*Dear folks,*

*This is disgusted Huff reporting in again. One of the kids who left the company last week came in today (on pass). He said no ships were expected in for 3 or four more days so he jumped the fence. Said he came back to get something to eat. He said the chow lines there were 3 blocks long. He also said he saw Hill down there. They're all expecting to leave Japan the 10th. He said he saw Rumain there. Rumain used to be in L Co. but was transferred to ordnance a few months ago. He has 2 weeks less time than I have but he's there and I'm still sitting here sweating it out.*

*I guess I'll get about a '38 Chevy when I get home. (If I ever get home.)*

*You asked if I ever saw anyone eat with chopsticks. Well, I never saw a Jap eat with anything else. In fact, they laugh at us eating with knife, fork & spoons.*

*Well, guess I'll quit.*
*Stan*
*P.S. I shouldn't have sent all those Jap flags home. Those crazy sailors in Yokohama are paying $15 a piece for them.*
*P.S.S. I may leave this month.*

～　　～

Postmark: February 9, 1946
Konosu, Japan
*Dear folks,*
*Got a few letters today so I might as well answer them. The main topic of conversation around here is—when am I going home?? All I know is I'll be on the next shipment out of here but when that'll be I don't know.*
*Bob, you better be there by now. The 54 points left here long ago. Old Mac is on the ball over here so far. I just hope he keeps it up. I hope to make it by March 20. A bunch of us from Indiana are planning on going to the state tourney in Indianapolis.*
*A Red Cross girl came down here yesterday and stayed here all day. You should have seen these guys. I almost fell over. I had to appoint someone to entertain her so I picked the most logical guy—myself. I took her around and introduced her to the guys, ate dinner with her etc. She was pretty nice. Said she went to Wellesley College.*
*Well there's nothing else to talk about so.*
*Bye, Stan*

～　　～

Postmark: February 16, 1946
Konosu, Japan
*Dear folks,*
*Well I'm still here wondering when I'll leave. I know I'll do something soon because the 97th is relieved of occupation duties Mar. 1. By April 1st it'll be completely deactivated.*
*It better be soon because between me & the company commander, we've got this company pretty well jazzed up. And the worst part is no one gives a damn. If the I.G. comes around we're up a creek.*

*I've got to start working on getting into a college as soon as I get there because they're really getting filled up.*

*I never was so fed up with anything as much as I am with this Army. I've got to leave here pretty soon. It's so dull. We aren't doing a thing worthwhile.*

*You should have seen us riding a rickshaw in Tokyo the other day.*

*Well guess I'll read awhile.*

*Bye now, Stan*

Postmark: February 20, 1946

Konosu, Japan

*Dear folks,*

*Well, I've got pretty good reason to expect that by the time you get this, I'll be on my way home. From the way things look, I'll probably leave around March 1-5.*

*That'll be a happy day for me when I step onto the U.S. soil again.*

*The mail service over here is getting lousy. It takes about 3 weeks. I guess you might as well stop writing. I probably won't be here to get them.*

*Well I'm not in the mood to write so.*

*Bye for tonight, Stan*

*P.S. The boys captured a bunch of officers from the 5th Air Force trying to steal some flying suits from one of our warehouses last night. They were going to sell them black market. Tough!*

*Bye*

On March 2, 1946, I finally left Yokohama on a small liberty ship. A little over two weeks later, we landed in Seattle. Two days after that I was on a train headed for Indiana. At Camp Atterbury in Indianapolis I signed some papers and picked up my mustering out pay. I was a civilian again. What a wonderful feeling!

*Photo by Affolder & Co., Decatur, Indiana 46733*

Stan with the medals and ribbons he earned during his 29 months of service during World War II: American Campaign Medal; Combat Infantryman Badge; Good Conduct Medal; Expert Qualifier Medal in the following: rifle, machine gun, B.A.R. (Browning Automatic Rifle), carbine, bayonet, and hand grenade; the Bronze Star Medal; Army of Occupation Medal; European Theatre Medal with two Battle Stars; and a World War II Victory Medal.

237

Stan on board ship for the return trip from Japan, April 1946.

Stan and Pat on the return trip
from Japan, April 1946.

238

# PART V

# REFLECTIONS

# WAR AND 25 ITS MYTHS

B Y 1939, THE GERMANS HAD GONE INTO THE RHINELAND, ANNEXED Austria, and taken over Czechoslovakia. Ominous war clouds were gathering. As I was discussing the situation with my friend, his father came into the room. He listened for awhile, then totally shocked me when he said, "My sons will never fight in a war. I fought in World War I. I was gassed by the Germans and I have suffered ever since. I'll take my sons to Canada before I will ever let them fight in another war."

As a fourteen-year-old, I was full of idealism and patriotism. My opinion of this man plummeted. I couldn't understand anyone who wouldn't be proud to fight for his family, his country, and his freedom. A few years later, I enlisted in the Army, eager to do my part to bring about the downfall of the evil enemy. I loved my family and I wanted to protect them, our freedom of thought, and other precious aspects of life in America in the 1940s.

I came home from World War II a different person. In a scant 29 months, I learned enough for a lifetime. I found out it was one thing to read in the paper that our forces had killed or captured a large number of enemy troops, but quite another to look into the face of a young, handsome, blonde German who had just been killed. His eyes wide open and his face showed the terror of his last minutes, while his body oozed blood from shrapnel and bullet holes. I wondered what mother, wife, or girlfriend would soon receive the tragic news that her loved one would not return.

As we drove deeper and deeper into Germany, we could hardly believe what we were seeing. With shock and revulsion we encountered Hitler's concentration camps, which imprisoned thousands of hapless inmates, not to mention the evidence of those who did not survive. In some places, gas chambers had been set up as shower rooms, with cyanide substituted for water. Although the victims were predominantly Jewish, there were also representatives of many other nations and faiths. They were killed in a variety of ways—gas, shooting, medical experiments, overwork, starvation, and exposure. Warehouses were full of shoes, clothing, dentures, and eyeglasses—all marked and sorted with meticulous efficiency.

Of the survivors, many suffered from diseases such as TB and typhoid, so while our hearts went out to them, we were constantly afraid of catching something. I don't believe that any of us who lived through those horrifying days can ever forget what we saw. We witnessed one of history's most successful mass murders. To me, it was a stunning fact that people of culture and religious faith committed these atrocities. I believe a small gang of fanatical gangsters got control of the country and decent Germans were either unable or unwilling to challenge them. Of course, many profited from the Nazi military expansion and were perfectly willing to accept the benefits and ignore the horrors. Could this happen in any society? Unfortunately, it has in many and probably can again.

I discovered that very little good can be said about war. It is best described as the lowest form of depravity participated in by humankind.

Unfortunately, some do benefit from war—politicians who gain and hold power; career military officers who get rapid promotions, public idolatry, and the opportunity to practice the craft they have spent a career training for; and businessmen who receive huge government contracts, handsome bonuses, and lucrative stock options.

But the benefits enjoyed by the few are far overshadowed by the tragedy of millions dead and wounded, and the immense suffering in concentration, slave labor, and POW camps. Add to this the misery of civilian populations, and of the countless young men who suffer psychologically for years, and sometimes for the rest of their lives.

I am not proud of having been a member of a combat division whose mission was to kill other human beings, even though in those days, they were just "Japs" or "Jerries."

On the other hand, I have reflected many times on the hapless human beings that we rescued. I have wondered who would have released the Jews, the slaves, the gypsies, the religious and political dissenters, and the elderly if we had not. Who would have saved the hundreds of thousands of prisoners of war who were so mistreated while in captivity? And how else would the decent Germans and Japanese who wanted to rid themselves of Nazism and Imperialism have been able to do so?

Now, with advancing years and a lifetime of experience, I look at things from a different perspective. I once had very strong feelings about who were the heroes and who were the villains in this greatest tragedy of the twentieth century. Now I feel that only Almighty God, in his wisdom, can make this determination.

I used to feel that conscientious objectors were cowards. Now, I believe it took as much courage for them to say, "No, I will not kill," as it did for me to enter battle.

I also have no hatred for the German and Japanese people—only for the gangsters who ran their governments during the war. Some of them were just as strongly opposed to their governments as we were, and most of them suffered tremendously. Hopefully, with God's help, humans will find a better way to settle their differences.

Early in the war, President Roosevelt ordered the relocation of Japanese-Americans from the Pacific Coast to inland camps. In retrospect, this was not our government's finest hour. Most of these Japanese-Americans were fiercely loyal to the United States, but at the time many in the government feared that some might still be loyal to their native country. Some Japanese-Americans did have relatives living in Japan—relatives who were in the Japanese military. Our government was apprehensive that some of them might provide important information to the Japanese. Following the shocking attack on Pearl Harbor, many West Coast residents feared bombing attacks and an invasion of the U.S. mainland. So, the order was given to relocate these American citizens of Japanese ancestry to detention camps.

Years later, in an attempt to right a wrong caused by war hysteria and fear, Congress authorized a payment of $20,000 to each Japanese-American citizen (or their heirs) that was relocated. It is interesting to contrast the experience of these Japanese-Americans, though, with the more than 300,000 American boys killed in the war. These young men, mostly draftees, were also forcibly removed from their homes. Many also lost businesses that were shut down when they went to fight. They would have preferred a detention camp here, in the States, compared to what they faced overseas. They lived through hard, painful times, which ended in their violent deaths. Their supreme sacrifice resulted in a $10,000 payment to their beneficiaries, not a direct payment from the government, but rather the payoff of an insurance policy that they were required to purchase out of their meager salaries when they became part of the military.

Many innocent people lost their lives during this war. I find it interesting, though, to see and hear people who were not even alive in the 1940s proclaim that World War II was more unfair to certain groups compared to others. Many people living at that time could make a good case for unfairness. War, itself, is unfair.

Many friends—from school, my neighborhood, my outfit—died in the war. I remember Baumgartner, my buddy from sixth grade through high school. Just a few weeks before he was killed invading Saipan, I received a letter from him that told about the living hell he had experienced invading Tarawa, where his Marine Division lost 40 percent of its men within a few days.

Homer has been dead now for well over 50 years. If he could come back to life today, he would see that the nation whose sons killed him is now one of the most prosperous in the world. He would find out that most of his fellow Americans had purchased an automobile or TV set manufactured by his old enemy. He would learn that the company that manufactured the Zero fighter plane that strafed him as he went into Saipan now has a big presence in the United States and employs many of his fellow Americans. What would he think about the thousands of former German soldiers who have immigrated to the United States to live the life that he and thousands of other boys never got to enjoy because they died protecting it?

My dead friends are not just statistics. To me, they were real kids with hopes, dreams, aspirations, and feelings. They wanted to come back, marry, have children, and enjoy the way of life they were fighting to protect—but they were denied this opportunity. May we never forget these boys and the sacrifices that they made.

American cemetery in Luxembourg that Stan and Alda visited in 1995.

# THE FOR**26**TE ONES

A S IT TURNS OUT, I WAS ONE OF THE FORTUNATE ONES WHO ULTI-mately benefited from the war. I wrote to and dated several girls while I was in the Army and after I got out. They were cute and intelligent, but I was not in love with any of them. It was not until I met Alda Jane Tibbitts in 1947 that I fell hopelessly in love. I knew immediately that she would be my wife. After we started dating, there was no else for either of us. We married on February 25, 1949.

After living through the Great Depression and fighting a long, cruel war, those of my generation who survived came home to a burgeoning, vibrant economy. Many of us were able to start busi-nesses or find good-paying jobs and enjoy a wonderful economic era.

Alda and I lived the American dream. We raised three children who have always been a source of happiness and pride to us. We traveled extensively, and we enjoyed homes on a lake in Michigan and on golf courses in Florida and Indiana. Our way of life was a world away from the depth of Depression in which we were raised.

But this good life turned into nightmare in 1992, when Alda was diagnosed with breast cancer. She fought it courageously, but we lost our fight in March 1998.

With all its horror, nothing I endured in World War II was as dif-ficult for me as losing my dear Alda. I have written this book because she encouraged me to do so. During the last days of her ill-ness, she was even able to help me begin it. I only hope I can live the rest of my life in a way that would make her as proud of me in death as she always was in life. Alda provided me with the quintessential American dream—a life of happiness with someone I loved with all my heart. I shall forever be grateful for the 49 years that I was privileged to be her husband.

Stan and Alda at their wedding reception, February 25, 1949.

Alda with Stan's mother, Dora E. Huff, 1963.

Alda at L Company reunion held in 1995.

# Epilogue
## MERTEN—50 YEARS OLDER

In May 1995, fifty years after V-E Day, my son Dave, who has developed a great interest in my World War II experiences, Alda, and I drove to the Sieg River area where I had been in combat.

We walked up to the top of the ridge where I had huddled, shivering in the rain overlooking the Sieg and Merten. How shocked we were to find the foxholes dug in 1945—filled with leaves—but still there. The last time I had seen those holes was the morning we assembled on the beach for the midday crossing of the river. Boys who did not survive that crossing had occupied some of them.

After a brief reckoning, I found the foxhole Vonksky and I had occupied. The village below looked just as pristine as it had on that spring morning half a century before. No traces of blood in the river.

When we drove into Merten, we could see repairs where buildings had been hit by machine gun and mortar fire. Otherwise, it seemed unchanged. We walked the streets of this small town, so heavy with memories for me I could not speak at times. Here friends had died as I might have.

Steeped in memories of youth and war, we drove to a beautiful restaurant and resort that had been recommended to us. After registering, we went to the dining room. While we were eating I remarked to Alda and Dave that I was sure Hernnstein Castle was nearby. I told them the story of its capture and my all-too-brief night of medieval splendor in a sleeping bag from which I was rousted at three in the morning to continue our attack.

Stan and his son Dave in Germany, 1995.

A German couple sitting at the next table overheard the name and the gentleman said to us in English, "Excuse me, sir. Did you mention Hernnstein Castle?"

"Yes, I did," I replied.

"Were you here fifty years ago, then?" the German asked.

I responded warily, not knowing how he would react, "Yes, I was an American soldier and we captured it."

"Well, I know where the old schloss is and I also know the Count who owns it and lives there," the gentleman said with a broad smile. "I will call him up and find out if you can see it." He left the room.

He returned laughing excitedly. When he had told him an American soldier who stayed in his castle during the war was in the restaurant, the Count had insisted he invite us to visit on the following Sunday afternoon. We accepted. Klemons—for that was his

Stan and Alda in foxhole overlooking Merten, Germany, 1995.

name—said he and his wife would pick us up on Sunday. This turned out to be only the first of several very pleasant and unexpected coincidences.

The next day, a Thursday, we toured the museum at Bastogne where the 101st Airborne refused to surrender to the Germans during the Battle of the Bulge, thus blunting their offensive and eventually causing it to fail. Afterwards, we drove the few miles to Luxembourg where, the following day, Alda and I went out to the huge American Cemetery. Since it was Memorial Day, a major program was scheduled and many cars were arriving for the special remembrance.

251

As the main building had a list of names of those buried there, we tried to go in but were stopped by a guard.

"Sorry," he said. "This building is not open to the public today because of the dignitaries participating in today's ceremony honoring the dead of World War II."

"That's okay," I replied. "I was just going to see if any of the guys I served with are buried here."

"Are you saying you were here fifty years ago?" he asked.

"Yes, I was in combat north of here."

"Wait a moment please," the guard said. "I'll be right back." He soon reappeared with a Luxembourg Army Colonel who asked me where I had served and in what capacity. He seemed quite excited with my answers and finally said, "Please come with me. There is someone I want you to meet." Pulling the rope aside, he ushered Alda and me into the building.

Once inside, he asked us to wait and disappeared. We were in a great ballroom filled with people, some civilians, and many military personnel. Soon the Colonel returned with an older gentleman and introduced us to the American Ambassador to Luxembourg. The Ambassador was very friendly and asked me many questions about my role as a combat infantryman. Then he excused himself saying he would return with someone that he wanted me to meet.

He soon reappeared, accompanied by the Prince and Princess of Luxembourg. The Princess took my hand and did not let go. She looked me in the eye and said, "On behalf of my people, I want to personally thank you for what you did here during World War II. Our people will be eternally grateful." I told her she was the first person in fifty years who had actually thanked me. She asked if she could take my picture, so Alda and I posed for the Princess of Luxembourg. She reciprocated and we took her picture.

The Ambassador then introduced us to the general in charge of all U.S. forces in Europe. He shook hands with me and said, "It's a real honor to meet you, sir." This was the first time I was ever addressed as "sir" by a general, but not the last, as several other generals were subsequently introduced. None was old enough to have been in World War II.

Stan and Alda meet the American Ambassador to Luxembourg during their 1995 trip to Germany.

They asked us to join them on the stage during the ceremony; however, we declined because Dave was waiting for us back at the hotel. Also, if the truth be told, Alda was pretty uncomfortable with the thought of sitting among all those dignitaries with thousands of people looking on. Thus ended one surprise adventure, but another was about to unfold.

As he had promised, Klemons and his wife picked up the three of us on Sunday. Approaching the entrance to the castle, I noticed cars parked everywhere. When we walked up to the main entrance, a German band broke out playing and we were greeted by the Count and Countess who, in turn, introduced us to a number of other people who were standing in a receiving line. Inside the castle was an elaborate reception, including hors d'oeuvres topped with little German and American flags. We were treated as special guests only because I had first come through that area fifty years earlier as an invading American soldier.

Although none of the German guests was invited to leave the first

Stan and Alda with Mr. and Mrs. Klemons, the kind German couple that escorted them through the Ruhr area in 1995.

floor, the Count offered us a tour of the rest of the castle, which were his private living quarters. As he took us through the magnificent rooms, I recalled my unescorted tour so many years before. I recognized the very spot where I had thrown my sleeping bag on the floor, climbed in, zipped it up, and shut out the war for a few hours. Only a healthy, exhausted 19-year-old could have drifted off to sleep ignoring the real possibility that he might never awake.

Showing us into his office, the Count pointed to a beautifully varnished plaque penetrated by a polished piece of shrapnel. They had found the imbedded metal in his forest, and when the tree was cut down, he had it made into a plaque for his office wall. It was American steel.

Later in the afternoon, the Countess handed me an envelope, saying she wanted me to have the contents. I opened it and found artists' renditions and photographs documenting the various remodelings of the castle dating back to the time of its original

A band reception greeted Stan, Alda, and Dave upon their arrival at Hernnstein Castle, 1995.

Stan and Dave, with the owner of Hernnstein Castle, surveying the room where Stan threw down his sleeping bag and fell asleep for a few hours in 1945.

Stan and Dave viewing the dining room of Hernnstein Castle, with the owner and her son in 1995.

construction in the twelfth century. It was a kind gift to a man who had enjoyed that castle in such diverse situations.

We met a lot of their friends that afternoon, and all treated us as honored guests. One man wanted to shake my hand. He explained that he was a German soldier captured by the Americans and sent to a prisoner of war camp in New Orleans, where he learned English. He wanted to emphasize to me his gratitude for the treatment he had received from his American captors. All in all, it was a delightful and moving afternoon.

Klemons offered to drive us along the route we infantrymen had followed. From the castle, we headed for Broscheid, the village I had innocently walked into on that long-ago morning. It, too, looked exactly as it had in 1945. Luckily, we met a lady who had been 16 years old at the time and remembered the day clearly. She told us it had been a communications center and was full of troops, but as our L Company marched through they stayed indoors, not knowing how large an American force they were dealing with.

We, of course, were new to the business of war and never checked the houses. She showed us where the German prisoners were kept after the battle. I also found the barn I had hidden behind, and the ditch where Jim and I had hugged the ground was still there. I got chills down my spine as I involuntarily clenched my fist as if it had a grenade in it, and remembered both my anxiety and my resolve when the German soldiers passed us by, running into the night.

As we drove away, Klemons told us his 91-year-old mother remembered the day we came into their little village. When he took me to her house, she threw her arms around me and, with tears in her eyes, told me how happy she had been to see us in 1945. Her son had run into the house and told her the soldiers coming down the road were not wearing German uniforms. She had said exactly what was on her mind at the time, "Thank God! The Americans are here!" She, like so many other Germans, was tired of war and wanted to get rid of Nazism and Hitler. They looked upon us as liberators—not invaders.

Klemons' mother also threw her arms around Alda and embraced her emotionally because she was my wife. This was very touching to Alda. She had actually been quite apprehensive about revealing to the Germans that I had gone through that area in 1945 as an enemy soldier. She certainly did not expect us to be treated in the manner in which we were received.

I did not know Alda when I was in the military. She was still in high school. Alda was a devout Christian and she abhorred war and killing. She looked only for the good in everyone and couldn't think of human beings trying to kill each other in battle. But she was greatly touched to have our former enemies embracing us and welcoming us to their homes fifty years later. She heard Germans thanking me for helping to overthrow and defeat the Nazi government that had ruled their lives for 12 years.

When we were alone in our hotel room that evening after the

Alda with German woman who saw the 97th Division of infantrymen arriving in1945, and exclaimed, "Thank God the Americans are
here."

encounter with Klemons' mother, Alda embraced me and said,
"Stan, I am so proud of you." Those words from Alda because of my
role in World War II meant more to me than all of the "thank you's"
I received from so many others—from ordinary Germans to the
Princess of Luxembourg—during that return to the land of our for-
mer enemy.

And so it seems fitting that when I returned to the scene of my
youthful dangers, the former enemy as well as allies treated me as a
liberator, and finally a friend. In the war I saw and did many things
I would rather not have done, but soldiers are put in situations
beyond their own control in which they must simply make the best
of what they must do and act as decently as they can. That is all I
tried to do at the time. I was fortunate enough to survive my unforgettable journey.